Canadian Multinationals

Canadian Multinationals

by Jorge Niosi

translated by Robert Chodos

Translated by: Robert Chodos
Published by: Between The Lines
                229 College Street
                Toronto, Ontario M5T 1R4
Typeset by: Dumont Press Graphix
                97 Victoria Street North
                Kitchener, Ontario N2H 5C1
Cover and interior design by: Margie Bruun-Meyer, *Artwork*
Printed by: Les Editions Marquis Ltée
Originally published as *Les multinationales canadiennes* by Boréal
Express, 1983.

Canadian Cataloguing in Publication Data

Niosi, Jorge, 1945-
    Canadian Multinationals

Translation of: Les Multinationales canadiennes.
Bibliography: p. 192
ISBN 0-919946-52-6 (bound). - ISBN 0-919946-53-4 (pbk.).

1. International business enterprises - Canada.
2. Investments, Canadian. 3. Corporations, Canadian.   I. Title.

HD2755.5.N5513 1985   338.8'8971   C85-098248-0

Between The Lines is a joint project of Dumont Press Graphix,
Kitchener, and the Development Education Centre, Toronto.

This book has been published with the help of a grant from the
Social Science Federation of Canada, using funds provided by the
Social Sciences and Humanities Research Council of Canada.

Table of Contents

Preface

There are not many works about Canadian multinational corporations. The team of Isaiah A. Litvak and Christopher J. Maule has written articles about them, as has G. Garnier.[1] Aside from these articles, there are only a few monographs about the international expansion of particular corporations.[2] A work edited by Professors Tamir Agmon and Charles P. Kindleberger, containing studies of multinational corporations based in such countries as Switzerland, Sweden and Australia, does not have a chapter on Canada.[3]

This lack of interest in Canadian multinationals is all the more surprising in light of the fact that in absolute terms Canada is one of the world's largest capital exporting countries. In 1971, it was in sixth place, behind the United States, Britain, France, West Germany and Switzerland.[4] Canada was also sixth in per capita foreign direct investment. And Canadian corporations were among the world leaders in a wide variety of industries including mining and refining, aluminum, distilling, rubber, telecommunications equipment, farm machinery, and shoes.

Because foreigners have such a large share of the Canadian manufacturing and mining industries, most economists have been more interested in foreign investment in Canada than in Canadian investment in other countries. Thus, even the best informed writers often underestimate the phenomenon of Canadian-based investment.[5] In addition, Canada has never had a colonial empire, and has had at most a small sphere of influence in the Commonwealth Caribbean. This situation leads writers who equate multinational corporations with imperialism to turn their attention away from Canada. And finally, a number of theories that endeavour to explain why companies become multinational stress the importance of being in the technological forefront, while Canada is known to be one of the world's leading importers of technology. In this area at least, Canada constitutes a paradox that the major theories of multinational corporations do not satisfactorily explain.

Thus, it is relevant to our study to examine these various theories, and the book begins with such a review before going on to measure the extent of Canadian direct investment in foreign countries and compare its development with that of American and Japanese investment as well as investment based in such countries as Australia and Argentina (Chapters 1 and 2). The next three chapters are devoted to a study of thirteen Canadian multinationals, divided into three sectors: utilities (Brascan and International Power), mining (Inco, Falconbridge, Noranda Mines, Alcan and Cominco), and manufacturing (Seagram, Hiram Walker, MacMillan Bloedel, Massey-Ferguson, Polysar and Northern Telecom). With a few exceptions, each of these corporations operates in at least five countries (including Canada) and had either assets of more than $1 billion or sales of more than $2 billion in 1979. Some of them are or have been foreign-controlled (such as International Power and Falconbridge) while others are under joint Canadian-American control (Alcan and Inco), but most of them are Canadian-controlled.

A Canadian multinational is defined as a multinational controlled by Canadian stockholders or directors. Thus, companies such as Ford of Canada, which is ultimately controlled by its parent corporation in Detroit (the Ford Motor Company), are excluded. Falconbridge, which has been American-controlled since 1967, is included in the study even though it violates this rule. Brascan also fails to fulfill one of the criteria outlined here, since most of its assets were concentrated in one country (Brazil), but is included nonetheless.

In organizing this book, I have borrowed substantially from the theories of Stephen Hymer, Raymond Vernon, Peter Buckley and Marc Casson. I have used Hymer's conception of the multinational corporation as belonging to national and international oligopolies, Vernon's thesis of the decline of the multinationals' bargaining power in the utility and mining sectors, and Buckley and Casson's central idea of the imperfection and "internalization" of technology markets. Luis Carlos Bresser Pereira, Philippe Faucher, Paul-André Linteau, Francisco Sercovich and Raymond Vernon read the manuscript and made very pertinent suggestions. The research was financed by the Social Sciences and Humanities Research Council of Canada and the Quebec Department of Education. Their help has been, and remains, very valuable to me. The University of Quebec at Montreal released me from my teaching obligations for a year to conduct the research and write the manuscript. I am grateful to all these people and institutions. As is customary, I bear full responsibility for the ideas, errors and omissions in the book.

Jorge Niosi

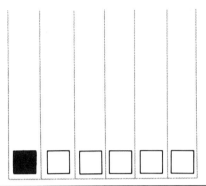

1 Theoretical Considerations

There is no firmly established theory of multinational corporations. Rather, there are many theories attempting to explain international direct investment; these theories complement and to a certain extent contradict one another. In this initial chapter, we will review the best known theories and the debates and criticism to which they have given rise. On this basis, we will be able to develop working hypotheses for studying the case of Canada.

Existing theories can be divided into two major groups — theories of multinational corporations and theories of imperialism and dependency. The division is, of course, not a strict one, and each set of theories borrows from the other. Nevertheless, academic economists representing the first group debate primarily with one another, while theoreticians in the second group rarely refer to writers in the first. In explaining the behaviour of Canadian multinational corporations, it may be valuable to look at analyses by writers in both groups. As our study will be the first group portrait of these corporations, there is a large quantity of material that we will not be able to cover. Thus, we will have to ignore the extensive literature dealing with the effects of the activities of multinational corporations on employment, income and growth in both their countries of origin and host countries.

A — THEORIES OF MULTINATIONAL CORPORATIONS

Special Advantages and International Operations

According to neo-classical theory, international direct investment is a function of interest rates: capital moves from countries where it is plentiful, and where as a consequence interest rates are low, to countries where it is scarce and interest rates are high. Taking a criticism of this theory as a starting point, the Canadian economist Stephen Hymer developed his own theory of multinational corporations in 1960.[1] In the first place, Hymer argued, a theory based on interest rates doesn't explain the fact that in the current period, capital usually moves from one country where it is plentiful to another such country; nor does it explain cross movements, such as American investment in Europe and European investment in the United States. Second, he said, firms that invest outside their countries of origin borrow most of their capital in the host countries; international movement of capital is thus highly limited and does not explain foreign direct investment. Third, most international direct investment is carried out by firms based in the United States, and almost all of it is accounted for by firms based in some ten countries in Europe and North America plus Japan. Thus, there is something inherent in the industrial structure of these countries that predisposes their corporations to international operations. And finally, foreign direct investment has always shown a marked industrial distribution, and the great majority of it is carried out by firms in a fairly small number of industrial sectors — chemicals, transportation equipment, metal processing.

Hymer noted that there is a particular dimension to direct investment that distinguishes it from portfolio investment — the dimension of control exercised by the parent corporation over its foreign subsidiary. Corporations seek control either to avoid competition between the subsidiary and other companies or to take full advantage of expertise or technology available to the parent firm. This latter advantage has to be substantial enough to compensate for the natural disadvantages (linguistic, cultural and legal barriers) from which a foreign company suffers. For a company has a nationality, as a result of the location of its head office, the nationality of its controlling shareholders and managers, and the discriminatory treatment of foreign-owned firms in many countries. In addition, a foreign company has to repatriate its profits and is therefore subject to the risks associated with exchange-rate fluctuations.

A company that carries out international operations must therefore have some technological, organizational or other advantage over its competitors based in the host country. But the existence of such an advantage is not a sufficient condition for foreign direct investment. For a firm possessing an advantage could serve the foreign market either by exporting its products or through a patent licensing agreement with an independent firm in the host country. However, the firm may be prevented from exporting to the host country by tariffs or non-tariff barriers such as the "Buy American Act." At the same time, patent licensing agreements raise the question of how to control the pricing, production and marketing policies of the local firm, which could end up competing with the company that licensed the patent. In addition, technology markets are highly imperfect and it is difficult to agree on a licensing fee satisfactory to both parties. The simplest way for a firm possessing an advantage to maximize its profit from the advantage and ensure that the local firm will not become a competitor is to control the local firm by making it a subsidiary. However, if it is anticipated that controlling the local firm will not be very profitable — if, for example, the local market is highly competitive — then it is clearly in the interest of the firm possessing the advantage to enter into a licensing agreement.

Industries in which multinational corporations operate are characterized by concentration and oligopolistic markets. If an advantage were possessed by many firms in the developed countries, this would indicate that it was not difficult to obtain and that companies in less developed countries could acquire it too. This explains why there are multinational corporations in the automobile and farm machinery industries but not in cotton or woollen textiles. Most foreign direct investment occurs in industries where technology is complex and barriers to entry due to economies of scale are significant.

In subsequent articles, Hymer made additional contributions to the analysis of the multinational corporation.[2] First, he wrote of the growing competition on a world scale coming from Japanese, European and, to a lesser extent, Canadian multinational corporations, and described the older industrial powers' "non-American challenge" to the established order of American multinational corporations. Hymer believed that the decline of the American transnationals was caused by the industrial recovery of Japan and western

Europe rather than competition from Third World companies. Thus, he predicted that there would be a lessening of concentration on a world scale but only a few competitors would benefit from it.

Hymer also believed that the multinationals were a relatively stable phenomenon within the capitalist world, and that they had established a relatively stable international division of labour. It was this international division of labour, through which the essential elements of machinery production, technology and organizational and management functions were limited to a few industrialized countries, that Hymer called "imperialism." In other words, the domination of the Third World by the industrial powers was based on industrial concentration and multinational expansion by oligopolists rather than on colonialism, a stable division of markets and spheres of influence or control of industry by banks. In addition, this domination occurred in the context of rivalry between powers experiencing a recovery — Japan and western Europe — and a power in decline, the United States.

In criticizing Hymer's theory, Peter J. Buckley and Marc Casson identified three weaknesses.[3] First, Hymer did not explain the advantages that lead to foreign direct investment, and didn't say how, why or at what cost some firms are in a position to obtain them. The second weakness is a consequence of the first: The theory as Hymer developed it is unable to predict which firms will invest in these advantages rather than in other assets. And finally, Hymer thought in terms of a single innovation or advantage while in reality some firms are characterized by an ability to innovate and develop a number of advantages.

The Theory of the Product Cycle

In Raymond Vernon's view, the life of a product goes through three stages. In the first stage, innovation and product development take place where demand and cost conditions permit. At the beginning the product is not standardized and producers serve only the market where the innovation took place. In his later writings, Vernon has emphasized the necessarily oligopolistic character of this stage of innovation.[4]

In the second stage, both the product and the oligopoly that created it mature. The product generally becomes standardized, but technology, scale of production and other barriers prevent other competitors from entering the industry. The firms responsible for the innovation become multinational to protect foreign markets for their creation.

In the third stage the product is completely standardized and uniform. The original firms are powerless to prevent competition from resuming and the oligopoly is eroded. Production is carried out wherever it is most economical; thus, for labour-intensive products, less developed countries take over production.

In its most recent version, Vernon's theory offers an explanation of the initial advantage enjoyed by multinational corporations and of the location of innovating firms. It also points out that the multinationals' initial advantage is relative and temporary rather than absolute and permanent. One particular case of the erosion of advantages is of special interest in studying Canadian firms since it affects the mining industry, utilities and agriculture. This is the process that Vernon calls the "obsolescing bargain" — the erosion of bargaining power. In industries with relatively simple technology, high initial investment and a risk stage limited to the beginning of operations, a multinational's bargaining power is rapidly eroded. Public and private enterprises in the host country quickly absorb the know-how that constituted the multinational's initial advantage. There is growing pressure on the multinational to transfer control of its subsidiary, in whole or in part, to local interests. This explains the slow but sure disappearance since the Second World War of multinational corporations in such sectors as electricity production, railways and plantation agriculture and the more recent proliferation of government takeovers in the mining and petroleum industries.

Vernon's theory is a good explanation of the structure of American direct investment in foreign countries in the twenty years immediately following the Second World War. It has also lent support to other theories and many empirical studies. However, some recent developments elude it — the creation by multinational corporations of products specifically intended for markets outside their countries of origin, the growing proportion of foreign direct investment that goes to produce goods already manufactured in the host country, and the purchase of firms in foreign countries to acquire advantages that the multinational does not possess (such as the acquisition by Minnesota Mining and Manufacturing of an Italian firm, Ferrania, to improve its photographic equipment). This last phenomenon must be taken into account in order to understand the way in which a number of Canadian multinationals have acquired technological advantages.

A disciple of Hymer, Ian Giddy, has criticized the product cycle theory.[5] In Giddy's opinion, Vernon's theory does not provide a good explanation of the growth of multinational corporations in the mining and petroleum industries; on the other hand, a theory based on industrial organization (that is, on technological advantages possessed by oligopolistic firms) accounts for international direct investment in extractive industries very well. In addition, it is becoming more and more common for multinational corporations to use their subsidiaries to bring products to third markets. Vernon has replied that innovation with distant markets in mind is a phenomenon more of the future than of the present; the "global scanner" is still far from being the norm among multinational corporations. Quite the contrary — multinationals still let themselves be guided by the home market in their countries of origin.[6]

A writer in the "dependency" school, Constantine Vaitsos, has offered a completely different kind of criticism. Vaitsos challenged the third stage of the product cycle, the senescent oligopoly and the resumption of competition. He argued that in the most technology-intensive sectors, industrialization based on foreign direct investment or imported technology does not lead to a resumption of competition. As a result of resource flows and restrictive clauses accompanying both direct investment and the sale of technology by the multinationals, the monopoly position of subsidiaries of multinationals or local companies operating under licence is preserved. Restrictive clauses generally oblige the firm in the host country to buy machinery, designs, technical services, intermediate goods and the like from the parent corporation. The effect of these arrangements is that technology is not dispersed, local companies are displaced, and the monopoly position of the multinational corporation or the licensee is strengthened.[7]

The Oligopolistic Reaction Theory

Frederick T. Knickerbocker has tried to explain the blossoming of American direct investment in foreign countries after the Second World War and its tendency to be distributed in "bunches" of firms in the same industry.[8] Knickerbocker noted that when the leading firms in an industry decide to establish foreign subsidiaries, rival corporations tend to follow them fairly soon afterwards. The loss of exports, the leading firm's potential for acquiring new capabilities through its subsidiary, and the profitability of international operations are all factors driving rival companies to follow the leader in establishing foreign subsidiaries. As a general rule, the more highly concentrated an industry, the stronger this "oligopolistic reaction" will be.

Knickerbocker's theory is thus an amplification of Vernon's, and, to a certain extent, of Hymer's as well. It contributes significant elements to an understanding of the phenomenon of multinational corporations. However, it has come under heavy criticism. In particular, Buckley and Casson have argued that the oligopolistic reaction theory does not clearly explain the goals of foreign direct investment, especially in the case of the leading firm. Why do innovative firms become multinational? Is it to maximize profits, to maximize growth, to maintain their share of the world market, or for other reasons.[9] Their criticism is valid, but it does not challenge the originality and coherence of Knickerbocker's argument or the solid empirical evidence on which it is based. At most, they point out some weaknesses in a work whose primary aim is to provide an empirical analysis of certain dimensions of the foreign expansion of American multinationals. Knickerbocker's goal is simply to develop Vernon's theory further and corroborate it in part.

The International "Pecking Order"

The phenomenon of multinational corporations based in "small countries" has been examined in a collection edited by Tamir Agmon and Charles Kindleberger.[10] In Agmon and Kindleberger's definition, a "small country" could be a highly industrialized country with a small population (Sweden, Switzerland, Holland, Belgium), an advanced country that developed very late (Australia, New Zealand, Canada), or a country that is rapidly becoming industrialized (Brazil, India, Mexico). The collection of articles is far from being homogeneous, and there is no overall theory proposed. Nevertheless, there are certain consistent themes running through Helen Hughes's article on Australia, Carlos F. Diaz Alejandro's contribution on Latin American multinationals, and Louis T. Wells, Jr.'s essay on the internationalization of firms from developing countries. Wells tries to reach a theoretical understanding of the advantages of multinational corporations based in developing countries.[11] Currently, most such corporations are in technologically mature industries. The specific advantages of these peripheral multinationals, with head offices in countries such as Argentina, Brazil, Mexico, Taiwan or Hong Kong, are the following:

a) They are able to adapt large-scale technologies from the industrialized world to smaller-scale production in their home countries. The resulting technology is often more labour-intensive and hence reduces production costs considerably. The example of Sociedad Industrial Americana di Maquinaries (SIAM), an Argentine multinational that produces refrigeration equipment in a number of

Latin American countries on the basis of licences purchased from
Kelvinator in 1937 and Westinghouse in 1940, is highly relevant.

b) Their managers are paid considerably less than the management personnel sent out by competing multinationals based in
developing countries, and their administrative costs are thus lower.

c) Most of them enter foreign markets through joint ventures
with host-country firms, because they lack sufficient capital or
because they are inexperienced in international operations or else to
avoid ruffling political feathers in the host country. This strategy
improves their competitiveness relative to multinationals based in
industrialized countries.

In general, multinationals based in less developed countries
appear to be better adapted in terms of both technology and the
products they offer to the less solvent markets found in the developing world. In addition, they offer better terms than advanced-
country multinationals. Wells sees these characteristics as part of a
more general phenomenon in the context of the product cycle — the
international "pecking order." Technology originating in the
United States is often picked up by European and Japanese firms,
adapted to serve lower-income markets and exported to semi-
industrialized countries which modify it in turn and introduce it in
less developed countries.

Wells's theory has two notable assets: It focuses attention on the
phenomenon of the existence of multinational corporations based in
semi-industrialized countries, about which little is known and to
which even less theoretical attention has been paid, and it identifies
the ways in which technology is disseminated in the context of the
product cycle.

The "Internalization" of Markets in Intermediate Goods

Peter J. Buckley and Marc Casson have tried to develop a general
theory encompassing the contributions of the writers discussed
above.[12] In their view, the key to understanding multinational corporations is the imperfection and "internalization" of markets in
intermediate goods. Before the Second World War, companies
became multinational to protect themselves against the imperfections of markets in raw materials; in other words, they "inter-
nalized" these markets to reduce the risk of supplies being interrupted. This explains why before 1940 multinationals were to a
large degree concentrated in the extractive industries, as companies

sought to become vertically integrated through their foreign operations. After the war, firms established foreign subsidiaries to "internalize" markets in know-how, technology and marketing, in order to derive greater profits from their innovations. This explains the growth of manufacturing multinationals since 1945.

Buckley and Casson began by noting that multinationals are found in the most concentrated industries and in those that are most intensive in research and development. They emphasized that the activities of modern companies go well beyond the routine production of goods and services. Companies also produce a large number of semi-finished goods through research, marketing, organization, the training of groups of managers and workers, and the like. With increasing frequency, these intermediate products take the form of knowledge and skills, which are incorporated in patents, personnel, or machines. When firms are faced with markets in all these intermediate products that are highly imperfect and difficult to organize, they get around this obstacle by resorting to international expansion. In a world where companies seek to maximize profits and come up against highly imperfect markets (at one time primarily in raw materials and now mostly in technology), the "internalization" of these markets across national borders creates multinational enterprises. Alcan Aluminium Ltd. is a good example of the internalization of markets in raw materials (in this case bauxite) across national borders. Polysar, a Canadian multinational that has produced synthetic rubber in Europe since the 1960s and in Latin America since the 1970s, illustrates the internalization of markets in technology.

Buckley and Casson's theory is consistent with Hymer's. It postulates that in the postwar era, the advantage that would explain international operations is typically an innovation resulting from prior research and development, and it recalls Hymer in its emphasis on the fact that technology markets are highly imperfect. It is also consistent with both Vernon's theory and the criticisms of it, as it takes into account situations where an innovative firm designs different products for the home market and for foreign markets. It answers the objections to Knickerbocker's theory by saying that multinationals seek to maximize the profits derived from their investment in innovation. Buckley and Casson's theory establishes a link among the major current explanations for multinational corporations. The question of whether it can be used to understand the multinationals based in the most advanced of the semi-industrial economies — Canada — remains.

The coalescence of banking and industry appears to be neither as universal nor as permanent as Lenin's definition suggested. This characteristic of modern capitalism appears to be limited to European countries that participated in the second wave of industrialization — Belgium, Italy, Germany, Austria. There is little evidence of it in France or the United States and none at all in England. Bank control of industry does not exist today in the United States, England or Canada.[17]

This leaves industrial concentration and the export of capital towards less developed countries. Both these observations retain their validity, and they amount to a brief summary of Hymer's theory of multinational corporations. But Lenin did not provide a good explanation of why firms in concentrated industries establish foreign subsidiaries, and thus did not go nearly as far as Hymer. In some places, Lenin attributed the export of capital to a lack of investment opportunities in metropolitan countries, but this blinds us to a central fact: each developed country carries out about 75 per cent of its foreign direct investment in other advanced countries. At other times, Lenin attributed the export of capital to a difference in the rate of profit between the centre and the periphery, which brings us to a theory based on interest rates of the sort criticized by Hymer. Finally, Lenin also partially attributed the export of capital to the search for raw materials. This explains direct investment in extractive industries but not in manufacturing, and manufacturing investment is now by far the more substantial of the two.

The usefulness of the classical Leninist theory for studying Canadian multinational corporations appears arguable. Canada never had a colonial empire, nor did it every have a "sphere of influence" outside the English-speaking West Indies. Canadian banks have not participated in the control of major industrial corporations, so that there is no coalescence of banking and industry. Only a few Canadian multinationals, such as Inco and Alcan, were at one time members of international cartels. Finally, the phenomenon of Canadian multinational corporations clashes with the tendency of classical Leninist theory to see the world economy as a dichotomy between countries that export capital and countries that receive it. Canada, having more often than not been described as part of the formal or informal empire of Britain and later of the United States, is generally classified as a neo-colony or a dependent country — a host country rather than an exporter of capital. In reality, however, it is difficult to classify Canada in terms of the Leninist dichotomy, and the dichotomy itself is, in any case, not very useful as a description of the present-day world economy.[18]

Dependency, Stagnation and Multinational Corporations

During the 1950s, it became clear that the classical Leninist theory was outdated. A number of writers developed theories linking multinational corporations with underdevelopment, but their picture of imperialism did not include colonialism, cartel agreements or the coalescence of banking and industry. In these new conceptions, responsibility for the Third World's economic stagnation and slow pace of industrialization was attributed to multinational corporations. Among the works belonging to this period in the development of the theory of imperialism are those of Paul Baran, André Gunder Frank, Meir Merhav, Samir Amin and Charles Bettelheim.[19]

Paul Baran's starting point was the concept of "economic surplus" — the part of production that is not needed for immediate personal consumption and can therefore be invested. He identified four major receivers of economic surplus in the Third World: local landowners, merchants and industrialists, and the transnationals. In Baran's view, all four contribute to economic stagnation. The multinationals fall into this category for a number of reasons. They bring little fresh capital to the host country; they repatriate most of their profits; plantation multinationals establish monoculture, while mining corporations export non-renewable resources on a massive scale; and they create few jobs as the technology they use is inappropriate to the distribution of factors of production in underdeveloped countries. It is important to note that Baran saw American multinationals as essentially concentrated in primary production. He quoted approvingly from another writer, Jacob Viner: "American investment abroad is largely concentrated in mining investments, notably in the petroleum field. . . . In the absence of very special circumstances no American private capital will now venture abroad."[20]

These few lines indicate the distance between Baran's position and my own. The share of manufacturing investment in total American direct investment in foreign countries has increased steadily throughout the postwar era, from 33 per cent of the total in 1946 to 45 per cent in 1978 (in terms of book value of accumulated capital). Baran's characterization of the manufacturing sector as a marginal one for foreign direct investment also failed to take into account the fact that almost 50 per cent of accumulated European, Japanese and Canadian direct investment has been concentrated in this sector.

We have reviewed the most significant current theories of multinational corporations — the theories that fit into the Hymer-Kindleberger tradition and those of the Vernon-Knickerbocker-Wells school. We have also looked at the fairly successful attempt by Buckley and Casson to integrate the two lines of thought into a single theory. Other theories have been deliberately omitted from consideration because they appear manifestly unsuitable to an explanation of the Canadian case.[13]

This theoretical review leads to a number of questions relevant to an analysis of Canadian multinationals. Since the theory of special advantages suggests that it is the most highly concentrated industries that carry out foreign direct investment, it will be necessary to look at the degree of concentration as a relevant variable. The same school of thought also points us towards an examination of the nature of the advantages that Canadian multinationals try to profit from through their foreign subsidiaries.

The product cycle theory leads us to consider the development of Canadian multinationals over time. On what innovations was their international expansion based? What are the characteristics of the process of erosion of these multinational firms in different sectors of the economy? Is there an oligopolistic reaction that impels the multinationalization of "bunches" of firms in the same industrial sector? What is Canada's place in the international pecking order that puts the United States at the top and the semi-industrialized countries at the bottom?

The questions raised by the theory of the "internalization" of markets touch on a number of areas: the origin of innovation in Canadian multinational corporations, the absorption and local adaptation of foreign technology, and the process by which innovations are generated in Canada and made profitable through international expansion. Where does the know-how of Canadian multinationals come from? Does it come from their own innovations, from buying and adapting foreign technology, or from advantages acquired through the purchase of foreign companies? These are some of the questions we will try to answer in order to explain the growth of foreign direct investment and Canadian multinational corporations.

B — IMPERIALISM, DEPENDENCY AND MULTINATIONAL CORPORATIONS

There is a very substantial economic literature in which the analysis of multinational corporations is put in a wider economic and political context — that of imperialism. There are at least three theories of imperialism: Rosa Luxembourg's, Arghiri Emmanuel's and the Hobson-Hilferding-Bukharin-Lenin tradition. As the first two do not emphasize foreign direct investment, it is not necessary to deal with them here.[14] The Leninist current has been the prevailing one and almost all works that link imperialism with multinational corporations have been coloured by it. It is with Lenin himself that we must begin.

Imperialism and the Export of Capital

In Lenin's definition, which became the classic one, imperialism consists of five elements: 1) industrial concentration; 2) the coalescence of banking and industry (in the form either of bank control of industry or of growing interpenetration and interdependence between the two); 3) the export of capital to peripheral countries; 4) a global division of markets among large corporations in the advanced countries; 5) a colonial division of the world among the great powers.[15]

This model provides a fairly good explanation of some aspects of relations between the developed capitalist countries and underdeveloped countries from the late nineteenth century to the Second World War. More recently, the model's validity has been seriously challenged, even by writers who are Marxists or close to Marxism.

The rapid decolonization that followed the Second World War led the French historian Catherine Coquery-Vidrovitch to conclude that colonialism should not have been part of the definition of imperialism. She demonstrated, with statistics to back her up, that colonial powers such as Britain and France have always carried out most of their direct investment not in their colonial empires but rather in regions that were part of their "informal empires" — eastern Europe for France, Latin America in the case of Britain.[16] In our own time, colonial empires have disappeared for all practical purposes and the lines of demarcation of the great industrial powers' "spheres of influence" are less clear.

The global division of markets has also ended. The era of international cartels that began in the late nineteenth century also came to a close with the Second World War. Today, large international firms based in metropolitan countries engage in vigorous competition for markets in both the underdeveloped and the industrialized world. The competition among American, Japanese and European multinationals for the American automobile market is only one example.

The link between dependency and stagnation is less relevant if the list of countries classified as stagnant is examined critically. Oil-producing countries such as Mexico, Algeria, Venezuela and Saudi Arabia can be removed from the list. So can Brazil, India, South Korea and Colombia, where nationalist industrial policies are combined with an influx of foreign capital. Taiwan and Singapore, which are also receiving a flood of foreign investment, can be taken off as well.

Baran and Paul Sweezy classified the internationalization of capital as one of the instruments used to relieve the increase in economic surplus in metropolitan countries. This increase in surplus was described in detail in their work *Monopoly Capital*.[21] They argued that it leads to excessive savings, which the metropolitan government uses in its world military effort and multinational corporations use in their foreign investments. This is close to Lenin's theory of the absence of investment opportunities in advanced capitalist countries and it leads to the same impasse — it doesn't explain the central fact that developed countries carry out almost three-quarters of their foreign direct investment in other developed countries.

A disciple of Baran's, Meir Merhav, has studied foreign direct investment in manufacturing in the same analytical framework.[22] Merhav's starting point is the concept of technological dependence, that is the inability of underdeveloped countries to produce the capital goods necessary for growth. Countries whose industrialization has been delayed have to import technology whose cost and complexity have increased considerably. In addition, this technology was developed for large advanced-country markets; when it is introduced into underdeveloped countries, either by a local firm operating under licence or by a multinational, it quickly leads to monopoly market structures that bring about stagnation. Merhav's theory of technological dependence is thus based in essence on the technical indivisibility of imported capital goods in underdeveloped countries and it is therefore fundamentally different from Vaitsos's explanation for the existence of monopoly, which is based on resource flows and restrictive clauses. Merhav appears to underestimate the possibility that technology developed in the industrialized countries can be adapted either by local firms or by transnationals. His system is thus incompatible with Wells's formulation in which Third World multinationals have specific advantages based on adapting imported technology.

André Gunder Frank is another writer in this current. In his view, Latin American economies are characterized by underdevelopment and chronic stagnation. Frank has argued that a number of factors have been responsible for this situation at different times: the pillage of natural resources (from the sixteenth to the twentieth century), the financing of imports by metropolitan banks (since the nineteenth century), and multinational corporations based in industrialized countries. The multinationals realize monopoly profits through their subsidiaries which produce in protected markets and are overbilled for machinery, technical services and intermediate goods imported from metropolitan countries. It should be noted that Frank did not go to the trouble of proving that underdevelopment and stagnation exist, but took their existence as a given. This made him an easy target for such writers as Bill Warren, who have demonstrated statistically that a number of Third World countries have been undergoing very rapid economic growth for more than a century.

Another theme that recurs frequently in works by writers in this current is that fewer and fewer multinational corporations are concentrating more and more of the world economy in their hands. In the same tradition, Harry Magdoff has argued that the long-term tendency is to growing industrial concentration on a world scale, but that it is held back by a number of factors, such as the support given by national governments to their own multinationals and the diversification of some giant corporations.[23] This is another aspect of the thesis of a growing polarization between the industrialized capitalist countries and the underdeveloped countries that is shared by these writers.

The thesis of growing industrial concentration on a world scale is worth noting, because not only is it directly opposed to the theoretical tradition spawned by Vernon but it also has a number of implications for the behaviour of multinational firms. If an industry such as aluminum production, copper or nickel mining and smelting, or the oil or petrochemical industry was becoming more and more concentrated on a world scale, then it would tend to impose bargains that were less favourable to host countries, joint ventures would become increasingly rare, and nationalist legislation would have less bite or would be abandoned outright because it couldn't be applied. In the following pages, we will see how concentration has declined on a world scale, at least in the major industries in which Canadian multinationals operate.

Dependency, Development and Multinational Corporations

Since the early 1970s, a number of Marxist writers have begun to develop models that combine dependency, development and multinational corporations. The Brazilian writer Fernando H. Cardoso was perhaps the first of these, but he was soon followed by others such as Bill Warren, Christian Palloix, Charles-Albert Michalet and Peter Evans.

In opposition to Baran's thesis, Cardoso has shown that American direct investment in foreign countries has increasingly tended to be in manufacturing.[24] He singled out André Gunder Frank's theory of development and underdevelopment as the very prototype of the kind of error to be avoided. In his view, however, situations in which development is combined with dependency are not universal but are limited to particular countries.

Bill Warren went further, arguing that since the Second World War the Third World has been experiencing significant industrial growth, in which a majority of countries on the three underdeveloped continents have shared. The conditions under which this industrialization has taken place have been independence from the old colonial empires, rivalries among the industrialized countries and the political and economic strengthening of the Third World.

In a way, Warren's theory, in which the multinationals and host-country governments are the principal agents of the industrialization of the Third World, is close to the ideas of Vernon and Wells (from whom Warren quotes at length), but in Marxist language. In addition, it constitutes a radical return to Marx, who saw the developed countries as the model that the underdeveloped countries would follow. Thus, Warren described a process in the mining and oil industries similar to the one Vernon calls the "obsolescing bargain."[25] He predicted that a similar erosion would take place in manufacturing in the not too distant future and criticized the thesis of a growing polarization in the world capitalist economy. Furthermore, he postulated that the nationalism emerging in a number of dependent countries such as Canada, Australia, Brazil and India is forcing multinationals to get rid of or reduce their percentage of control over their subsidiaries, export manufactured products, and buy a growing proportion of their inputs in goods and services in the host country.

Warren also had no room for the idea of technological dependence in the sense of a self-supporting, permanent inability to generate innovation. He argued that, on the contrary, despite some obstacles and restrictive clauses, the technology associated with developed capitalism is disseminated in the Third World. The extent to which this dissemination occurs varies with the capacity of underdeveloped countries to absorb and learn the technology, and the multinationals constitute one of the main factors facilitating it.

In sum, Warren departed radically from the idea that dependence and stagnation are two sides of the same equation, with multinational corporations based in the industrialized countries providing the link. He said that the major industries are becoming steadily less concentrated on a world scale, argued that host-country governments are becoming increasingly stronger and denied that technological dependence is a self-regenerating and permanent process.

In a posthumous work, Warren demonstrated that the empirical foundation of the stagnation theories was a weak one. A number of countries in Latin America (Brazil, Mexico), Asia (South Korea, Taiwan) and Africa (Egypt, Ghana) have much higher long-term growth rates than the industrialized countries. If the results of this growth are not more conspicuous, that is in large part because of the population explosion brought about by improvements in health and nutrition. In addition, these countries account for a growing proportion of world manufacturing — largely as a result of the industrializing activity of multinational corporations. The colonialist imperialism described by Lenin is a thing of the past. The world expansion of capitalism, far from creating stagnation and dependency, has speeded up the industrialization of the Third World. Here, Warren stands diametrically opposed to the ideas of André Gunder Frank.[26]

Christian Palloix represents a link between the Baran-Frank-Merhav-Amin current and the new theories of the dependent industrialization of underdeveloped countries. His most significant theoretical contribution is the concept of the internationalization of industrial branches.[27] Palloix argued that multinationalization cannot be analyzed in terms of individual firms; instead, groups of firms in the same branch reach the stage of international expansion simultaneously. To a certain extent, this thesis converges with Knickerbocker's theory of the oligopolistic reaction, discussed above. However, it has two notable weaknesses: The empirical demonstration supporting it is trivial and unsystematic (in contrast to Knickerbocker's empirical discussion) and it offers no explanation of the imitative behaviour of firms in the same branch. Despite these weaknesses, Palloix did contribute a new element to the theory of the oligopolistic reaction: When industrial branches become international, so do the engineering firms operating in the same industry.

Charles-Albert Michalet, meanwhile, argued that the relocation of industries to the Third World is bringing about its industrialization.[28] In Michalet's view, Lenin made a great contribution to the study of the world economy, notably in linking corporate concentration and the export of capital. However, he wrote, Lenin appears to have limited the export of capital to the export of money capital; in fact, it is well known that multinational corporations borrow in the host countries on a massive scale and that the profits they repatriate are at least equal to the capital they invest. In addition, Lenin argued primarily in terms of investment in the primary sector (extraction, plantations) and utilities (railways, harbours), while since the Second World War most direct investment by multinational corporations in foreign countries has been in manufacturing.

Nor did Michalet accept the analysis of his more recent Marxist predecessors. For example, by linking the central capitalist countries with the peripheral ones through the world market, Samir Amin and André Gunder Frank identified the international division of labour with that of the industrial revolution and ignored the industrialization of the Third World.[29] Michalet also criticized Palloix's theory of the drift of industrial branches on the grounds that it did not fit into an overall model of the world economy and that its definition of a branch — on the basis either of the multinationals that constitute it or of the commodity it produces — was unsatisfactory.

According to Michalet, there is no one reason why firms become multinational, but rather a number of reasons. He began by eliminating from the discussion such explanations as the geographical location of ore deposits and particular climatic conditions, as these circumstances affect only mining and agricultural multinationals, which are of declining significance in relative terms. Then he noted a number of explanations found in the economic literature, ranging from protectionist measures through the technological advantages of oligopolistic firms to the low wages paid in certain underdeveloped countries. He endeavoured to group these interpretations around two major poles or principles of explanation:

a) Commercial strategy: Circumstances such as protectionist measures, transportation costs, and competition from local firms or a third country force some multinationals to undertake production in a market they have hitherto served through exports or neglected. The subsidiary is supposed to sell its product in the market where it is established. This is the most widespread form of multinational.

b) Production strategy: Here the multinational tries to take advantage of unequal production costs between one region and another. The subsidiary's output is exported either to third markets or to other subsidiaries of the same multinational. This strategy is much less common than the first one.

Michalet's explanation is only a synthesis of other writers' explanations, and his original contribution is limited. Michalet also does not believe that there are multinationals from semi-industrial or underdeveloped countries; while there are deficiencies in the data on these multinationals and the theoretical examination of them, their existence has been demonstrated.[30] This is a serious weakness in Michalet's work, for one of the major questions we can ask in analyzing Canadian multinationals is whether they can be placed in the international "pecking order" defined by Wells, in which American multinationals rank at the top and the emerging ones of India and Brazil are at the bottom.

As the world economic system has evolved over the last century, theories that place multinational corporations in the wider context of imperialism or dependency have changed radically. In this process there have been some remarkable convergences, notably between recent Marxist writers and non-Marxists. Thus, Palloix's doctrine of the multinationalization of industrial branches resembles Knickerbocker's theory of the oligopolistic reaction, while the product cycle theory has common features with Warren's thesis of dependent industrialization and the erosion of the multinationals. The Marxist theories of the Leninist and Baran-Frank-Merhav-Amin currents on the one hand and the theses of the Vernon school on the other show the clearest opposition. For example, Magdoff's thesis of increasing industrial concentration on a world scale contrasts sharply with Vernon's concept of the senescent oligopoly, while Merhav's theory of technological dependence is opposed to Wells's analysis of technological adaptation by Third World multinationals.

In general, Marxist analysis of multinational corporations has its own weaknesses, which are peculiar to it and which it is unable to escape. The first of these weaknesses is the lack of a convincing explanation of the conditions under which firms undertake international expansion. Neither Lenin's thesis of the abundance of money capital or the absence of investment opportunities in capitalist countries nor Baran and Sweezy's theory of the increase in surplus nor Michalet's strategies of multinationalization constitute a solid and coherent explanation. Almost all writers agree in identifying industrial concentration and the quest for maximum profits as conditions of internationalization. But these conditions are not enough to explain the superiority of multinational corporations over their competitors in the host countries, especially in the case of multinationals from one developed country operating in another. In understanding the advantages of a multinational over its local competitors, the contributions of Hymer, Kindleberger, Vernon, Buckley and Casson appear essential.

Nor is there a solid Marxist explanation of the erosion of multinationals' market power, conditions of disinvestment, and the learning or adaptation of technology. This last deficiency is especially remarkable in an era in which a number of socialist countries are becoming open to foreign direct investment in the hope of acquiring technology that they don't have.

In the absence of an adequate empirical basis or a clear examination of the evolution of the world economic system, there is a juxtaposition of theses rather than theoretical development. Theories proliferate, largely unconnected to one another and loosely confirmed by the facts.

C — WORKING HYPOTHESES

While there is no theory of multinational corporations capable of gaining unanimous approval, a certain consensus in favour of a few major propositions is beginning to emerge. These propositions provide the conceptual framework for this study; it is an eclectic and composite framework but, it is to be hoped, not a contradictory one. The following are among the propositions that constitute it:

a) *Capital travels primarily among countries where it is plentiful rather than to regions where it is scarce.* In other words, most foreign direct investment takes place between one developed country and another. Neither orthodox economic theories of the international movement of capital nor classical theories of imperialism explain this essential phenomenon.

b) Some industries breed multinational enterprises more prolifically than others. *Most manufacturing multinationals are found in the most concentrated industries and in those where research and development and technological barriers play the largest role.*

c) *Multinational corporations are most often the largest firms in each industry, the "leaders" of the branches in which multinationalization has occurred.* As a general rule, they have a "special asset" which is often a technological advantage (new products or processes) but can also be an organizational advantage, better vertical integration, or any other advantage. It is the existence and variety of such advantages that explains cross investment in the same industry in advanced countries. In this study, we will inquire into the nature of the special advantage of the major Canadian multinationals in three sectors where such firms have been active — utilities, mining and manufacturing. These three sectors account for the majority of Canadian direct investment in foreign countries. They also all involve a technological element, and this element forms part of most theories of multinational corporations.

d) *The products manufactured by large companies follow a cycle* that goes from innovation by a small oligopoly to gradual standardization by firms that by now have become multinational, and then to complete standardization of the product. At this last stage, as writers in the tradition of Vernon see it, the market becomes competitive. Others, such as Harry Magdoff, argue that concentration on a world scale does not diminish and barriers to entry are not reduced with the standardization of the product. Vaitsos takes a middle position in this debate. This point is of the utmost importance, as declining concentration would create conditions favourable to the erosion of the multinationals' power while continuing concentration would imply a long-term strengthening of the multinationals' bargaining position relative to host country governments.

It can, however, be postulated that the multinationals' advantage is subject to erosion. In sectors where technology is relatively simple and the initial investment is significant (plantation agriculture, utilities, transportation, mining), private or government-owned corporations in the host country end up acquiring the outside investor's know-how and the relationship between the multinational and the receiving country changes. The host country consolidates its bargaining power after the company's plant is set up; once the risk stage has passed, the process of the "obsolescing bargain" as defined by Vernon begins.

An analogous process takes place in manufacturing — local companies end up being able to make a product once it becomes standardized and its technology can be purchased easily. However, we know that the process of erosion varies in speed and intensity depending on the industrial policy of the host country. Japan and Canada, two countries in which industrialization occurred late, can be seen as remarkable illustrations of the results of different attitudes towards multinational corporations on the part of host country governments. Japan succeeded in preventing foreign control of its economy while rapidly acquiring and assimilating the technology of foreign multinationals. On the other hand, Canada, after a century of pursuing a liberal policy towards foreign direct investment and the transfer of technology, now finds itself (although this has begun to change) with half of its industry under outside control — one of the highest percentages of foreign control in the world. The ways in which Canadian capital has undertaken industrialization and become multinational have been greatly affected by this situation.

We will analyze the process of expansion, maturation and erosion of Canadian multinationals in the three sectors we have chosen to look at, as well as the companies' strategies in the face of the erosion of their share of the world or local market. The role of host country governments will also be briefly analyzed.

e) *As late-developing countries undertake the process of industrialization, they become home to their own local multinationals.* The main asset of these multinationals may be their adaptation of technology developed in an advanced country to a smaller market or a more labour-intensive production process. However, these multinationals based in semi-industrialized countries are little known and have undergone still less theoretical examination. Louis T. Wells, Jr.'s thesis of the international "pecking order" and the adaptation of technology by countries whose industrialization has been delayed is worth considering as a possible explanation of the emergence of Canadian multinationals. We will ask, however, whether Canadian multinationals fit this model of absorbing and creating advantages.

f) Imitation of a leading firm by other large companies in an industry is another thesis that will be discussed in this study. The theory of the multinationalization of industrial branches has been stated in different forms by writers as widely separated as Frederick T. Knickerbocker and Christian Palloix. We will measure the extent of the phenomenon in the main branches where Canadian multinationals operate, such as distilling and nickel mining and smelting.

The study of the international operations of Canadian firms is still in its early stages, and the goals of this work are simply to come to terms with the extent and development of these operations and begin to trace an explanation for them. The economic and social consequences of the activity of Canadian multinationals on the host countries and on Canada will not be examined here. Aspects such as how the income of Canadian multinationals is distributed, their effect on growth in both the host countries and Canada, and their contribution to the scientific and technical potential of the receiving countries will not be part of this study. There is a very large theoretical and empirical literature on these questions and an examination of it could take us far from our initial goal. In any case such a study should come after the more general one outlined here.

This work could appropriately be accompanied by an analytical study of a different nature. If Canadian multinationals appear to be responsible for few "major" innovations (in the sense of the word used by Schumpeter), they probably initiate a significant number of "adaptive" innovations — innovations whose purpose is to modify already established processes, make machines faster or larger, find new uses for products introduced elsewhere, and the like. It is possible that a stage of adaptive innovation precedes the multi-nationalization of Canadian firms. To look into this process, a separate study of firms within Canada should be carried out. It is important to note that in this work we are interested only in "major" inventions — innovations that give birth to or completely revolutionize an industry.

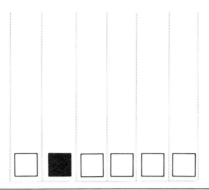

2 The International Expansion of the Canadian Economy

The major features of the model according to which the Canadian economy has become industrialized over the last century are a high degree of foreign control, intense economic concentration and pronounced technological underdevelopment. The characteristics of Canadian direct investment in foreign countries can be explained in the light of this model. As will be seen, because of their size and concentration Canada's giant corporations have been in a position to absorb technological innovations originating in other advanced economies, especially the United States and Britain. Another factor that deserves examination is the significant role played by the government in the international expansion of large Canadian companies.

A Case of Dependent Industrialization

Canada's belated industrialization, which began during the second half of the nineteenth century, was affected from the 1870s on by the northward expansion of large American mining and manufacturing corporations. At the time this process began, Canadian industry was far behind that of the United States. There were numerous obstacles to the development of manufacturing in Canada — a limited market, scattered over a huge area; a protracted colonial link to Britain, the foremost industrial power of the era; a small population. But soon after Confederation, American direct investment was attracted by a series of measures taken by the various levels of government in Canada. The first of these was the Canadian Patent

Act of 1872, which declared null and void any patent that was not used within two years of being registered in Canada. The effect of this legislation was to attract a number of American firms that wanted to make a profit from their technology and avoid imitation by Canadian competitors. The protective tariff introduced in the National Policy of 1879 forced many American corporations to hurdle the tariff wall in order to preserve their share of the Canadian market. When Canada inaugurated a system of preferences for British products in 1897, American firms envisioned the possibility that Britain might reciprocate and hence that they would be able to manufacture in Canada for the British and Empire markets. Finally, the system of subsidies established by municipalities to attract industrial investment — interest-free or guaranteed loans, free industrial sites, tax breaks and gifts — did not discriminate against American companies.

At the same time, the Canadian market was an easy place for American companies that were ripe for international expansion to get started, as language, geographical proximity, income levels and consumer habits made the Canadian economy a natural extension of the American. Thus, many an American corporation undertook its first foreign endeavour in Canada.[1] Let us look at a few examples.

We will focus first on the utility sector. The Bell Telephone Company of Canada was established in 1880 under the minority control of American Bell Telephone, and immediately became the dominant telephone company in Canada, a status it retains today. A few years after its creation, it began to manufacture telephone equipment in Canada to protect its patents. American control lasted until the 1950s, when the parent corporation — which had become American Telephone and Telegraph — gradually sold off its shares to Canadian investors. Other parts of the utility sector also experienced a high degree of American control. In 1930, for instance, 34 per cent of Canada's electricity and 74 per cent of its natural gas were produced by American-controlled corporations.[2] These proportions have declined steadily over the last fifty years, notably as a result of the activity of Canadian provincial governments, which have brought many utility companies under public ownership. In 1980, American subsidiaries owned only 5 per cent of total assets in the utility sector in Canada.[3] It is in this sector that the acquisition of know-how and the "obsolescing bargain" have contributed most to buying back the Canadian economy.

The invasion of American companies in the mining industry began at about the same time as it did in the utility sector — in the late 1870s. Several objectives were served by this northward move-

34

ment. Companies sought raw materials to sell on the American and world markets, protection for their patents and, in the case of a number of manufacturing firms, upstream vertical integration. Around 1880, the companies that would later constitute International Nickel (Inco) were established in Canada by American entrepreneurs; Inco was organized in New Jersey in 1902 and became the world's largest nickel company, the largest Canadian producer of nickel and copper and the number one mining company in Canada. In 1930, about 40 per cent of Canadian copper production was under American control, through such companies as Noranda Mines (founded in 1922), Hudson Bay Mining and Smelting and Inco. From the early twentieth century on, other minerals occupying a significant place in the Canadian economy were also developed under American control. Among these was asbestos, where Canadian Johns Manville, founded in 1910, gained a position of dominance; the second largest producer, the Asbestos Corporation, did not become American-controlled until the 1950s. Canada has been the capitalist world's leading producer of asbestos since the early part of the century.

Mining developments in Canada since the Second World War have been almost entirely the work of American corporations, and this has contributed to raising the percentage of foreign control in the sector. Among the noteworthy new ventures has been iron ore mining in northern Quebec, which began in 1948 and has been carried out almost exclusively by subsidiaries of large American steel companies such as United States Steel, Bethlehem Steel and National Steel. In 1980, 70 per cent of Canada's iron ore production capacity was under American control, and Canada was the fifth largest iron ore producer in the world.

The other major postwar development has been petroleum production, which began after the discovery of extensive reserves in Alberta in 1946. Within a few years the industry had become almost entirely foreign- and mostly American-controlled, although since 1971 a movement to buy back the industry has existed under the leadership of a few Canadian companies such as the privately-owned Dome Petroleum Ltd. and ·the federal crown corporation Petro-Canada. Nevertheless, 70 per cent of Canadian oil production in 1980 was carried out by foreign-owned companies, among them Imperial Oil (a subsidiary of Exxon), Gulf Oil and Texaco.

Looking at the trends in foreign control of the Canadian mining industry as a whole, a continuous rise until 1970 and a rapid decline since that date can be seen. In 1930, 39 per cent of Canada's mining and petroleum production was carried out by subsidiaries of American companies. By 1970, 58 per cent of the assets in the mining industry were under American control, while as of 1980 this proportion had fallen to 40 per cent. Also by 1980, an additional 9 per cent of the assets in the industry belonged to subsidiaries of corporations based in other foreign countries. Foreign control over the Canadian mining industry has undoubtedly been further reduced since 1980, judging by the remarkable number of purchases of subsidiaries of foreign corporations carried out by federal and provincial crown corporations such as Petro-Canada and the Quebec National Asbestos Corporation as well as private Canadian corporations for which a favourable climate has been created by increasingly nationalist legislation.

Meanwhile, soon after American direct investment in Canada began on a significant scale, manufacturing became its main area of concentration. As early as 1908, 38 per cent of American direct investment in Canada was in manufacturing, as compared with 34 per cent in mining and 4 per cent in oil and gas.[4] Some of the industrial branches that are most intensive in research and development were established under foreign and especially American control. In the automobile industry, the Ford Motor Company first expanded into Canada in 1904, and was followed a few years later by General Motors, Chrysler and a number of other companies. Around 1932, more than 83 per cent of Canadian car and truck production was carried out by subsidiaries of American corporations and this percentage has become steadily higher since then.[5] The Canadian chemical industry was also invaded by American multinationals very early on, and quickly became dominated by Du Pont (1910), Union Carbide, Procter and Gamble, Colgate-Palmolive and Sherwin-Williams, among others. In 1932, American corporations accounted for more than 41 per cent of the value of production in the chemical industry, and forty-five years later they controlled 63 per cent of the industry's sales and 54 per cent of its assets. Finally, in the electrical industry, companies such as Canadian General Electric (1892), Westinghouse of Canada (1896), Northern Electric (1882) and Canadian Marconi rapidly achieved a position of dominance in the Canadian market. American companies accounted for 68 per cent of the gross value of production in the industry in 1932, and their share of its sales was still as high as 53 per cent in 1980.

According to Herbert Marshall's estimates, in 1932 subsidiaries of American corporations accounted for 24 per cent of gross value of manufacturing production in Canada.[6] This percentage continued to rise until 1970, and then began to decline slowly. In 1980, subsidiaries of American multinationals accounted for 40 per cent of the sales and 41 per cent of the assets in manufacturing in Canada, while subsidiaries of companies based in other foreign countries accounted for 10 per cent of the sales and 13 per cent of the assets. Some overall statistics on foreign control in Canada between 1926 and 1977 are summarized in Table 1.

TABLE 1

Foreign Control in Canada, Selected Years, 1926-1977

Sector	1926	1939	1948	1958	1967	1977
	Control by non-residents of Canada as a percentage of total					
Manufacturing	35	38	43	57	58	54
Oil and gas*	—	—	—	73	74	64
Mining and smelting	38	42	40	60	65	53
Railways	3	3	3	2	2	1
Other utilities	20	26	24	5	5	4
Total of above industries plus commerce	17	21	25	32	35	30
	Control by United States residents as a percentage of total					
Manufacturing	30	32	39	44	46	42
Oil and gas*	—	—	—	67	60	51
Mining and smelting	32	38	37	51	56	40
Railways	3	3	3	2	2	1
Other utilities	20	26	24	4	5	4
Total of above industries plus commerce	15	19	22	26	28	24

* Oil and gas industry data were included in mining before 1954.
Source: Statistics Canada, Cat. 67-202, annual, 1971, pp. 150-51, and 1982, p. 110.

As Table 2 shows, within the manufacturing sector the most sophisticated branches have the highest degree of foreign control. Canadian businessmen have most effectively resisted foreign competition in sectors with little technological complexity — finance, commerce, services, construction and agriculture. These data are confirmation of the central role of the technological factor in foreign control in Canada. The entry of Canadian firms into such industries as rubber products, oil and coal products, transportation equipment, electrical products, machinery, and chemical products appears to have been prevented by technological barriers. Similar barriers would also initially have played a key role in mining industries, but Canadian firms are no longer deterred by this obstacle and are entering the mining sector at a rapid rate.

In almost all theories that endeavour to explain why corporations become multinational, technology is one of the central elements: Hymer spoke of "technological advantages," Vernon of innovation, and Buckley and Casson of the "internalization" of markets in technology. Hence, the flow of foreign capital into Canada and the country's technological weakness have a strong bearing on Canadian multinationals, and it is worth looking more closely at the role of the 1872 Patent Act in encouraging these developments. According to the economic historian Tom Naylor, Canadian dependence on American technology has manifested itself historically in four distinct ways. Before 1872, the dominant means were the theft by Canadian entrepreneurs of American techniques, processes and patterns and the immigration into Canada of American technicians and entrepreneurs; after the Patent Act, these were superseded by two other mechanisms: the licensing of American patents to Canadian firms and direct investment in Canada by American companies.[7] The first two methods resulted in an increase in Canada's technological capabilities, while the latter two (which were mutually reinforcing) brought with them the long-term subjugation of the Canadian economy to American technology.

The Patent Act required American companies to obtain a Canadian patent and render it operational within two years, either through a licensing arrangement or through a subsidiary. The effect of this measure was to impede Canadian ownership in every industrial branch that was at all technologically complex. While all patents issued in Canada were awarded to Canadians in 1870, Canadians obtained only 35 per cent of patents issued in Canada in 1880, 26 per cent in 1890 and 16 per cent in 1900. Meanwhile, the percentage of Canadian patents issued to Americans, which was zero in 1870, grew to 60 per cent of the total in 1880, 67 per cent in 1890

Table 2

Foreign Control of Corporations
in Percentage of Assets, 1980

	Control (%)		
Industry	American	Other foreign	Total foreign
Tobacco products	24	76	100
Rubber products	65	26	91
Chemical products	59	18	77
Transportation equipment	64	6	70
Non-metallic mineral products	17	54	71
Petroleum and coal products	49	21	70
Textile mills	43	11	54
Electrical products	44	10	54
Machinery	43	9	52
Other manufacturing	34	9	43
Paper	28	7	35
Metal fabricating	28	7	34
Beverages	22	10	32
Food	23	7	29
Leather products	21	1	23
Wood products	15	4	20
Knitting mills	14	1	15
Clothing industries	14	—	14
Primary metals	5	8	13
Printing and publishing	8	3	12
Total manufacturing	35%	13%	48%

Source: Statistics Canada, Cat. 61-210, annual, p. 149 (Ottawa, 1983).

and 77 per cent in 1900.[8] Since the turn of the century, Canadians' share of the patents awarded in the country each year has continued to decline. In 1968-69, Canadians obtained only 5 per cent of the patents issued, while Americans obtained 67 per cent and residents of other countries obtained 28 per cent.[9]

This percentage of patents awarded to local residents is one of the lowest in the world. It is lower than the percentage in such developing countries as Australia, Argentina, India and Mexico, or in small industrialized countries such as Sweden, Belgium, the Netherlands, Norway and Denmark.[10] An outstanding example of a country that followed a different policy, and achieved different results, is Japan. It can be concluded that Canada's legislation concerning the ownership of technology has been one of the major obstacles to the emergence of an independent capacity for innovation in Canadian industry.

The effects of this technology policy quickly bécame clear in areas that went well beyond the simple question of control of industry. Canadian manufacturers export few industrial products and import considerable quantities of machinery, intermediate goods and technological services, so that the structure of Canada's international trade resembles that of an underdeveloped country: 80 per cent of Canadian exports are raw materials, ores, agricultural products, and semi-finished goods, while Canada imports capital goods and intermediate products.[11] In addition, Canadian industry does little research and development, as the innovation done bÿ subsidiaries of foreign companies — which constitute half of the Canadian manufacturing and mining industries — consists mostly of making slight modifications in products and manufacturing processes to adapt them to Canadian market, climatic and legislative conditions. Although the Canadian government has tried to rectify this situation by increasing its own investment in R&D, the result has been that Canada is one of the few members of the Organization for Economic Co-operation and Development (consisting of the developed countries of North America, Europe and Japan) in which private industry accounts for less than 50 per cent of expenditures on research and development.[12]

The clear negative effects of Canada's patent policy on the country's capacity for innovation have been reinforced by other factors — the limited scale of the economy, the absence of risk capital, regional and industrial fragmentation of the home market and the lack of significant export markets.[13] All analysts come to the same conclusion: Canadian industrial firms, whether Canadian- or foreign-owned, are not very innovative.

How, then, has Canada been able to become the world's seventh largest international investing country? On what "technological advantages" have Canadian multinationals been based? Is there an "innovative oligopoly" at the root of the international expansion of

Canadian firms? What is the source of the know-how that Canadian multinationals seek to protect through "internalization"?

Before answering these questions it is necessary to look at the market structure of Canadian industries, because the various theories in which we are interested (Hymer, Vernon, Buckley-Casson, Kindleberger) presume that capital-exporting firms will occur in industries in which there is a high degree of concentration. It can be seen that this condition is fulfilled in almost all sectors of economic activity in Canada except for agriculture and retail trade. In fact, if there is one feature that characterizes the Canadian economy, it is precisely the high level of industrial concentration in the production of goods and services.

Thus, the chartered banks became concentrated between Confederation and the First World War; today, the five largest chartered banks control almost 95 per cent of the assets of all banks.[14] The trust sector has been dominated by two companies, Royal Trust and Montreal Trust, since the late nineteenth century. In the life insurance industry, a small number of companies, among them Confederation Life, Sun Life, Metropolitan Life and National Life, took control of a majority of the assets very early on.

The same process can be seen in manufacturing, and it occurred at an accelerated rate during the merger waves of 1909-13 and 1924-31. By the end of the First World War, there was a Canadian steel oligopoly made up of four companies: Stelco, Dofasco, Algoma Steel and Dosco. The first three of these today account for more than 80 per cent of Canadian production of pig iron and steel. Alcan Aluminium had a monopoly of Canadian aluminum production from its formation in 1902 until the late 1950s, and its share since then has remained over 80 per cent. In the pulp and paper industry, six companies have accounted for two-thirds of Canadian production since the 1926-29 merger wave. The production of synthetic rubber has been dominated by a federally-owned corporation, Polysar, since the beginnings of the industry in 1942. The production of telecommunications equipment is largely controlled by Northern Telecom. Table 3 presents a picture of concentration in a variety of Canadian manufacturing industries in 1980.

The Canadian mining industry has been controlled by a small number of large corporations since the turn of the century. Thus, nickel mining has been dominated by International Nickel (Inco); copper by Inco, Noranda and Hudson Bay Mining and Smelting; asbestos by Canadian Johns Manville and the Asbestos Corporation; petroleum by Imperial Oil, Texaco, Gulf Oil and Mobil Oil; uranium by Denison Mines and Eldorado Nuclear; iron ore by

TABLE 3

Concentration in the Manufacturing Sector in Canada, Selected Industries, 1980

Industry	4-firm concentration ratio*
Distilling	74.9
Brewing	99.0
Winemaking	72.0
Tobacco products	99.6
Rubber products	56.6
Pulp and paper	30.9
Steel	77.9
Smelting and refining	72.0
Aluminum rolling, casting, etc.	88.1
Copper rolling, casting, etc.	79.3
Agricultural implements	61.9
Office machines	75.1
Motor vehicles	93.7
Telecommunications equipment	52.4
Cement manufacturing	84.4
Petroleum refining	61.7
Plastics and synthetic resins	57.3
Manufacturing sector average	46.0

* Value of the shipments of the four largest firms as a percentage of the industry total.
Source: Statistics Canada, Cat. 31-402 (Ottawa, 1983).

Quebec Cartier Mining, the Iron Ore Company of Canada, Quebec Iron & Titanium and Wabush Mines; and so forth. In the mining sector, however, there has been a trend towards reduced concentration with the entry of new competitors, both Canadian and foreign. In the nickel industry, for example, Inco obtained a monopoly in 1928, but its share has been reduced by the entry of Falconbridge Nickel in the 1930s and Sherritt Gordon Mines in the 1950s. In the copper, petroleum, asbestos, and uranium industries concentration has been reduced slightly but remains very strong, and these industries are still in the hands of a few multinational firms, both Cana-

TABLE 4

Concentration in the Mining Sector in Canada, Selected Industries, 1980

Industry	4-firm concentration ratio*
Gold-bearing quartz mines	75.0
Uranium mines	*
Iron mines	86.7
Nickel/copper/gold/silver mines	73.8
Silver/lead/zinc mines	81.6
Coal mines	77.0
Asbestos mines	**
Potash mines	**
Mining sector average	79.3

* Value of the shipments of the four largest firms as a percentage of the industry total.
** Close to 100%; exact figure not divulged for reasons of confidentiality.
Source: Statistics Canada, Cat. 31-402 (Ottawa, 1983).

dian and foreign. Table 4 presents a picture of concentration in this sector.

Corporate concentration appears to be significantly stronger in Canada than in the United States. Major reasons for this are the limited scale of the Canadian market in the manufacturing sector and the penetration of foreign capital in both mining and manufacturing.[15] But despite the higher degree of concentration in Canada, Canadian companies are smaller than their American counterparts; they are, on the other hand, comparable in size to European and Japanese companies.

If concentration were a sufficient condition for international expansion, the Canadian economy would have spawned a large number of multinational firms. However, the potential of Canadian industry for multinational expansion has of necessity been limited by the frequency with which the technology used in Canada has been of foreign origin and the large proportion of companies in Canada that are foreign-controlled.

CANADIAN DIRECT INVESTMENT IN FOREIGN COUNTRIES IN THE TWENTIETH CENTURY

Although it was late in becoming industrialized and never had a colonial empire, in the first half of the twentieth century Canada quickly became one of the world's major exporters of capital; by 1930, it was ahead of such countries as Germany, Italy and Japan.[16] Immediately after the Second World War Canada was in third place, ahead of old powers such as France and the Netherlands, but as Europe became reindustrialized Canada slipped down a few rungs. In their calculation for 1966, Stefan H. Robock and Kenneth Simmonds placed Canada sixth among capital-exporting countries with 4 per cent of the world total.[17] The famous United Nations study for 1971 also placed Canada sixth, behind the United States, the United Kingdom, France, West Germany and Switzerland. A new version of the same study calculated that Canada was in seventh place in 1976 (see Table 5).

From Table 5, the United States appears to have an unassailable lead over western Europe, Canada and Japan. However', its margin has been steadily reduced over the last twenty years. Thus, in 1967 the United States had sixteen dollars of direct investment in foreign countries for every dollar of foreign direct investment held by Canada, while in 1980 this ratio was only nine to one. In other words, Canada's direct investment in foreign countries — like that of Europe and Japan — has developed more rapidly than American direct investment.

There has been a significant constant in the distribution by region of Canadian direct investment in foreign countries: the United States has always been the host country for more than half of this investment. Western Europe was the second largest site of Canadian investment until the late 1950s, but Latin America caught up to it in the 1960s. Table 6 shows the distribution by region of Canadian direct investment over the last fifty years. The Third World accounts for about a quarter of Canadian capital invested in foreign countries.

An analysis of growth rates by region since the Second World War confirms the trends shown by Table 6. Thus, between 1967 and 1977, Canadian direct investment in underdeveloped countries grew at an annual rate of 15.6 per cent, while in developed countries the rate was only 12 per cent. Canadian capital, which was heavily concentrated in the United States immediately after the war, is now spread all over the globe. Thus, the annual rate of growth of Cana-

TABLE 5

Corresponding Assets Invested in Foreign Countries, Direct Investment, Developed Market-Economy Countries, 1976

Country	billions of US$	%
United States	137.2	47.6
United Kingdom	32.1	11.2
West Germany	19.9	6.9
Japan	19.4	6.7
Switzerland	18.6	6.5
France	11.9	4.1
Canada	11.1	3.9
Netherlands	9.8	3.4
Sweden	5.0	1.7
Belgium/Luxembourg	3.6	1.2
Italy	2.9	1.0
Total, above countries	270.4	94.2
Other Countries	16.8	5.8
Total	287.2	100.0

Source: United Nations, Centre for Transnational Corporations, *Transnational Corporations in World Development: Second Survey* (New York, 1978), p. 262.

TABLE 6

Percentage Distribution of Canadian Foreign Investment by Geographic Area, 1926-79

Year	United States	United Kingdom	Other Europe	Latin America*	Other**
1926	63.0	1.8	—	—	35.2
1939	61.4	8.8	—	—	21.8
1949	77.9	6.4	2.1	7.8	5.9
1959	65.1	10.3	3.4	14.4	6.8
1969	54.8	12.3	9.3	14.1	9.5
1979	60.9	10.4	8.1	12.3	8.3

* Mexico, the Caribbean, Central America and South America
** Africa, Asia and Oceania. Before 1949 also included continental Europe and Latin America.
Source: Statistics Canada, Cat. 67-202, 1971 and 1983.

dian direct investment between 1946 and 1976 was 8.7 per cent in the United States, while in the world as a whole it was 9.4 per cent.[18]

For decades, Canada was the second largest foreign investor in the United States, after Britain. In recent years, there has been a substantial increase in the share of foreign investment in the United States held by a number of western European countries and Japan, and the British and Canadian shares have been correspondingly reduced. In 1978 the Netherlands was the largest foreign investor in the United States with 25 per cent of foreign direct investment, followed by Britain with 18 per cent and Canada with 15 per cent. Table 7 shows the rise of continental European and Japanese multinationals in the United States and the relative decline of British and Canadian investment.

TABLE 7

Foreign Direct Investment in the United States, 1950 and 1981

	1950		1981	
Country	millions of US$	%	millions of US$	%
Britain	1,168	34.4	15,527	17.3
Canada	1,029	30.3	12,212	13.6
Continental Europe	1,059	31.2	42,178	47.0
Japan	—	—	6,887	7.7
Other countries	134	4.0	12,955	14.4
Total	3,390	100.0	89,759	100.0

Source: U.S. Department of Commerce, Survey of Current Business, October 1961, August 1982.

The distribution of Canadian direct investment by major sectors of economic activity has exhibited two significant trends since the Second World War — the decline of investment in the utility and commercial sectors as a proportion of total foreign direct investment and a relative increase in investment in the industrial and financial sectors. In the 1970s, however, there was a remarkable resurgence of investment in the mining and petroleum industries, a relative decline in investment in manufacturing and a rapid increase in direct investment in the financial sector. Thus, the overall average annual rate of growth of Canadian direct investment in foreign countries between 1967 and 1977 was 12.7 per cent, but the rate was 22.8 per cent in the oil and gas sector, 21.7 per cent in the financial sector, 15.7 per cent in mining and refining, 15.1 per cent in the utility sector, 10.2 per cent in manufacturing, and only 5.3 per cent in the commercial sector. Table 8 gives a picture of the same phenomenon over a longer time period, summarizing the distribution of Canadian direct investment by sector of activity over the last forty years.

TABLE 8

Canadian Direct Investment in Foreign Countries, Percentage Distribution by Sector, 1939-79

Sector	1939	1949	1959	1969	1979
Manufacturing	43	60	59	58	50
Commerce				6	5
Mining and refining	18	10	11	7	10
Oil and gas			7	6	15
Utilities	37	30	20	15	6
Finance	2	1	1	6	13
Others			2	3	2

Source: Statistics Canada, Cat. 67-202, 1971 and 1983.

The distribution of Canadian direct investment by sector of activity varies significantly in different categories of host countries (see Table 9). Direct investment in the manufacturing sector is concentrated in the industrialized countries, while direct investment in mining is more likely to occur in developing countries. An exception to this rule is the concentration in the United States of Canadian direct investment in the petroleum sector.

Let us look at the place occupied by Canadian investment in each of the major host countries and the distribution in these countries by sector of activity. We have already seen that Canada is currently the third largest foreign investing country in the United States. In 1980 Canadian investment in the U.S. was heavily concentrated in industrial activities: 40 per cent in manufacturing, 26 per cent in the petroleum industry and 7 per cent in mining. A similar situation existed in Britain, the second largest host country for Canadian investment: 64 per cent of Canadian investment was in manufacturing, and 13 per cent was in the oil and gas industry.

TABLE 9

Distribution of Canadian Foreign Direct Investment by
Country, Broad Sectors, 1980

	Percentage		
Sector	United States	United Kingdom	Other countries
Manufacturing	61	14	25
Commerce	55	5	40
Mining and smelting	45	1	54
Oil and gas	77	6	17
Utilities	44	4	52
Finance	74	10	16
Others	67	11	22
Total	64	9	27

Source: Statistics Canada, Cat. 67-202 (Ottawa, 1983).

Canada was the second largest investing country in Britain, after the United States. Seagram, Hiram Walker, Inco, Massey-Ferguson and Alcan are among the leading Canadian investors.

Brazil was in fifth place among host countries for Canadian investment in 1977, with 2 per cent of the total. Canada was the fifth largest foreign investing country in Brazil in 1976, after the United States, West Germany, Japan and Switzerland. In that year Brascan was the largest foreign company in Brazil, through its subsidiary, Light-Serviços de Eletriciade (which would be nationalized in late 1978). Other Canadian companies such as Alcan Aluminium, Polysar, Acres International, Montreal Engineering and the Royal Bank were also active in Brazil.

The Caribbean is the third of the major host areas for Canadian direct investment. Among the more significant host countries within this region are Bermuda (the third largest host country), the Bahamas, Jamaica, and Trinidad and Tobago. Canadian banks and insurance companies along with a few industrial corporations such as Alcan in Jamaica stand out among Canadian investors. In a number of Caribbean countries Canada is the second largest foreign investing country after the United States.

Fourth among host countries for Canadian direct investment in

1980 was Australia, with 3 per cent of the total. Alcan Aluminium, Inco, Noranda Mines, Placer Development, Ford of Canada, Canada Packers and Moore Corporation were among the seventy Canadian companies with subsidiaries in Australia. Canada was one of the leading foreign investing countries in Australia after the United States and Britain.

In the most heavily industrialized countries of Europe and Latin America, Canadian direct investment occupies a much smaller place, although it is significant in some specific industries.

One question that has often been asked is: Does Canadian direct investment in foreign countries genuinely belong to Canadians, or is it really American investment carried out through subsidiaries in Canada? The example of the Ford Motor Company of Canada and its foreign operations is often mentioned in this regard. However, statistics show that the degree of Canadian ownership and control of Canada's foreign direct investment is increasing. In 1965, Canadian firms owned 56 per cent and controlled 64 per cent of Canadian direct investment in foreign countries. Fifteen years later, the proportion of Canadian ownership was 65 per cent while Canadian control had risen to 84 per cent. This increase in the ownership and control of foreign direct investment by Canadians is a reflection of Canadians' increased control over their own economy, a process that began in 1970 and has accelerated since then.

TABLE 10

Foreign Direct Investment in Brazil, Percentage Distribution by Investing Country, 1976

Country	%
United States	32.2
West Germany	12.4
Japan	11.2
Switzerland	10.8
Canada	5.4
United Kingdom	4.7
France	3.6
Others	19.7

Source: Central Bank of Brazil, 1977.

Canadian direct investment in foreign countries exhibits a high degree of corporate concentration. In 1976, sixteen firms, each with more than $100 million invested outside Canada, accounted for 65 per cent of total Canadian direct investment in foreign countries. An additional forty-nine firms, each with investments of between $25 million and $100 million outside Canada, accounted for another 21 per cent. Thus, more than 86 per cent of the total was in the hands of sixty-five firms. The sixteen leading firms each had an average of $466 million invested outside Canada, while the average for the second group of forty-nine firms was $50 million. It is safe to say that these sixty-five corporations are the real Canadian multinationals. The other 830 firms with investments outside Canada account for only 14 per cent of the total.

The sixteen giant Canadian multinationals, accounting for a very large proportion of Canadian direct investment in foreign countries, are: Alcan Aluminium, Bata Shoes, Brascan, Canada Packers, Cominco, Falconbridge Nickel, the Ford Motor Company of Canada, Inco, MacMillan Bloedel, Massey-Ferguson, Moore Corp., Noranda Mines (along with its wholly-owned subsidiary Canada Wire and Cable), Northern Telecom, Polysar, Seagram and Hiram Walker. Two of these companies, Falconbridge and Ford of Canada, are controlled in the United States. In the group of smaller Canadian multinationals are companies with major investments in either the United States or Britain. Among these are pulp and paper firms such as Domtar, Abitibi-Price and Consolidated-Bathurst; breweries such as Molson, John Labatt and Carling-O'Keefe; and steel companies such as Stelco, Dofasco and Algoma Steel. It should be remembered, however, that in 1978 there were no fewer than 535 industrial subsidiaries of 243 Canadian corporations in the United States.[19]

The Role of the Canadian Government

In general, it can be said that before 1970 Canadian capital became multinational with only minor intervention by the Canadian government. Starting in the late 1960s, however, the government's role became an increasingly active one. The main instrument of government intervention was the Export Development Corporation (EDC).

The EDC was established in October 1969 to succeed the Export Credits Insurance Corporation (ECIC), a crown corporation created by an act of parliament in 1945. The ECIC's original goal was to insure export credits so that exporters would be protected against non-payment by foreign buyers. In this way, the program facilitated bank financing of Canadian exports. A 1960 amendment to the ECIC's charter allowed it to undertake long-term financing services to help exporters of capital goods and firms of consulting engineers. Subsequent amendments eventually led to a complete rewriting of the act and the establishment of a new corporation in 1969. At this time, foreign investment insurance was added to the services offered by the corporation.

The EDC currently offers fourteen different services to Canadian corporations. Foreign investment insurance is one of the most infrequently used of these services. In 1979, for example, only two foreign investment insurance policies were underwritten for a total of $1.8 million,[20] while export insurance and guarantees amounted to more than $2 billion.

The investment insurance program is intended for investors in high-risk countries — in other words, in the Third World. Three major risks are covered: inconvertibility (the inability to repatriate profits or capital), expropriation, and war or revolution. An example of the kind of insurance policy provided by the EDC is the $25 million guarantee obtained by Canadian Superior Oil, a Calgary-based subsidiary of Superior Oil of Houston, against political risks incurred in oil production and exploration in the Dominican Republic.[21] As of April 1979, twenty-six countries had signed agreements with the EDC in connection with this program: eleven in the Caribbean (Antigua, Barbados, Belize, the Dominican Republic, Grenada, Jamaica, Montserrat, St. Kitts-Nevis, St. Lucia, St. Vincent, and Trinidad and Tobago), eight in Africa (Ghana, Gambia, Guinea, Liberia, Malawi, Morocco, Rwanda, and Senegal), five in Asia (Indonesia, Israel, Malaysia, Pakistan, and Singapore), and two in Oceania (Fiji and Western Samoa). This list of countries shows that it is not the major host countries for Canadian capital that are involved but rather a number of small Third World countries. Thus, it is not surprising that only 5.6 per cent of the $3.2 billion in Canadian direct investment in developing countries in 1977 was insured by the EDC. This program appears to have had only a marginal effect on the expansion of Canadian firms into the Third World.

The EDC also indirectly aids Canadian multinationals in another way — by financing the sale of Canadian equipment and services to their subsidiaries. For example, Inco subsidiaries in Guatemala and Indonesia obtained $26 million and $56 million respectively in EDC credits to buy Canadian-made capital goods.[22] It is difficult to quantify the significance of this form of EDC assistance to the international expansion of Canadian firms, but at first glance it does not appear to play a major role.

Another program of assistance to Canadian direct investment in foreign countries was established in October 1970 by the Canadian International Development Agency (CIDA). That year, CIDA set up a Business and Industry Division to encourage Canadian firms to invest in foreign countries. This division had two main programs. The first provided grants of up to $2,500 for "starter studies" (exploratory market surveys), while under the second program firms could obtain up to $25,000 for feasibility studies. CIDA's programs appear to have had an even smaller impact than the EDC's. Three years after the establishment of the division, CIDA has approved seventy-three starter studies and thirteen feasibility studies, on which it had spent a total of $310,000. Only one of these projects had come to fruition.[23] In September 1978, the business and industry program was replaced by a new and only slightly more ambitious industrial co-operation program. In eight years of operation, the original program had consumed $2 million, an infinitesimal sum compared to CIDA's total aid budget of $1.165 billion for 1978-79. This $2 million total was divided among some 300 starter and feasibility studies. Because of the small size of the grants, the clientele of the program — which was limited to companies whose stock was at least 51 per cent owned by Canadians — consisted of middle-sized firms.

The same division of CIDA also gathers and collates information on investment opportunities in developing countries and disseminates this information to potential Canadian investors. In addition, it stages conferences on investment opportunities in the Third World.

In the area of tax law and legislation concerning capital movements, Canada is one of the most liberal countries in the world. Companies investing in foreign countries escape the risk of double taxation because income taxes paid to a foreign government are deductible from Canadian income tax. This provision along with other complementary ones guarantees favourable tax treatment of foreign direct investment. In addition, Canada has never imposed exchange controls for investors or legislation restricting capital exports. Through these policies, the Canadian government has demonstrated an attitude of passive encouragement to foreign direct investment.[24]

Unlike other advanced countries such as the United States, Britain, France, West Germany and Belgium, Canada has no public agency that finances international development by providing direct financial co-operation with private investment. On the other hand, Canada does participate along with these same countries in a number of multilateral financial agencies, including the World Bank Group, the Asian Development Bank, the Caribbean Development Bank, and others.

The International Bank for Reconstruction and Development, or World Bank as it is generally known, was established in 1946. Its capital was made up of subscriptions from the member countries. The size of a country's subscription was based on its gross national product, and its vote was proportional to its subscription. As of the fall of 1971, the United States had 24.5 per cent of the vote, Britain had 10.1 per cent, West Germany 5.02 per cent, France 4.14 per cent, India 3.2 per cent, Canada 3.1 per cent and Japan 3.07 per cent. At that time, the vast majority of the bank's loans had been issued in the electricity and transportation sectors, and the beneficiaries of its aid were governments and publicly-owned corporations in developing countries.

In 1956, the World Bank established an affiliated institution, the International Finance Corporation (IFC), with the aim of lending money to private enterprise without government guarantees. The IFC's membership is the same as the World Bank's. In 1980 Canada's subscription to the IFC amounted to 4.58 per cent of its capital, while that of the United States was 33.35 per cent, Britain 12.38 per cent, West Germany 6.99 per cent and Japan 3.88 per cent. As of that date the IFC had approved 535 projects since its creation, for a total of $1.159 billion in loans and $245 million in equity investments. This aid went to private and joint public-private corporations in developing countries, including both locally-controlled firms and subsidiaries of multinationals.[25] Table 11 is a summary of the IFC's contributions to some Canadian multinationals.

A number of observations are in order about Table 11. First, these six projects account for only 1 per cent of the total number of projects approved by the IFC in its twenty-four years of existence. Second, the amount provided to Canadian multinationals represents only 2.4 per cent of the total committed by the IFC in loans and equity investments from 1956 to 1980. Third, the amounts provided by the IFC were substantial and covered a significant proportion of the cost of the projects. For example, the Bata SA Malagache project (Madagascar) had a total cost of US $5.23 million, of which $1.25 million was covered by the IFC loan. The estimated cost of Inco's Guatemala project was $100 million, of which $15 million was financed by the IFC. Only the largest Canadian multinationals

TABLE 11

Funds Committed by the International Finance Corporation to Projects Involving Canadian Multinationals, 1972-80

Year	Multinational	Country	Project	IFC commitment (US$ 000)
1972	Sherritt Gordon Mines	Philippines	Nickel mine	15,000
1972	Bata Shoes	Zambia	Shoe mfg.	1,100
1973	Bata Shoes	Zambia	Tanning	1,200
1974	Inco	Guatemala	Nickel mine	15,000
1975	Bata Shoes	Cameroon	Shoes	469
1980	Bata Shoes	Madagascar	Shoe mfg.	1,250

Source: International Finance Corporation, Annual Reports, 1956-1980.

appear willing or able to use the services of this international financial institution.

The situation is similar for the other international agencies mentioned. The Asian Development Bank was established in 1966. Two-thirds of its capital comes from twenty-nine Asian member countries while the other third comes from fourteen developed countries. Japan subscribes 17 per cent of its capital while Canada subscribes 7 per cent. However, of the $2.95 billion the bank has spent since its creation for the purchase of goods and services, only $83 million in contracts — or 2.77 per cent of the total — has gone to Canadian institutions. The major beneficiaries have been the large Canadian consulting engineering firms.[26]

The general impression that arises out of this overview is that the Canadian government places a wide range of direct and indirect incentives at the disposal of companies that want to expand outside Canada, although these incentives do not include loan financing or equity investment in subsidiaries. These public incentives to multinational expansion appear to be underutilized by Canadian corporations, and the role of the government does not appear to have been an essential one.

In other countries, governments have played a much more important role in encouraging corporations to expand internationally. Before the Second World War, Japanese firms had foreign subsidiaries, but they were largely concentrated in the Japanese colonies of Manchuria, Taiwan and Korea. After the loss of these colonies, Japan did not undertake direct capital exports again until 1951. Between 1951 and 1967 Japanese direct investment in foreign countries grew very slowly as the government encouraged domestic investment to reduce unemployment and increase exports. In 1968, however, the rapid growth of foreign direct investment by Japanese companies began. The manpower shortage in Japan, ecological considerations, trade barriers imposed by countries to which Japanese products were exported, and difficulties in obtaining raw materials all led the Japanese government first to remove the restrictions that had hindered the growth of Japanese firms in foreign countries and then actively to encourage their multinational expansion. It established a number of public agencies aimed at financing the expansion of Japanese companies abroad: the Overseas Economic Co-operation Fund, the Japan International Co-operation Agency, the Japan Overseas Development Corporation, the Japan Petroleum Development Corporation, and others. All these agencies supplied companies that wanted to invest abroad with a significant portion of the risk capital they needed. The Japanese government also provided highly attractive tax incentives to firms wishing to invest outside Japan. But financial incentives, important as they are, have not been the only means by which the Japanese government has encouraged foreign investment. It has also intervened in the negotiations between Japanese multinationals and host countries concerning large integrated projects such as the aluminum production schemes in Amazonia (Brazil) and Asahan (Indonesia), with the aim of protecting the national interest of Japan and the interests of its transnational corporations.

Canadian Multinationals in Perspective

Canada has always resisted being placed in the usual economic categories. Is it developed or underdeveloped? Industrialized or semi-industrialized? These questions can also be asked for the particular case of Canadian multinationals. Are Canadian multinationals like the multinationals based in developed countries, or are they more like the emerging multinationals of the semi-industrialized countries of the Third World? In other words, what is Canada's place in the "international pecking order" identified by Louis T. Wells, Jr.?

The first observation that must be made is that in the distribution of its foreign direct investment by geographical area and by economic sector, Canada is similar to the advanced industrial countries, and especially the United States. Thus, in 1980, Canada had 17 per cent of its foreign direct investment in developing countries, as compared to 25 per cent for the United States; the percentages for Britain, France and West Germany were all in the same range. Japan was the only industrialized country with more than 50 per cent of its foreign direct investment in developing countries, and this is consistent with the late date of Japanese multinational expansion and its concentration in light industry.[27] In other words, the geographical profile of Canadian capital in foreign countries shows us that it is competitive in major industrial markets. In this, Canadian multinationals are very different from those of other semi-industrialized countries such as Australia, India and Brazil, which spill over into less advanced economies such as Indonesia, Thailand or Ecuador.

In the distribution of its foreign direct investment by sector, Canada is again similar to the United States and the industrialized countries of Europe. Table 12 shows the distribution by sector of Canadian and American direct investment in 1980. The two distributions are remarkably close to each other, and the parallel is even more striking in the light of the almost identical figures for per capita foreign direct investment based in the two countries: US$940 for the United States, C$1,075 for Canada in 1980. By contrast, Japan had only US$275 per capita invested abroad in 1979, and 22 per cent of its foreign direct investment was in resource extraction while only 35 per cent was in manufacturing.[28]

Most of Canada's large multinationals are on *Fortune*'s list of the 500 largest industrial corporations outside the Untied States (and others, such as Bata Shoes and Polysar, should be on the list). The number of large corporations based in Canada clearly places it closer to small industrialized countries such as Sweden or Switzerland than to typical semi-industrialized countries (see Table 13).

Based on their size (both absolute and relative), their presence in the large American and European markets, their number, and the position they occupy in the industries in which they operate, Canadian multinationals resemble those of the advanced industrial countries much more than those of the major Latin American or Asian countries. In a 1980 article, Wells sketched the typical Third World multinational in the following terms: It has become skilled in serving small markets, it uses local capital goods, it modifies its products depending on the preferences of the particular market in which it is operating, it uses few well-known brand names, and it is

56

TABLE 12
Canadian and American Direct Investment in Foreign Countries by Sector, 1980

Sector	Percentage	
	Canada	U.S.
Manufacturing	42	42
Commerce	4	12
Mining and smelting	10	3
Oil and gas	21	22
Utilities	6	2
Finance	14	16
Others	2	2
Total (%)	100	100
Total ($ million)	25,800 (C$)	213,648 (US$)

Sources: U.S. Department of Commerce, *Survey of Current Business*, August 1981; Statistics Canada, Cat. 67-202 (Ottawa, 1983).

TABLE 13
Distribution of the 500 Largest Non-American Industrial Corporations by Country, Selected Countries, 1981

Country	number of corporations	Country	number of corporations
Japan	130	Australia	7
Britain	92	South Africa	7
West Germany	58	Finaland	6
France	38	Belgium	6
Canada	33*	Mexico	6
Sweden	22	Austria	3
Italy	14	Norway	3
Switzerland	11	India	2
Spain	11	Turkey	2
South Korea	10	Portugal	1
Netherlands	10	Argentina	1
Brazil	7	Venezuela	1

* Including 10 subsidiaries of foreign-owned companies.
Source: Fortune, August 23, 1982, p. 194.

quick to go into partnership with interests in the host country.[29] This description applies, for example, to such Argentinian multinationals as Siam Di Tella and Alpargatas, which operate in a number of Latin American countries.

It is not accurate, however, for Canadian multinationals, which include the world's second largest aluminum producer (Alcan), the world's largest shoe manufacturer (Bata Shoes), the world's largest and third largest distilleries (Seagram and Hiram Walker), North America's second largest telecommunications equipment manufacturer (Northern Telecom), the world's largest producer of business forms (Moore Corp.), the world's fourth largest producer of farm machinery (Massey-Ferguson), a corporation that produces 10 per cent of the world's synthetic rubber (Polysar Corp.), the world's largest and second largest nickel producers (Inco and Falconbridge), and the world's largest lead-zinc producer (Cominco). In other words, Canadian multinationals are not third-rate imitators, but are often at or near the top of their respective industries.

On the other hand, Canadian multinationals are most commonly found in industries with relatively little technological content. Buckley and Casson ranked the multinationals of nine industrialized countries according to the level of research performed by their subsidiaries.[30] West German multinationals headed the list: 88 per cent of their subsidiaries were in R&D-intensive industries such as chemicals, electrical and non-electrical machinery, and transportation equipment. At the bottom of the list were Japanese and Canadian multinationals, with only 50.5 and 50 per cent respectively of their subsidiaries in high-technology industries.

Let us compare Canadian multinationals with those of a typical semi-industrialized country. While Argentina does not publish statistics on its foreign direct investment, it is clear that only one Argentinian multinational, Bunge & Born, is comparable in size to the major Canadian multinationals. Bunge & Born is a private company that was founded in 1884 to export Argentinian grain. In the 1920s and 1930s it diversified within Argentina, expanding into the production of edible oils, cans, textiles, paints and chemical products. At the same time its grain-trading division became multinational, as it became active in Brazil, the United States, Australia, western Europe and Asia as well as Argentina. Later, its other operations became multinational as well, as it undertook the production of food, textiles and chemicals in Uruguay, Brazil, the United States and elsewhere. There are varying estimates of its total sales. In 1964, according to the journal *International Management,* they stood at US$2 billion. In 1974, the Buenos Aires periodical

Realidad Economica calculated the sales of the thirty-nine companies of the Bunge & Born group in Argentina at US$3.8 billion. Another Buenos Aires periodical, *Mercado,* placed the sales of the group's five major subsidiaries in Argentina at US$923 million. The group's American subsidiary, the Bunge Corporation, is the third largest American grain exporter. In the 1970s the Bunge Corporation became vertically integrated, buying and building edible oil factories and other food products plants in the United States at a rapid rate. [31]

Other Argentinian multinationals, such as Alpargatas and Siam Di Tella, are Third World multinationals in the sense defined by Wells. Alpargatas, founded in 1886 to manufacture shoes, established subsidiaries in Uruguay (1890), Brazil (1935) and elsewhere in Latin America. In 1971 the group's four leading subsidiaries had sales of US$141 million and employed 18,600 people in Argentina, Uruguay and Brazil. Alpargatas Argentina was the twenty-third largest company in Argentina in 1980 with sales of US$371 million, while the group's subsidiaries in Brazil and Uruguay were among the fifty largest firms in each of those countries. [32] Siam Di Tella, founded at the turn of the century to manufacture bread ovens, diversified into the production of household electrical appliances, metal pipes and heavy electrical equipment. Starting in 1928, it expanded into Brazil, Chile and Uruguay. Its expansion both inside and outside Argentina was based on imported technology. In 1970 its total sales were US$80 million; by 1980 its sales in Argentina alone were US$94 million. [33] Although Alpargatas and Siam Di Tella are the second and third largest Argentinian multinationals, they are much smaller than the major Canadian multinationals, and neither of them is active in any of the advanced industrial countries.

In this chapter, we have seen that despite the late date and dependent nature of Canadian industrialization, Canada has as many multinationals in proportion to its population as the advanced industrial countries. When we examined some of the characteristics of Canadian industry more carefully, we observed a high degree of foreign control, massive imports of technology in all its forms, and a low level of innovation. According to Raymond Vernon's product cycle theory, multinational expansion is the product of industrial invention. However, the evidence shows that there is little innovation in Canadian industry. Vernon's primary condition for international growth is not fulfilled.

On the other hand, Hymer's main condition for multinational expansion — corporate concentration — is fulfilled. Canada has one of the most heavily concentrated industrial structures of all the high-income countries. But the Hymer school does not see concentration as a sufficient condition in itself. Concentration only leads to transnational expansion if it produces certain advantages over potential competitors in the host countries. What kind of advantages do Canadian multinationals have that make them different from multinationals based in other recently industrialized countries? The thesis that underlies the observations in the remainder of this book is the following: Canadian multinationals are characterized by their capacity for quickly absorbing innovations originating in the United States and Britain, Canada's two leading trade partners.

This special capacity of Canadian multinationals is due to Canada's high degree of corporate concentration and the similarity between Canada's home market (high incomes, consumer tastes, etc.) and those of other advanced countries. Because Canada's industry is so concentrated, its corporations are on a scale comparable to European and Japanese companies. As a result, they are able to buy or imitate processes and products resulting from innovation in other countries. There is no semi-industrialized country whose firms have a similar ability. In addition, Canada's affinity with the United States and Britain in the areas of culture, language and trade and its geographical proximity to those countries give Canadian multinationals further advantages over firms based in semi-industrialized countries.

According to this thesis, Canada ranks with the semi-industrialized countries by virtue of its low level of innovation (which has been amply demonstrated by the Science Council of Canada) and with the advanced industrial countries by virtue of its foreign direct investment.

In the following chapters, this explanation will be confirmed by an analysis of the major Canadian multinationals in the utility, mining and manufacturing sectors. In conclusion, the specific ways in which Canadian multinationals absorb foreign technology will be characterized.

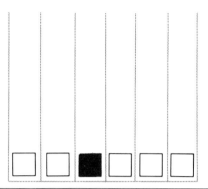

3 The Rise and Fall of the Utility Multinationals

At the end of the nineteenth century, Canadian promoters began to organize a remarkable group of transnational corporations in the utility sector, operating in Latin America and elsewhere. These corporations were concentrated in what are generally referred to as utilities in the narrow sense — street lighting, streetcars, gas, and the like — but were also frequently involved in steam railways and telephone service. Established between 1899 and 1914, they were among the largest foreign companies active in Mexico, Brazil and several other Latin American and Caribbean countries.

A number of questions can be asked about these companies. Their need for capital was very great, primarily because of the large scale of their fixed assets, and they met almost all of their capital needs by issuing bonds and preferred shares, a method of financing that was open to them because of their very stable return on investment. Hence, they resorted to the major capital markets for funds. In addition, the utility multinationals used technology from outside Canada (heavy electrical equipment, transmission lines, telephone exchanges and equipment, etc.). The main question these circumstances raise is the following: How were Canadian promoters able to build such large corporations when the major capital markets and technology they needed were not available in Canada? There is a simple answer to this question: The founders of the utility multinationals built their empires by resorting to foreign capital markets — especially the London and New York markets — and foreign (primarily American) technology. Actually bringing this about, however, was not such a simple matter.

In this chapter, some important aspects of the economics of the utility sector in North America that bear on the development of multinationals will be examined, and the growth and decline of Canadian and American multinationals over the twentieth century will be studied. Then, the development of the two major Canadian utility multinationals — Brazilian Traction, Light and Power and International Power — will be traced. Finally, the main conclusions that can be drawn from these case studies will be looked at. This discussion will focus on the generation and distribution of electricity, for while these corporations were marginally involved in such services as telephones, railways and water distribution, their main activity was electricity production and related services.

Multinationals and the Utility Sector

Modern electrical equipment for lighting, urban transit and industry had its beginnings in the late nineteenth century. Before 1880, cities were lit by gas, urban transportation was based on animal power, and the steam engine was used in industry. In the United States, voltaic arc lighting started to replace gas in the late 1870s. A few years later, Thomas Edison's incandescent bulb began to compete with the voltaic arc. The Edison system of electric lighting was first put into practice in the Wall Street district of New York City in 1882 by a subsidiary of the inventor's own company (founded in 1878). Technological innovations appeared at a rapid rate. The turbine, a European invention that was adopted and improved in the United States in the 1880s and 1890s, increased the capacity of electrical generating systems. Work on the large hydroelectric project at Niagara Falls began in 1893, and it led to a series of innovations. Between 1884 and 1887, Frank J. Sprague developed electric motors for industry and urban transportation. The first street railway run by electric power was established in 1888, and the innovation spread in spectacular fashion; by 1890, there were 180 electric streetcar systems operating or under construction in the United States.

That same year, Sprague's company was absorbed by Edison General Electric, which had grown out of Edison's original company. In 1892, Edison General Electric merged with the second largest American electricity producer to form General Electric, the world leader in the industry. Another company, Westinghouse Electric, appeared on the scene in 1886; the Westinghouse system was based on alternating current, and was able to compete with Edison's direct current systems. Finally, in 1901, the third and last of the major American heavy electrical equipment producers, Allis-Chalmers, was founded.

Protected by patents and taking advantage of the sector's technological complexity, these companies succeeded in preserving their market shares over a long period of time. Thus, in the period between 1900 and 1925, General Electric installed 65 per cent of the generating capacity in the United States, Westinghouse 25 per cent and Allis-Chalmers 9 per cent. These percentages were essentially the same for the period 1948 to 1963.[1]

The Canadian heavy electrical equipment industry quickly came under the control of the American manufacturing giants. When the two leading American companies merged to form General Electric in 1892, there was a corresponding merger of their subsidiaries in Canada. Between 1895 and 1923 Canadian General Electric was controlled in Canada and operated under licence, but GE subsequently regained control. Westinghouse began operations in Canada in 1896, while Canadian Allis-Chalmers was absorbed by Canadian General Electric in 1913. Thus, production in Canada of heavy electrical equipment (turbines, generators, circuit breakers and switches for generating stations) became wholly foreign-controlled, and Canadian utility multinationals could not grow except by using foreign technology.[2] Even on a world scale, there have never been many challengers to the American giants. At the turn of the century a German company, Halske, was the main competitor, while today, only a handful of companies — notably Brown Boveri of Switzerland, Kraftwerk Union of West Germany and General Electric Co. Ltd. of England — compete with the American manufacturers. In the U.S. market itself, these non-American companies have only a marginal share.[3]

In addition to the manufacturing giants and the utility companies, engineering firms have also played a significant role in developing the technology of providing electricity service. When the international growth of the utility multinationals was in its early stages, projects were often planned and executed by individual engineers. At the end of the nineteenth century, however, firms of consulting engineers began to appear, first in the United States and Europe and later in Canada. A consulting engineering firm would be placed in charge of planning and managing the civil construction aspects of a project (buildings, embankments, dikes, bridges, and so forth) and choosing the necessary heavy equipment. A number of these firms also provided technical advice to existing utility companies. The first firm of consulting engineers in the electrical services sector was founded in the United States in 1889,[4] while the leading Canadian firm, Montreal Engineering, was not established until 1907. In the course of the twentieth century, these engineering firms have become international, extending their operations into many countries through subsidiaries and agents.

The relationship among the three components of the electrical services industry has been a constantly changing one. From the time it was founded, General Electric established utility companies to assure itself of a captive market for electrical equipment. Its most important creation in this area was the Electric Bond and Share Company, which was incorporated in 1905 and became the largest American holding company in the electrical services field. For its part, Bond and Share established American & Foreign Power, a holding company for utilities operating outside the United States. This company will be discussed in more detail further on. Bond and Share also established Ebasco Services to provide the technical expertise the group needed. In 1924, under pressure from the U.S. government, General Electric sold its interest in Bond and Share, but the commercial link remained.

General Electric's utility interests helped it retain its leadership position, ahead of its rival Westinghouse which did not establish significant subsidiaries in the utility field. Meanwhile, some American consulting engineering firms, notably that of Samuel Insull, established utility companies in both the United States and Latin America. Ownership links between equipment manufacturers and utility companies were outlawed by the Public Utility Companies Act in 1935, but informal commercial links still persisted.

In Canada, the equipment manufacturers did not play any role in the establishment of the utility multinationals. The Canadian utility multinationals initially used the services of foreign consulting engineering firms, while later they contributed to the creation of Canadian engineering firms and sometimes founded such firms themselves, as we shall see further on. First, however, let us look at the North American utility multinationals as a group.

To understand these companies, it will be useful to identify a number of relevant characteristics that were common to American and Canadian utility multinationals. First, they were holding companies that controlled subsidiaries operating primarily outside their country of origin. Thus, Brazilian Traction was a Canadian holding company whose two main subsidiaries, Sao Paulo Tramway, Light and Power and Rio de Janeiro Tramway, Light and Power, provided a variety of services to the two largest cities in Brazil; Brazilian Traction did not provide any similar service in Canada. International Power had a variety of subsidiaries in a number of Latin

American countries and one in Newfoundland, which was not yet part of Canada. Almost all of American and Foreign Power's operations were in Latin America.

In other words, the parent companies were essentially financial institutions. Their main function was to provide capital to their subsidiaries by selling securities, shares and bonds on the financial markets in the advanced capitalist countries. They floated these issues in London, New York, Brussels, Paris or Berlin and invested the proceeds in securities of their subsidiaries. The utility multinationals' ability to raise capital provided them with a decisive advantage over their local competitors, as a result of two imperfections in capital markets. In the first place, the major financial markets were the only ones that could provide utilities with capital in the quantities and time frame required for them to build their huge structures and put their vast systems into operation, and between 1890 and 1914 it would have been difficult if not impossible for companies based in underdeveloped countries to gain access to these markets. The creation of large holding companies was encouraged by a second imperfection: Giant corporations were necessarily endowed with greater credibility and financial stability — and as a result had greater borrowing capacity — than small corporations based either in the economic centre or in the periphery.

The second function that the utility holding company performed was the provision of technical services to its foreign subsidiaries. The holding company recruited the technicians whom the subsidiaries needed to bring their projects to completion, plan the expansion of their networks and negotiate the purchase of machinery and equipment. In the late nineteenth century, these services were often provided by individual engineers who joined the company as executives or even as partners. In the twentieth century, a holding company either relied on firms of consulting engineers, or, more often, established a group of experts in electrical engineering affiliated with the company. These engineers or engineering firms were familiar with the turbines, generators, transmission lines, electric motors, telephone equipment, rolling stock and other equipment manufactured in the major industrialized countries and could draw up plans with a view towards using or adapting these products in new markets. The engineers were, of course, based in the same countries that produced the equipment, and the host countries for the utility multinationals' investments had no similar technical personnel. This easy access to a technology that did not exist in the host countries constituted the second advantage held by utility multinationals based in the advanced countries.

Another significant characteristic of these holding companies was the key role of their founders in providing access to capital markets. The utility multinationals came to these markets as new companies seeking vast quantities of capital for overseas investment, and such companies needed the backing of businessmen who enjoyed considerable prestige and were well known to the brokerage houses, the financial community and the investing public. In Canada, this role was filled by such business people as Sir William Van Horne, Sir William Mackenzie and Max Aitken (later Lord Beaverbrook). These Canadian promotors faced an especially tough challenge, for their companies were foreign in a dual sense to investors in London and other major financial centres; not only did they invest in Latin America, but they also had their head offices in Toronto or Montreal. In compensation for this challenge, promoters could reap considerable profit by establishing new companies, especially utility holding companies organized as large and complicated pyramids with most of their assets far away from the investors. All indications are that it was common practice to water stock and give assets inflated values. These practices entailed a very substantial profit margin for the holding companies' founders, who became rich through what amounted to a translation of the advantages we have noted into personal capital.[5]

In sum, the "specific advantages" (to use Hymer's term) enjoyed by multinational corporations based in the advanced countries in the utility sector consisted of their access to the major financial markets and the necessary technology. After the Second World War, these advantages steadily eroded in Latin America, where Canadian and American direct investment in the utility sector was concentrated. The larger countries in the region — Argentina, Brazil, Mexico, Colombia, Venezuela — eventually mastered the technology, and now have most of the engineering services they need to plan, build, maintain and expand their electrical systems and related services, even if they still have to import most of the heavy equipment. In addition, new financial institutions — international ones such as the World Bank and the Inter-American Development Bank and national ones such as the U.S. Agency for International Development, the Canadian International Development Agency and publicly-controlled development banks in the host countries — place capital at the service of local utility companies, which are generally government-owned corporations.

As a result, the advantages enjoyed by the multinationals based in the advanced countries have eroded, and the door has been opened to both the establishment of local competitors and nationalization.

This process of erosion is essentially complete in Latin America. The model of the obsolescing bargain helps us to understand the cycle that has seen the utility multinationals rise and then decline. In the utility sector, the fixed assets are huge, the risk stage is concentrated at the beginning of operations, and the host country can buy the material elements of the technology so long as it has a minimum of engineering capability. All these factors combine to erode the multinationals' negotiating power after a few decades of operation. In this sense, utility miltinationals are similar to mining and oil companies and undergo a comparable cycle of expansion, maturity and decline. The period of the cycle depends on the learning capacity and degree of industrialization of the host country. In Latin America, this period has been shortest in Argentina, somewhat longer in Mexico and Brazil, and longer still in Venezuela and Ecuador, while in Bolivia the cycle has still not been completed.

We have noted that the parent corporations were financial institutions and their main advantage was their access to major capital markets. These characteristics of the utility multinationals made it impossible for them to devise a fall-back plan once their bargaining power eroded. They could not depend on either a stream of innovations or a protected technological monopoly, and as a result they were doomed to disappear. In 1967, American & Foreign Power was absorbed by Electric Bond and Share, which became a closed-end investment company. Brazilian Traction remained a holding company, but it gradually withdrew from Brazil and reinvested its funds in Canada. International Power was dissolved in 1977. In other words, the only strategy open to the utility multinationals to deal with the erosion of their bargaining power was a defensive one.

The Growth and Decline of the Utility Multinationals

From the turn of the century until the late 1960s, Latin America was the major host region for American and Canadian direct investment in the utility sector. In 1914, for example, Latin America accounted for 74 per cent of American direct investment in the utility sector outside the United States. Mexico and Cuba were the leading host countries, and retained that status despite increasing amounts of American capital invested in Argentina, Brazil, Chile, Ecuador, Colombia and Venezuela.[6] In 1960, the lion's share of American direct investment in the utility sector still went to Latin

America. After 1960, however, the level of investment in this sector began to decline, both in absolute terms (net disinvestment) and relative to other activities. While in 1960 American investment in Latin American utilities totalled $1.18 billion, this total was only $610 million in 1970 and $287 million in 1977.[7] And while investment in utilities represented 12 per cent of total American direct investment in foreign countries in 1950, this proportion was only 2 per cent in 1978. All the evidence suggests that in the 1960s and 1970s the American utility multinationals were undergoing a process of erosion and coming to the end of their cycle.

Canadian utility multinationals followed a similar course, although the decline phase of the cycle came later. Canadian companies began to provide utility services in Latin America and the Caribbean at the turn of the century — Mexican Light and Power (incorporated in 1902); Sao Paulo Tramway, Light and Power (1899); Rio de Janeiro Tramway, Light and Power (1904); Barcelona Traction, Light and Power (1911); and a myriad of smaller companies in Cuba, Jamaica, Bolivia, Trinidad and Tobago, Venezuela, British Guiana and Mexico. Before examining the development of the two largest Canadian multinationals, we will look at the general characteristics of the cycle undergone by the utility multinationals in Latin America.

The first steam railways in Cuba, Peru, Colombia and Mexico were built in the 1830s, but the railway construction boom in the major Latin American countries took place only in the years 1880-1914.[8] The railways were built with the help of British, American or, less often, French or German capital and technology. In the same era, Canada was building its three transcontinental railways, also with the help of imported capital and technology. It played a marginal role in Latin American railway development — notably in Cuba — but was in no position to do more.

The electric age began in Latin America around 1900, about twenty years later than in North America, and by this time Canada had built its first electric generating stations and Canadian urban transit had become electrified. The great railway promoters (such as Sir William Van Horne of the Canadian Pacific and William Mackenzie and Donald Mann of the Canadian Northern) and a few financiers such as Max Aitken quickly learned the art of combining local resources with foreign equipment and capital. Their previous activities had given them the necessary contacts in the London and New York financial markets to float bond issues for international utility companies. This small group of promoters, surrounded by their lawyers, financial advisers and engineers, was responsible for a great majority of Canada's transnational utility corporations.

At the end of the nineteenth century, Canadians began to compete with German, Italian, British, American and Belgian entrepreneurs in the installation of electric generating stations, lighting systems and streetcar networks in Latin America. Four major groups of Canadian promoters were involved in this activity. In Toronto, Mackenzie and Mann, with the help of the American engineer F.S. Pearson, formed companies that obtained hydroelectric, lighting and tramway concessions for Mexico City, the Brazilian cities of Sao Paulo and Rio de Janeiro, and Barcelona, Spain. From Montreal, Max Aitken ran operations in the Caribbean and later in Latin America; initially he used the services of the New York firm J.G. White Engineers, but he subsequently established his own firm of consulting engineers. Also from Montreal, Sir William Van Horne controlled a number of electricity and railway companies in Cuba and elsewhere in the Caribbean. And a group of Halifax financiers including John F. Stairs and R.E. Harris was active in Trinidad and other Caribbean islands.

Meanwhile, German interests had obtained utility concessions in Buenos Aires, Santiago de Chile and Valparaiso; the Italians controlled the utilities of Lima and competed with the Germans in Buenos Aires; the British were entrenched in Caracas, La Paz and elsewhere; and the Americans were in Havana and the middle-sized cities of Mexico. The First World War eliminated the German companies and weakened the other European interests, and the major American companies came on the scene at this time. In 1913 the Germans were the leading exporters of electrical equipment to Argentina, Chile and Mexico. Ten years later the American manufacturers were the leaders in Chile and Mexico, although in Argentina the Germans had recovered from the ravages of the war and caught up to the Americans again. In the years between the wars, Germany remained the world's leading exporter of utility equipment, followed by Britain and the United States; these three countries supplied at least three-quarters of the world market. Europe was the Germans' primary market, while the British supplied their own empire and the Americans sold to Latin America and Canada.[9] This situation reflected the control of utilities in the less developed countries by multinational corporations based in the manufacturing nations, since each electrical services multinational tended to use machinery produced in its home country. An exception to this pattern, of course, was Canada, which was not listed among electrical equipment exporting countries before the Second World War.

We have already mentioned the establishment in 1923 of American & Foreign Power, a subsidiary of Electric Bond and Share, itself a holding company controlled by the American giant General Electric. American & Foreign Power promoted the electrification of a number of Latin American cities and took control of several European and American utility companies. When American & Foreign Power was founded, Bond and Share turned over companies in Cuba, Panama and Guatemala to its new subsidiary. Four years later, American & Foreign Power had acquired interests in Ecuador, Mexico, Brazil, Colombia and Venezuela.[10] Thus, in a few years American & Foreign Power became the largest foreign multinational in Latin America. Table 1 is a summary of American & Foreign Power's activities when the company was at its height.

In 1941, American & Foreign Power had total assets of $706 million, while the assets of Brazilian Traction, the largest Canadian company in Latin America, amounted to $481 million. But while American & Foreign Power's holdings were dispersed over eleven Latin American countries (including the capitals of seven of them), Brazilian Traction's were concentrated in Brazil.

Unlike their rivals based in other countries, the Canadian companies were based on the use of foreign technology and capital. Only the control of these companies was Canadian. Thus, as of 1913 the *Monetary Times* estimated that the capital of Canadian utility companies in Mexico was $240 million (shares and bonds outstanding) of which almost $200 million was held by British investors.[11] And in the course of the year 1911, Canadian international utility companies issued a total of $26.8 million in shares and bonds, 98.8 per cent of which were sold in Britain.[12] During the First World War, however, Canadian financiers began to turn more towards the American and Canadian capital markets.

It has already been noted that before 1940 Canada was not an exporter of technology to Latin America except on a marginal basis. Thus, the expansion phase of the Canadian multinationals was of necessity based on foreign and especially American technology. More detailed information for each company shows the same picture. All the equipment for Sao Paulo Tramway, Light and Power, for both electricity production and urban transport, was supplied by General Electric in the United States.[13] In 1905 Mexican Light and Power (Mexlight) built its hydroelectric plant at Nexaca, one of the largest of its time, with turbogenerators built by Escher, Wyss & Co. of Zurich, alternators from Siemens in Berlin, and transfor-

TABLE 1
American & Foreign Power in Latin America, 1941

Country	Number of cities, towns & villages served	Major cities	Regional population
Argentina	170	Cordoba, Santa Fé Tucuman, Mondoza, Parana, Mar del Plata	2,580,000
Brazil	304	Pernambuco, Porto Alegre, Bahia, Belo Horizonte, Campinas, Niteroi, Curitiba	5,165,000
Chile	38	Santiago, Valparaiso, Via del Mar, Nunoa, Providencia	1,484,000
Colombia	24	Barranquilla, Cali, Palmira, Buga, Santa Marta	577,000
Costa Rica	36	San José, Cartago	193,000
Cuba	215	Havana, Santiago, Camagüey, Matanzas, Cienfuegos	1,662,000
Ecuador	2	Guayaquil, Riobamba	164,000
Guatemala	12	Guatemala City, Antigua, Escuintla	228,000
Mexico	226	Puebla, Mérida, Orizaba, San Luis Potosi, Tampico, Veracruz, Leon	1,926,000
Panama	8	Panama City, Colon, Cristabal	218,000
Venezuela	12	Caracas, Victoria, Los Teques	344,000
Total	1,047		14,541,000

Source: Moody's Manual of Investments, New York, 1942, p. 1440.

mers and circuit breakers from General Electric in Schenectady, N.Y.[14] West India Electric, which supplied Kingston, Jamaica with electricity, bought its turbines from Stilwell-Bierce & Smith-Vaile Co. of Dayton, Ohio and its generators from General Electric in 1901.[15] S. Morgan Smith, a turbine manufacturer in York, Pennsylvania, supplied several Canadian companies operating in Latin America on a number of occasions.[16] There is no instance before 1940 in which Canadian equipment manufacturers are listed as suppliers to any Canadian utility multinationals. Thus, foreign technology was at the root of the expansion phase of these multinationals. And in addition, most of the engineers who planned these companies' projects and were in charge of their construction were either American or British, at least in the first decade of the companies' existence.

After the Second World War, Canada became one of the suppliers of equipment to its own electricity generation multinationals. But even then the orders went to subsidiaries of American corporations, which were the only companies in Canada that manufactured the equipment in question. Thus, between 1947 and 1951, Brazilian Traction spent $160 million to supply its Brazilian operations. Of this total, 39 per cent was spent in Brazil, 31 per cent in Canada, 23 per cent in the United States, 4 per cent in the United Kingdom and 3 per cent in other countries. In Brazil, the company bought lumber, construction materials, office equipment, fuel, and the like, while in Canada it bought heavy equipment such as generators, turbines, large transformers, and circuit breakers for generating stations. Its two largest suppliers in Canada were Canadian Westinghouse and Canadian General Electric.[17]

Having shown that the Canadian utility multinationals grew on the basis of foreign technology and capital, let us look at the distribution of their operations at their height, at the end of the Second World War. Most of the electricity generated in Brazil, Mexico, Bolivia, El Salvador and Jamaica was produced under the control of Canadian companies. In Brazil, subsidiaries of Brazilian Traction and American & Foreign Power accounted for almost 80 per cent of electricity production. The Canadian firm Mexlight generated about 55 per cent of Mexico's electricity while American & Foreign Power supplied 30 per cent. In Argentina Buenos Aires was supplied by European interests while American & Foreign Power was the largest producer in Venezuela, followed by the Canadian-based International Power. In Chile, American & Foreign Power was the dominant company.[18]

The decline of the utility multinationals began in the 1940s when Argentina nationalized about a third of American & Foreign Power's plants. In 1950, American & Foreign Power entered into negotiations with a view to selling all its holdings in Argentina to that country's government. Argentina was at the time the most highly industrialized country in Latin America and it was technologically capable of running its own electric companies, tramways and other utilities. In the 1950s and 1960s, the remaining foreign utility companies in Argentina were nationalized. In 1960 the government of Mexico — which already generated 40 per cent of the country's electricity — nationalized Mexlight and the Mexican operations of American & Foreign Power.[19] In Brazil, the federal government established Eletrobras in 1954 and developed its own electric production facilities, which existed side by side with the systems owned by the governments of the large industrial states and private foreign companies. Eletrobras bought American & Foreign Power's holdings in 1965 and those of the Light (Brazilian Traction) in 1978.[20]

Similar developments occurred in other Latin American countries. American & Foreign Power's holdings in Cuba were confiscated in 1960 while its Colombian interests were purchased by the government in 1961-62. Venezuela bought American & Foreign Power's assets in 1964 and International Power's in 1975. American & Foreign Power sold its properties in Chile to the government of that country in 1965. By the time American & Foreign Power merged with Bond and Share in December 1967, bringing down the final curtain on its activities, the one-time utility multinational no longer controlled a single electric company.

Brazilian Traction, Light and Power

The largest Canadian utility company operating outside Canada was Brazilian Traction, Light and Power, renamed Brascan in 1969. Brazilian Traction was the product of a 1912 merger of two Canadian electric companies active in Brazil's two largest cities — Sao Paulo Tramway, Light and Power and Rio de Janeiro Tramway, Light and Power.

Sao Paulo Tramway was the older of these two companies. Its founders included William Mackenzie of the Canadian Northern Railway: Frederick Nicholls, another Toronto financier who from 1903 was involved along with Mackenzie in Electrical Development, one of the electric companies operating at Niagara Falls; Dr. F.S. Pearson, an American engineer; Senator George A. Cox of Canada Life; lawyers from the Toronto firm of Blake, Lash and Cassel;

and J.R. Plummer of the Canadian Bank of Commerce. This group was involved in the establishment of a number of companies in Canada in railways, electricity and the industrial sector.

Sao Paulo, which in the twentieth century has become the industrial and commercial centre of Brazil, was already one of the largest cities in Latin America in 1900, with a population of 240,000. However, its electric service was limited to a few small thermal stations and its urban transit consisted of animal-drawn streetcars. Sao Paulo Tramway hired an American engineer, H. Cooper, and opened an electric streetcar service in 1900 and a hydroelectric generating station in 1901. Most of the equipment was supplied by General Electric in the United States. The first hydroelectric station was built on the Tiete River, thirty-seven kilometres from Sao Paulo. Construction began on another hydroelectric station, eighty-eight kilometres from the city, in 1908; it was inaugurated in 1914. Meanwhile, the capacity of the first station was doubled. By this time, the company had acquired a monopoly of electricity service and urban transit in Sao Paulo.

Soon afterwards, the same group of Toronto promoters bought the German and Belgian companies that provided electricity, lighting, streetcar and telephone service to Rio, then the capital of Brazil and a city of 750,000 people in 1900. Although the major European companies had been established for decades, they were absorbed by Rio de Janeiro Tramway, founded in Canada in 1904. Four years later the Canadian company inaugurated its first hydroelectric station, built under the direction of another American engineer. The company also electrified the streetcar lines and built a new gas plant. These developments were again accomplished with American-made equipment, as was the improvement of Rio's telephone system.[21]

These enterprises were financed through the sale of bonds and shares, principally on the London market and to a lesser extent in Paris and Brussels. Thus, all of the $10.5 million in securities issued by the two companies in 1912 was sold in Britain, while in 1909 Rio de Janeiro Tramway issues appeared on the Paris and Brussels markets.[22] This method of financing explains why each of the companies occasionally included English, French or Belgian financiers on its board of directors, although the Toronto group retained a majority on the board, the key administrative posts, and control of the companies.

The two companies were merged into Brazilian Traction, Light and Power in 1912. The new company was incorporated in Canada, and its capitalization, at $120 million, brought a large profit to the promoters, especially Mackenzie and Pearson. Under the presidency of a Toronto lawyer, Sir Alexander Mackenzie, Brazilian Traction issued no securities between 1915 and 1928. Instead, it financed its expansion from undistributed profits, so that the company's real assets could catch up to their book value, which had been inflated at the time of the merger.[23] Between 1924 and 1944 Brazilian Traction increased the size of the Sao Paulo system by building the huge Cubatao hydroelectric station, which was conceived by A.W.K. Billings, an American engineer who joined the company in 1922. In 1929, Brazilian Traction bought the utility company in the port city of Santos, which owned electricity, lighting, gas, water and urban transit concessions and equipment in Sao Paulo's Outlet to the sea. The company also began to enlarge the Rio electric generating plant in 1938; three turbines — two made in Switzerland and the third in Canada — and an American generator were installed during the Second World War.

After one last stock issue in 1928, Brazilian Traction followed a policy of internal financing. In 1948, it received a $75 million loan from the World Bank. This was the first loan by the bank to a private utility company, and it was increased to $90 million in 1951. In addition, the company floated a $10 million bond issue on the Canadian market in 1950. At that time, it had an electric capacity of 932,265 kilowatts, some 400,000 telephones in operation, 220,000 customers for its gas and 29,000 for its water service. It was the largest company in Brazil with more than 45,000 employees, and one of the largest utility companies in the world.[24] The money it raised was used to buy equipment; 9 per cent of the funds were spent in Brazil, 31 per cent in Canada and 60 per cent elsewhere. The major "Canadian" suppliers were subsidiaries of foreign (mostly American) companies: the list was headed by Canadian General Electric and Canadian Westinghouse and included other American-owned firms such as Northern Electric, Dominion Engineering, Canadian Allis-Chalmers, Ford of Canada and General Motors of Canada, and British-owned ones such as Canadian Vickers, English Electric and British Metal Corp.[25] In 1965, the company again received a loan to finance its expansion; this loan totalled $40 million, of which $25 million was to be spent in the United States and the rest in Brazil.[26] The pattern of growth based on foreign capital and technology never changed throughout the company's history.

Public authorities in Brazil began to take over Brazilian Traction's interests in the late 1940s. The company turned its Sao Paulo streetcar service over to the city in 1947 and did the same in Santos in 1952; both services were unprofitable. Meanwhile, there was growing discontent among Brazilians with two aspects of the company's electricity service. First, from 1946 on, even though the company continued expanding, it was unable to meet demand, and there was a growing waiting list for service. Throughout the postwar period, electricity was rationed, the quality of service declined and blackouts were common. Judith Tendler has shown that these problems were partly due to the rapid growth of the Brazilian economy, which was concentrated primarily in the Rio-Sao Paulo corridor.[27] Second, Brazilians increasingly complained about the company's rates. Brazilian Traction had won acceptance for its rates between 1900 and the Second World War, but after 1945 resistance to its rate increases became more active. On the one hand, the company maintained that it was not making enough profit to expand its system to meet demand; on the other hand, customers were reluctant to pay higher electric bills for deteriorating service. The result was a highly involved rate system, which a variety of forms of compensation provided by the Brazilian government only made even more complicated.[28]

With the creation of Eletrobras in 1954, the Canadian-American electricity monopoly in Brazil came to an end. From 1956 on, Brazilian Traction raised no objection as the Brazilian federal government and the governments of the states encompassing its concession area (Sao Paulo, Minas Gerais and Rio) became involved in electricity generation. And after 1963, Brazilian Traction no longer expanded its generating facilities and concentrated on the distribution sector. The Brazilian companies were now capable of planning and running electric generating stations and related services, although most of the heavy equipment was still imported. American & Foreign Power was nationalized by Eletrobras in 1965, and the next year Brazilian Traction sold its telephone service for $96 million. It was required to reinvest 75 per cent of this amount in Brazil, and it established three Brazilian holding companies as umbrellas for a number of firms operating in the financial, manufacturing and mining sectors in Brazil.[29] In 1967, Brazilian Traction incorporated its electricity services subsidiaries in Brazil under the name of Light-Serviços de Eletricidade, of which it held 83 per cent. The same year, the Toronto holding company began to acquire Canadian subsidiaries.[30] It sold its gas service to the Brazilian government in 1969, and in December 1978 Eletrobras bought the Light for $380 million. At that time, the book value of Brascan's shares in the Light was $840 million, and the Light's total assets were carried on the books at $2.2 billion.[31]

The sale of the Light to Eletrobras marked both the end of the cycle for utility multinationals in Brazil and the last act for Canadian transnationals in this sector. Brazilians had acquired the necessary expertise in engineering and management, the bargaining power of foreign interests in the sector had steadily declined, and the advantages enjoyed by the Canadian multinational had ultimately eroded.

International Power

Another group of Latin American utility companies owed its beginnings to the Montreal financier Max Aitken, later Lord Beaverbrook. Aitken was a banker and the owner of Royal Securities, one of the leading Canadian brokerage houses, founded in Montreal in 1902. Through Royal Securities, he bought and refinanced a number of utility companies, including one in Canada (Calgary Power) and others in the Caribbean (West Indies Electric, Porto Rico Railways, Trinidad Electric, Demerara Electric, Camagüey Electric).[32] After initially employing American consulting engineers, Aitken also established his own consulting engineering firm, Montreal Engineering, in 1907. Today known as Monenco, it is Canada's second largest firm of consulting experts and managers in the energy field, and one of the foremost such firms in the world. Aitken capped his Montreal career by bringing about some of the most spectacular mergers in the history of Canadian industry — including the creation of Canada Cement, which gained an absolute monopoly of Canadian cement production, and that of Stelco, which a few years later became the leading firm in the Canadian steel oligopoly — and then left for England in 1910.

In 1919, Aitken sold Royal Securities, Montreal Engineering, Calgary Power and some Caribbean electric companies to his associate Izaak W. Killam. Seven years later, Killam established a holding company to control some of the firms acquired by Royal Securities through its refinancing arrangements. A number of Halifax, Saint John, N.B., and Montreal financiers became minority partners in this new holding company, International Power, although Killam remained its president and controlling shareholder until his death thirty years later.

At the time of its founding the group included six Latin American companies. The oldest of these was Demerara Electric, founded in 1899, which owned the electric generating station and provided lighting and electric streetcar service in Georgetown, the capital of British Guiana. Porto Rico Railways had been founded in 1907 with the aim of purchasing a number of companies providing electricity, lighting and streetcar services to the Puerto Rican capital, San Juan. It also supplied electricity to a number of other towns in the eastern part of the island and owned a steam railway. Bolivia Power, purchased from British interests, had operated a hydroelectric generating station since 1910 and provided lighting, streetcar and telephone service to La Paz, the Bolivian capital and a city of 110,000 people. Newfoundland Light and Power had been established in 1900 to provide electricity, lighting and streetcar service to the Newfoundland capital, St. John's, which had a population of 38,000 in 1926. Venezuela Power provided electricity through thermal generation to Maracaibo (which with a population of 75,000 was Venezuela's second largest city) and through gas generation to Barquisimeto. Finally, San Salvador Electric Light provided electricity and lighting service to San Salvador, the capital of El Salvador with a population of 70,000, and to sixteen other communities (with populations totalling 50,000) in the Central American country. All these firms were under the absolute or majority control of the Montreal holding company. In 1928, International Power also purchased a controlling interest in Oruro Light and Power, which provided electricity and lighting services to Oruro, the third largest city in Bolivia with a population of 40,000.[33]

International Power differed from Brazilian Traction in a number of ways. First of all, it was much smaller, with assets in 1929 of $28 million, about one-tenth of the size of its Toronto rival. Second, it had a more diversified base of operations, with subsidiaries in five Latin American countries and Newfoundland from the time of its establishment (Calgary Power, although controlled by the same owners, was never part of the holding company). Third, because of its size it did not need as much capital, and it used the growing Canadian capital market to a greater extent (although not exclusively); its shares were listed only on the Montreal and New York exchanges. Fourth, International Power was organized at a time when Canada was developing a degree of technological capability in the hydroelectric field, although it depended on American and European manufacturers — and later their Canadian subsidiaries — for all of its heavy equipment supplies. Thus, it put Montreal Engineering in charge of developing its hydroelectric generating stations in Bolivia in 1926. The growth of Montreal Engineering paralleled that of International Power, and it was only during the Second World War that the engineering firm received its first contract (from the Canadian government) outside the confines of the holding company.[34] Twenty years later Montreal Engineering was a firm of consulting engineers with an international reputation, and in 1962 the United Nations entrusted it with the responsibility for a study of electricity production in the industrial heart of Brazil.[35]

Three new companies were added to the International Power group during its expansion phase. It took control of a company in Venezuela in 1930, one in El Salvador in 1931, and finally, Monterrey Railway, Light and Power in 1935. This last company, originally a German venture, had in 1905 fallen under the control of Mackenzie and Mann, who had established its head office in Toronto. It supplied electricity, lighting, streetcar, gas and water service to Monterrey, one of the largest cities in Mexico.

This expansion through foreign capital and technology had a number of ramifications. First of all, several multinationals organized by Canadians soon fell under foreign control. Barcelona Traction and Mexican Light and Power passed into the hands of Belgian financiers, while Canadian-promoted electric companies in Cuba were bought by American interests after a few years of existence. Only two of the five large international groups organized by Canadians — Brazilian Traction and International Power — remained under Canadian control. In addition, in the period before the second World War, while the Canadian subsidiaries of American and British manufacturers supplied the Canadian domestic market, the existence of the Canadian utility companies did not lead to the creation of a local heavy equipment exporting industry. On the other hand, the Canadian utility multinationals did help create some of the largest firms of consulting experts and managers in North America in the field of electrical energy. These consulting firms played an essential role in the management of the international electrical services companies. We noted how Montreal Engineering was a product of the multinational expansion of International Power.

The specific advantages of the utility multinationals eroded rapidly after the Second World War. Their expansion had been related to imperfections in the capital and technology markets: Latin American companies, whether publicly or privately owned, could not obtain the large sums of money they needed to finance electricity projects, and equipment manufacturers were often connected to the multinationals either through ownership ties or through well-established commercial links. And finally, underdeveloped countries did not have the technical personnel they needed to run utility companies.

After the Second World War, a number of international financial institutions — the World Bank, the Inter-American Development Bank, the Asian Development Bank — helped eliminate the imperfection in the capital market and provided government-owned corporations in the Third World with the funds they needed to allow their utilities to grow. As these countries became more and more industrialized and an increasing number of their citizens gained experience by working for the subsidiaries of the multinationals, they acquired the technical and administrative personnel they needed. In some cases they succeeded remarkably well: Today, Brazilian consulting engineering firms compete with Canadian ones, not only in Brazil but also in other Latin American countries and in Africa.

Finally, utility multinationals have been subject to the "obsolescing bargain"; we will see the same process at work in the next chapter in relation to mining multinationals. Because fixed assets are large, the risk stage is concentrated at the beginning of operations, and the engineering and administrative knowledge these enterprises require can be learned quickly, utility multinationals are an easy target for local competition and later for expropriation. Most Latin American countries started by establishing their own electric companies to provide electrical services (Mexico in 1937, Argentina in the 1940s, Brazil between 1953 and 1964), and later resorted to nationalization.

Our study of Canadian utility multinationals constitutes a development of Hymer's theory of special advantages. Hymer applied his thesis to manufacturing multinationals, and we began with the proposition that utility multinationals must also have one or more advantages that would serve as a shield against local competition. We found these advantages in the areas of access to major capital markets and electricity technology — that is, in imperfections in the financial and technological markets on an international scale. As these imperfections were reduced, the advantages of the utility multinationals eroded after the Second World War. These companies began to feel the effects of local production and then of nationalization.

We have also found that Vernon's model of the obsolescing bargain is valid for firms of this kind. And finally, we noted that the Canadian case presents some unusual features. The three large producers and exporters of electrical equipment between 1880 and 1940 were Germany, Britain and the United States, and utility multinationals based in these countries used equipment produced by the own domestic manufacturers. Canadians, on the other hand, built multinational corporations on the basis of technology that they purchased outside Canada. In conclusion, it should be noted that Canada does not appear to have been the only example of this phenomenon. Neither Belgium (which was home to the Sofina group, for instance) nor Italy produced heavy equipment during this era, and yet Belgian and Italian utility multinationals, while not as large as the Canadian ones, operated in a number of Latin American and African countries. Thus, Belgian and Italian companies could be other examples of international expansion based on foreign technology.

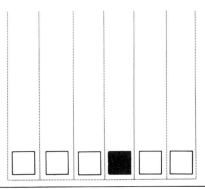

4 Multinationals and the Mining Sector

Canada is one of the world's leading mineral producers, ranking third in terms of the overall value of its output of metallic and non-metallic minerals and construction materials. It is the world's largest producer of nickel, potash and asbestos and among the leaders in copper, zinc, lead, iron ore and uranium. Canada's abundance of hydroelectric energy makes possible the electrolytic reduction of a number of metals — aluminum (for which the raw material, bauxite, is imported), nickel, copper, zinc, and lead. Because of the small size of Canada's domestic market, a large part of this output of minerals and metals is exported, primarily to the United States. In this context, it is not surprising that large Canadian mining companies are in a dominant position in a number of major industries within the mining sector.

We saw in Chapter 2 that a large proportion of Canadian mineral production takes place under foreign control, and in some industries with a very high degree of foreign control — notably iron ore — the creation of multinational firms has clearly been impeded by this circumstance. However, in other industries that have been established in Canada for a longer time, such as nickel and copper, Canadian ownership and control have grown over the years and a number of Canadian companies have become involved in international activities. At the same time, a number of American-controlled multinationals, such as Alcan and Inco, have fallen under Canadian or joint Canadian/American control. And during the 1970s, foreign control in the mining sector in Canada was substantially reduced, especially in asbestos, petroleum and potash. This may turn out to have even greater effects on the creation of Canadian multinationals, as a number of new Canadian companies — formerly subsidiaries of foreign-owned firms — have the size, experience and technological capability to be candidates for international expansion in the near future.

In the first part of this chapter, we will look at the development on a world scale of the industries within the mining sector in which Canadian multinationals are most prominent — nickel, aluminum, copper, zinc and lead. While the oil and gas industries are missing from this list, this does not indicate that Canadian direct investment in foreign countries in these industries is not significant. Rather, even though such Canadian oil companies as Husky Oil, PanCanadian Petroleum, Westburne International Industries and Petro-Canada International, have undertaken international investments, Canadian multinationals are still not a major force in the world hydrocarbon industry.

In the second part of the chapter we will take a closer look at the principal Canadian multinationals that extract or refine minerals outside Canada: Inco, Falconbridge Nickel, Alcan, Cominco and Noranda.

A: THE MAJOR INDUSTRIES

Most theories of multinational corporations are directed primarily at explaining the international expansion of manufacturing firms. The multinationalization of mining companies is either not explained at all or else quickly passed over in the context of efforts by manufacturing firms to control raw materials or become vertically integrated. Some writers — notably Stephen Hymer — make no distinction between mining companies and manufacturing companies in explaining international expansion.

Raymond Vernon is one of the few writers who offer a specific explanation of the expansion and decline of mining multinationals. This cycle that mining companies undergo is treated in his thesis of the obsolescing bargain, which is complementary to his product cycle theory for the manufacturing sector. In Vernon's view, for mining companies based in an industrialized country to expand internationally, the necessary conditions are corporate concentration and the development of an oligopolistic market in that country. Under these conditions, companies have the capacity to ship ores from one country to another and bring about significant technological improvements in mining, smelting and refining. Thus, they become multinationals, both to control major ore deposits in foreign countries and to serve expanding markets outside their home base.

A mining multinational enjoys advantages over its local competitor in three areas — technological, financial and commercial. Patented process, technicians and know-how are at the disposal of the multinational at every stage of producing and refining the mineral. Starting a new mine is a very risky endeavour, and the presence of a multinational makes it possible for this endeavour to be funded by the international financial markets. The multinational's commercial or industrial networks also allow it to process and sell the mineral in the major markets of the world. However, once the size of the orebody has been determined, production has begun and financing has been secured, the risk stage is over and the multinational's bargaining power quickly erodes. Mining technology is relatively simple, widely accessible, available for purchase, and thus within reach of most host countries. The equipment is in place, ore reserves are known, and distribution networks have been set up. On the other hand, private companies in the host countries are rarely in a position to take advantage of the deterioration in the multinational's bargaining position. The purchase price of a subsidiary is very high, and the know-how gained in the host countries is concentrated in the public sector. As a result, most of the benefit from the obsolescing bargain of the multinationals is reaped by host-country governments. This process of decline also takes place in the context of a worldwide deconcentration of the industry as its technology becomes standardized and disseminated. Nationalization as such generally occurs only after one or more intermediate stages: increased smelting, refining and semi-finishing in the host country; legislation forcing the multinational to sell shares in its subsidiary to local private interests; or stricter tax laws.

With this general picture in mind, we will analyze the major industries within the mining sector in which Canadian multinationals operate on a world scale.

The World Nickel Industry

The industrial use of nickel is relatively new. It was not until the last twenty years of the nineteenth century that the processes by which nickel is refined and combined into alloys were invented by a very small group of European and American companies. The first processes were developed in Europe to refine the small quantities of nickel ore mined on the continent. In 1882, the Rothschild family created Société Le Nickel in France, through which they established a virtual monopoly of nickel refining in Europe and gained control of the large nickel deposits of New Caledonia, a French colony since 1853. The world's other large known reserve of nickel was discovered in Sudbury, Ontario in 1883, and a number of American companies exploring for copper obtained concessions there. In the twenty years following the discovery of the reserve, one of these companies, Canadian Copper, succeeded in gaining control of the best deposits in the Sudbury region. It sold the nickel-copper matte it produced to an American copper refiner, Orford Copper, which eventually succeeded in mastering the techniques of reducing nickel by pyrolysis and electrolysis.

Canadian Copper and Orford Copper were merged in 1902 under the direction of J.P. Morgan & Co., and the resulting company, International Nickel (Inco), quickly became the world's largest nickel mining and processing company, a status it retains today. Inco and Le Nickel constituted a world oligopoly that remained remarkably stable until the Second World War, as a result of the size of the deposits controlled by the two companies, the very small number of patented refining processes, and the close commercial ties between the nickel producers and consumers of the metal, notably the steel and arms industries.

Inco replaced Le Nickel as the world's leading producer soon after its founding and in 1913 Canada accounted for 75 per cent of world nickel production, as compared with 20 per cent in New Caledonia. Inco's competitors in Sudbury were eliminated one by one. Some companies disappeared because they could not refine the matte, others were underfinanced, and still others had inferior orebodies that made their operating costs too high. The only company besides Inco that succeeded in the nickel industry in Canada was a British firm established in 1900, Mond Nickel. Its founder, Ludwig Mond, had invented an original nickel refining process in 1889, and later purchased some Sudbury deposits. Mond's market was Europe while Inco's was the United States and other western hemisphere countries; the presence of another company, far from representing a threat to Inco, was a form of security for the giant producer. In any case, Inco absorbed Mond in a share exchange in 1928.

Meanwhile, another small producer went into the business of mining and refining nickel; this was Falconbridge Nickel Mines, which bought a reduction plant in Norway and ore reserves in Sudbury. Because Falconbridge was small and sold to the European market and because Inco feared antitrust suits, no attempt was made to eliminate this new competitor. Meanwhile, Inco had begun to move part of its refining operations from the United States to Canada in 1918. With the purchase of Mond, it obtained increased reserves in Sudbury, plants in England and access to the British company's distribution networks in Europe. When France and Norway were occupied by the Germans during the Second World War, Inco's Canadian, American and British plants constituted a near-monopoly of allied nickel refining capacity. Inco agreed to refine the matte produced by Falconbridge and the American government gave subsidies to Freeport Sulphur to reactivate Cuba's nickel mines.

Inco's monopoly position was placed in sharp focus by the Second World War. In 1946 the American government began anti-trust proceedings against Inco, but the company escaped unscathed two years later. During the Korean War, Washington undertook more energetic measures to increase competition. It signed a supply contract with Falconbridge in 1951, followed by another one for a longer term in 1953. Under this contract, Falconbridge received a premium of forty cents over the market price for the first 100 million pounds of nickel, to be delivered over nine years. The 1953 agreement made it possible for Falconbridge to set in motion a vigorous international expansion program. In 1954 a third Canadian producer, Sherritt Gordon Mines, entered the market, using its own refining process at its Fort Saskatchewan, Alberta, plant, which it supplied from mines at Lynn Lake, Manitoba.[1]

New competitors continued to appear all through the post-war period. While Inco still accounted for 85 per cent of the capitalist world's nickel production in 1950, this proportion had declined to two-thirds by 1960, just over half by 1970, and only about 30 per cent by 1980. Falconbridge climbed to second place in the world industry with a little over 10 per cent in 1960 and almost 20 per cent in 1975. The decline in Inco's share of the world nickel oligopoly has been the result not only of the growth of its Canadian competitors but also of the entry of new American producers (such as Amax, Kaiser, Freeport Minerals and Hanna Mining), a number of Japanese groups that have appeared on the scene more recently, and some European companies, notably Patino Mines. In this process of deconcentration, the beneficiaries have not been publicly- or privately-owned companies in the host countries but new competitors based in the industrialized world. There are, however, a few exceptions to this rule, such as Western Mining, an Australian company, and the Filipino firm Marinduque Mining and Industrial, which uses Sherritt Gordon's process under licence to refine domestic nickel ores.[2]

How can this rapid reduction in the concentration of the industry in the last thirty years be explained? The intervention of the American government with its supply contracts has already been noted, but this factor would not have been sufficient without the presence of a number of other elements. Before 1950, almost all the nickel ore available consisted of sulfide ore deposits in the cold regions of the world. But these deposits — which included the Canadian reserves — were quickly becoming insufficient to satisfy world demand. Companies had to turn to tropical deposits of lateritic ores, which constituted almost 80 per cent of known reserves. The large tropical orebodies, however, were not under Inco's control. New arrivals could enter the market by obtaining and developing new deposits, either on their own or in association with older companies.

In addition, the technology monopoly enjoyed by Inco, Le Nickel and Falconbridge was subject to erosion. Sherritt Gordon Mines played a major role in the dissemination of nickel technology. Its refining process, although developed for Canadian ores, was easily modified to produce pure nickel from lateritic deposits. Sherritt Gordon granted licences to a number of independent producers that brought new mines in tropical countries into operation. Finally, large producers of other minerals in the industrialized countries had easy access to international financial markets and could absorb the technology of nickel production without difficulty, and these companies were the most important agents in reducing concentration in the nickel industry.

At the same time, the companies in this new, wider oligopoly preserved some of their bargaining power by organizing joint ventures in which the participation of the host countries was only symbolic. In Guatemala, for example, Inco holds 80 per cent of the local mining company, Exmibal, while the U.S.-based Hanna Mining Company holds the other 20 per cent. However, the Guatemalan government has an option on 30 per cent of the share capital; if it exercised that option Inco's share would be reduced to 56 per cent and Hanna's to 14 per cent.

The industry has also become less concentrated geographically. By 1979, only 28 per cent of the world's nickel was mined in Canada. New Caledonia, with 16 per cent, was now tied for second place with Australia, while the Philippines and Indonesia each had 8 per cent of the world total.[3] This diversification was the result of international expansion by companies based in the industrialized countries and Canada. Relatively little international expansion had occurred before 1960. Inco did most of its mining, smelting and refining in Canada and had refining, alloying and research subsidiaries in the United States and England. Le Nickel had mines in New Caledonia and reduction plants in France. Falconbridge produced matte in Canada and refined it in Norway. Sherritt Gordon had its mines and plants in Canada.

The first company to expand internationally was Falconbridge, which developed nickel mines in the Dominican Republic. Falconbridge bought the mines in 1955, but construction did not take place until the years 1968-72. During the 1970s, Inco imitated its rival by undertaking projects based on lateritic ores in Indonesia and Guatemala. With larger Canadian reserves than Falconbridge, Inco was reluctant to set the pace in the move towards multinationalization, and it ended up following the lead of the industry's number-two company. The new American entries in the industry are involved in New Caledonia in association with Le Nickel, in the Dominican Republic in association with Le Nickel, in the Dominican Republic in association with Falconbridge and in Guatemala in association with Inco. Sherritt Gordon is doing feasibility studies in Indonesia along with an American company and a Dutch firm. Thus, between 1970 and 1980, the world nickel map changed somewhat, but this process did not include the shift of a significant share of the market to Third World enterprises. Canadian companies' share of the capitalist world's nickel production was only a little over 40 per cent in 1979, which represented a considerable loss of ground, although the low figure was partly due to lengthy strikes suffered by Inco between 1977 and 1979.

Le Nickel and the three Canadian nickel producers have been innovators in the technology of mining, smelting and refining the metal. Each of the three Canadian multinationals has its own patented processes. The control of technology at all stages of production has certainly been one of the major advantages enjoyed by the Canadian nickel multinationals, even if some of this technology has been shared with new competitors in the various joint ventures and, in the case of Sherritt Gordon, with a number of other producers through licencing arrangements.[4]

In sum, one of the conditions of the obsolescing bargain — a decline in economic and geographical concentration of production — has been fulfilled in the nickel industry. However, no host country has nationalized the assets of any of the multinationals and there has been no participation by private companies in these countries, except for a few Australian companies and one in the Philippines.

A number of factors have delayed the erosion of the multi-nationals' bargaining power in the nickel industry. First, a large proportion of the world's nickel ore is supplied by rich semi-industrialized countries (Canada and Australia), a colony (New Caledonia), and countries with military regimes (Guatemala and Indonesia). Second, there has been only a partial reduction in the major producers' technology monopoly, and what reduction there has been has occurred at the mining and smelting stages rather than in refining, which is technically more complex and has remained concentrated in its traditional locations. Thus, any country that nationalized its nickel mines would be vulnerable to potentially costly retaliatory measures; the multinationals could, for instance, refuse to refine its matte.

Third, the developed countries, and especially the arms, steel, automobile and aircraft industries in those countries, represent the main market for nickel. These industries' commercial ties with the nickel multinationals are sufficiently old and solid that a nation-alized company could find these markets closed to it. In addition, because of nickel's strategic importance, no government in a devel-oped capitalist country would establish commercial ties with a supplier that had nationalized the assets of a multinational. And finally, access to international financing is always difficult for a Third World mining company and could be closed completely to a nickel enterprise because of its dubious profitability. Lateritic nickel consumes large quantities of energy and has proved a fairly expensive substitute for the sulfide ores of Canada and Australia. Thus, tropical mines have involved additional costs and this has weakened the position of the new producing countries. For all these reasons, it is unlikely that reduced concentration will lead to a take-over by the host countries of the subsidiaries of multinationals oper-ating in their territory, except perhaps in the long run.

The World Copper Industry

Human beings have used copper since prehistoric times, but it is only in the last century that an industrial technology and industrial uses for the metal have been developed. Britain was the world's largest copper producer until 1850, after which Chile held the lead for thirty years and then lost it to the United States, which remains the leading producer today. Demand from the new electrical indus-try, the leading consumer of copper, stimulated exploration for copper mines and technical developments in smelting and refining.

American companies quickly established a dominant position in the industry. During the first world war, American firms produced 60 per cent of the world's copper ore in the United States and another 20 per cent in their mines in Chile, Canada, Mexico and elsewhere. After a series of mergers and consolidations, three dominant firms emerged. Anaconda Copper was organized in 1910 out of another, identically-named mining company. It controlled rich deposits in Montana, bought the Chuquicamata reserves in Chile in 1923, and also owned deposits in Mexico, Canada and other countries. Kennecott, founded in 1915, owned mines in Utah and Alaska and the Braden mine in Chile. Unlike Anaconda, which had its own smelters and refineries, Kennecott had its ore processed in plants owned by the world's leading lead producer, Asarco. The third major producer was Phelps Dodge. Founded in 1909, it had no international interests but owned integrated facilities encompassing all stages of production within the United States. In 1929, these three leading producers accounted for 66 per cent of the copper mined in the United States and 31 per cent of world production.[5] The world's other large copper producers were Union Minière de Haut Katanga, a publicly-owned Belgian company that was founded in 1906 and began mining copper in the Belgian Congo (now Zaïre) during the First World War; and Rio Tinto, founded in 1972, which developed mines near Seville in Spain and later in Northern Rhodesia (now Zambia). The industry also included a number of smaller American companies.[6]

In Canada, copper production was developed almost entirely under American control. At the time of the First World War, less than 5 per cent of world copper ore production took place in Canada. Two American companies, Howe Sound and International Nickel, and the Canadian-owned Consolidated Mining and Smelting Company (Cominco) controlled the major deposits.[7] It was only much later that Canada became a significant copper producer; in 1926 it still accounted for only 4 per cent of world mine production. However, the relative positions of the producing countries changed radically during the Depression and the Second World War. American companies lost ground while Canadian firms developed rapidly. In the postwar period Canada became the world's fourth largest producer, behind the United States, the Soviet Union and Chile.[8]

The other major development in the industry was a decline in concentration on a world scale. Two factors were primarily responsible for this: the entry of new American, Canadian, Australian, European and Japanese competitors, and the nationalization of a large part of the multinationals' assets in Third World countries, notably Chile, Peru, Zaïre and Zambia. The new American entries included Asarco (which began mining copper during the Second World War), Duval (which began copper operations in 1959), American Metals, and Newmont Mining; while in Canada Canterra entered the industry in the early 1970s.

Meanwhile, a number of the major Third World producing countries established government-owned corporations to bring the assets of multinational firms operating on their territory under local public control. Between 1967 and 1974 Chile expropriated the local subsidiaries of Anaconda and Kennecott to establish Codelco, which became the world's largest copper mining company and the second largest in terms of refining capacity. In 1970, Zambia nationalized the Amax mines and created a joint public/private company under public control, Zimco, which became the second largest copper mining company in the world. Zaïre took control of the Union Minière mines within its jurisdiction in 1967 and its new government-owned company, Gecamines, became the world's third largest copper mining firm. In 1973 the government of Peru expropriated the country's largest mining company, Cerro de Pasco, a producer of copper, lead and zinc, and established a publicly-owned company, Centromin. The government of Mexico adopted legislation in 1961 granting significant tax advantages to mining companies that were at least 51 per cent owned by Mexicans. Anaconda and Asarco found buyers for their copper mines and withdrew from the country.

Thus within a few years, between 1967 and 1974, almost all the Third World's copper mines were either nationalized or purchased by local private interests. In 1978, government-owned corporations — notably Codelco, Zimco, Gecamines and Centromin — accounted for 35 per cent of the non-communist world's copper production. The share held by American and Canadian companies had declined to 45 per cent.[9]

The establishment in 1967 of the Intergovernmental Council of Copper Exporting Countries (known by the initials of its French title, CIPEC) on the model of the Organization of Petroleum Exporting Countries buttressed the producing countries' bargaining power. The countries that had nationalized their copper mines took the initiative in forming CIPEC, and in 1975 Indonesia joined the organization while Australia and Papua-New Guinea became associate members. However, CIPEC has not been as effective as OPEC in controlling prices or production. First of all, the member countries accounted for only 30 per cent of world copper ore production in 1974 (this percentage has increased slightly since then); two of the leading producers, the United States and Canada, have not joined the organization, and their ore production is almost as large as the total produced by the member countries. Second, in the major uses of copper, notably in electrical cable and wire production, aluminum is an adequate substitute; an overly large increase in the price of copper ore would encourage the use of aluminum instead. And third, copper represents more than 60 per cent of the value of the exports of the three leading Third World producers (Chile, Zambia and Zaïre). These countries need foreign exchange to finance their debt and their development, and are not in a good position to negotiate voluntary production cuts in an effort to stabilize or increase prices.

Despite the scale of Canadian copper output, Canadian companies have never played more than a secondary role in the world industry. The largest Canadian producer is Noranda Mines, a multinational corporation which in 1979 accounted for almost 25 per cent of Canadian copper ore production, but only 2 per cent of world output. In second place was Inco with 11 per cent of Canadian production and 1 per cent of world output. (These figures do not indicate Inco's true place in the industry, as the company was paralyzed by work stoppages a number of times between 1977 and 1979.) Canterra is the third largest producer, with a share of Canadian and world output approximately equal to Inco's. Then comes Hudson Bay Mining and Smelting, a subsidiary of the Anglo-American Corporation of South Africa, and Lornex Mining, part of the London-based Rio Tinto-Zinc group, each with 10 per cent of Canadian production. In 1979, these five companies accounted for two-thirds of Canada's output.[10] Inco, Noranda and Hudson Bay have clearly lost part of their share of the world copper market in the last thirty years, but that share was never as large as the proportion of the world nickel market held by Inco and Falconbridge. Among the leading Canadian copper companies, only Noranda produces copper and has plans in progress outside Canada. Inco, for which copper has always been secondary to nickel, has never considered producing it in other countries, while both Hudson Bay and Lornex are subsidiaries of foreign-owned companies.

Reduced concentration on a world scale, nationalization in the Third World and the formation of a producing countries' cartel superficially appear to indicate that the copper industry is an excellent illustration of Vernon's thesis of the eroding bargaining power of multinational corporations. Some writers, however, argue that this trend will not be able to continue. Dorothea Mezger argues that the changes in the world copper industry have not fundamentally modified its structure.[11] In her view, there are a number of factors operating to stop the transfer of bargaining power to the producing countries. One of these factors is the continuing control of technology by large corporations in the industrialized countries. Mezger has observed that the new government-owned corporations in the Third World still buy their technology from the old parent corporations.

In addition, they refine only part of their output locally, and send a considerable portion of their ore to refineries in the industrialized countries. The tendency for the higher stages of production to be concentrated in the advanced countries has been further enhanced by some recent technological developments — notably the process of continuous casting of refined copper for cable production. The vertical integration of the multinationals into semi-finished products and wire and cable manufacturing has prevented the Third World mining companies from having access to the genuinely industrial stages of copper production. Interestingly, Codelco is a shareholder along with two West German refining companies in a continuous casting plant at Emmerich, West Germany, which processes Chilean copper.[12]

However, the dissemination of copper mining, smelting and refining technology has been going on for sixty years. In 1920, American corporations had a virtual monopoly of this technology, while today it is shared among firms in some ten countries. The technology was brought into Canada by American producers. Inco's copper refinery was built in 1926 by American Metals, which operated it for many years. A similar long-term relationship existed between Canadian Copper Refiners, Noranda's refining subsidiary, and Nichols Engineering and Research, a subsidiary of Nichols Copper of New York, which built the Noranda smelter between 1929 and 1931 and then operated it.[13] These were the only copper refineries operating in Canada in 1980; Canterra's refinery, using technology acquired from Mitsubishi Metals, was scheduled to open in 1981.

But while Canadian companies have always been importers of technology in the highly oligopolistic copper refining industry, at the smelting stage three Canadian companies — Inco, Noranda and Sherritt Gordon — have their own patented processes. Inco's process was first put into practice in 1953 and Noranda's in 1964, while there has as yet been no commercial application for Sherritt Gordon's process.[14] The Canadian example shows that copper technology is disseminated slowly but surely, and its adoption by a producing country depends partly on the country's capacity for absorbing and learning the technology, along with the location of the major consumer markets. Canadian copper multinationals have exported technology to countries other than Canada on only a few occasions.

Not counting oil, the decline of the multinationals' bargaining power has been more unambiguous in copper production than in any other mining industry. The five-company oligopoly of the 1920s and 1930s began to erode after the Second World War. As part of this process the industry was redistributed geographically, so that almost 30 per cent of the world's copper is now refined in the Third World producing countries and Australia. Most copper ore in underdeveloped countries is mined either by government-owned corporations or by local private companies. However, a number of producing countries that had nationalized their copper industries — notably Chile and Peru — have more recently called on the multinationals to bring new mines into production. These developments show that in addition to the technological, financial and commercial obstacles to the multinationals' obsolescing bargain, political factors can come into play. When a country is ruled by a totalitarian regime, firms are under absolutely no pressure from public opinion and governments to turn their subsidiaires over to local interests. As in the case of the nickel industry, the presence of military dictatorships can cancel out the effect of purely economic variables that in the long run operate in favour of underdeveloped countries.

The World Aluminum Industry

The aluminum industry consists of four distinct stages. The first is bauxite mining, which is largely concentrated in a small number of tropical and semi-tropical countries, notably Australia, Guinea, Jamaica and Guyana, which among them account for two-thirds of the bauxite production capacity in the capitalist world. The second stage is the chemical refining of bauxite to produce alumina. This stage can be carried out either near a bauxite mine or near an aluminum reduction plant, depending on such factors as transportation, labour and energy costs, the tariff policies of the industrialized countries (where the transformation of alumina into aluminum generally takes place), and demands by the bauxite producing countries. The third stage is primary aluminum production (the smelting of aluminum from alumina, as opposed to secondary production, the raw material for which is aluminum waste and scrap). Primary aluminum production consumes large quantities of electricity, and the smelters in which aluminum is produced are generally located near sources of electrical energy. Ever since the beginnings of the industry, the bulk of the energy needed for the electrolytic reduction of alumina into aluminum has been provided by hydroelectricity. These primary stages are complemented by the aluminum products industry. The aluminum smelting companies themselves process some of their output of aluminum ingots into tubes, sheets, electric wires and construction materials, while the rest is purchased by other industrial sectors such as the transportation equipment and machine tool industries.

The electrolytic reduction process for making alumina into aluminum was invented simultaneously in 1886 by Paul Héroult in France and Charles M. Hall in the United States. The first European and American companies developed as monopolies protected by the patents granted to the inventors. These companies were also able to build other barriers to the entry of new competitors: complete vertical integration covering all stages of production, a monopoly of the major known bauxite deposits, and the development of new uses and alloys. Until the Second World War, the world aluminum industry was a stable oligopoly based on control of natural resources and vertical integration requiring very large amounts of capital. According to Joe S. Bain, the capital requirements for entry into integrated aluminum production are as high as for automobile manufacturing.[15]

Within a few years of the invention of the electrolytic process by Hall and Héroult, a number of companies were established in Europe and North America to produce aluminum commercially. In the United States, Hall founded Pittsburgh Reduction in 1888 in association with the Mellon family bankers of Pittsburgh and a metallurgist, A.E. Hunt. This company established a Canadian subsidiary in 1902 to run a reduction plant and hydroelectric dam on the St. Maurice River in Quebec. The parent company was renamed the Aluminum Company of America (Alcoa) in 1907, while the Canadian subsidiary would later be known as Alcan. Alcoa retained its monopoly position as the only integrated aluminum producer in the United States by purchasing the best American bauxite deposits, gaining control of excellent hydroelectric sites within the United States, developing new products, and closely following the growth of demand with a corresponding growth in supply. Alcan — until 1955 the only Canadian aluminum producer — remained a wholly-owned subsidiary of Alcoa until 1928. In that year the shares of Alcan were distributed to the holders of Alcoa shares, so that the two companies were controlled by the same group of stockholders. A U.S. court injunction in 1950 ordered the stockholders to sell their shares in one or the other of the companies. The Mellons, Hunts and Dukes kept their shares in Alcoa, while the Davis family retained its Alcan shares.

In Europe, four independent firms produced aluminum before 1914 on the basis of the Héroult patents. The Swiss-based Aluminium Industrie A.G. (AIAG) was founded in 1889 by Swiss and German interests. This company, the forerunner of today's Alussuisse, was the largest producer in Europe in 1914. It produced bauxite in France, alumina in France and Germany, and aluminum in Switzerland and Germany. When the Héroult patents expired in 1914, it was a fully integrated producer on a European scale. La Société Electro-Métallurgique Française (SEF) was founded in 1888 and for the next eight years was the only French producer. It conducted all its operations in France. The Pechiney family's Compagnie Alais began producing aluminum in 1896 and became fully integrated within France over the next few years. Also in 1896, British Aluminium was incorporated in the United Kingdom to produce aluminum in Britain from French bauxite. After the patents expired, four marginal companies began operations in Europe but did not threaten the position of the four leaders. In 1914 half the world's aluminum was produced in Europe and the other half in North America (the United States and Canada).

Before 1914 the industry was, by and large, confined within national borders, and the few transnational operations took place within the confines of the industrialized countries. The French bauxite reserves were sufficient for the European producers, while the American reserves constituted an adequate supply for production in North America. During the First World War, however, the industry became genuinely multinational. Alcoa established a subsidiary in British Guiana in 1916 to exploit the bauxite deposits in that British colony. It also took control of reserves in Dutch Guiana, France, Italy and Yugoslavia and had a majority interest in a new aluminum smelter in Norway. In 1925 Alcoa increased its production capacity in Canada, and three years later it legally separated its Canadian and international operations from the parent corporation by establishing a holding company, Aluminium Limited, which took charge of Alcoa's operations outside the United States. This reorganization allowed Alcoa to continue its indirect penetration of the British Empire and to participate, through Alcan, in international cartels without running the risk of antitrust suits in the United States.

New national aluminum monopolies were established in Europe between 1914 and 1939, notably in Germany, the Soviet Union and

Italy. The German government established a publicly-owned corporation, the Vereinigte Aluminium-Werke (VAW), which within a few years had become an integrated producer on a European scale. In 1936 Germany was the world's second largest aluminum producer after the United States. Between the two world wars the majors and the national monopolies grew in strength. Alcoa's monopoly in the United States and Alcan's in Canada have already been noted. British Aluminium produced 93 per cent of Britain's aluminum, the Pechineys' Compagnie Alais accounted for almost 90 per cent of the aluminum produced in France, AIAG controlled 95 per cent of Swiss production capacity, and VAW had a virtual monopoly in Germany. These six companies, each controlling at least one significant market, accounted for almost 90 per cent of the capitalist world's production capacity. Periodic cartels fixing prices, markets and output strengthened this world oligopoly.[16]

This market structure prevailed for half a century, but it was changed substantially by the Second World War. Demand for aluminum increased rapidly all over the world, but only in the United States and Canada could this demand be met by increased production. Output increased sevenfold in the United States and fivefold in Canada during the war. New markets opened up for the aluminum companies, and they were now operating at levels of production that were matched only by the very largest corporations. Meanwhile, American bauxite reserves were rapidly becoming depleted, and they were clearly insufficient to support the new production volumes, so that it was necessary to resort to reserves in the Caribbean and South America. This meant that the Alcoa-Alcan monopoly lost part of its base, as these companies did not control reserves outside the United States as tightly as they did American bauxite. Thus, the increased demand meant that the barriers to entry due to economies of scale in integrated aluminum production could now be overcome. Financial obstacles were also removed in this period as a result of money loaned by the U.S. government, the sale of government-owned aluminum plants at a loss after the war, and the presence of new competitors with financial resources of their own. In these conditions, two companies undertook integrated aluminum production in the United States between 1942 and 1946 — Reynolds Metals and Kaiser Aluminum and Chemical. These two companies broke most of the national monopolies and near-monopolies in North America and Europe.

When the Second World War began, the Reynolds group was a producer of cigarettes and aluminum foil. Then the government lent it money to build its first aluminum reduction plant, and during the war it leased plants from the government and purchased bauxite deposits in Arkansas and Jamaica. After the war it purchased its leased plants and gained control of reserves in Haiti and British and Dutch Guiana. Through these acquisitions it became the second largest aluminum producer in the United States and the third largest in the world. It purchased British Aluminium in 1958 and in 1970 gained absolute control of British Aluminium's fifteen-year-old Canadian subsidiary, which it renamed Canadian Reynolds Metals. Reynolds currently produces bauxite in Jamaica, the United States, Haiti and Ghana, alumina in the United States, Jamaica, West Germany and England, and aluminum in the United States, Canada, West Germany, England, Ghana and Venezuela.

The Kaiser group became involved in primary metal production during the Second World War but did not enter the aluminum industry until 1946, when it bought aluminum plants from the U.S. government. Kaiser's bauxite supplies come from Australia and Jamaica; it produces more than half its alumina in the United States and another quarter in Australia; and it produces aluminum in the United States, West Germany, England, Ghana, India and Bahrein. Two-thirds of its aluminum production capacity is in the United States.

The large European producers have followed a different course. VAW has remained under government control, but many of its installations were destroyed during the Second World War. It is no longer one of the majors, and several of the surviving majors produce aluminum in West Germany. British Aluminium also came out of the Second World War in a greatly weakened state, and as noted above was purchased by Reynolds. Alcan and Kaiser have also entered the British market. The Compagnie Alais, renamed Pechiney-Ugine-Kuhlmann (PUK), has become the only primary aluminum producer in France and the largest producer in Europe. PUK has aluminum smelters in Holland, Spain and Cameroon, alumina refineries in Guinea and Australia, and bauxite mines in Guinea, France and Greece. AIAG, renamed Alussuisse, began to invest outside Europe after the war. It is still one of the majors and produces aluminum in Switzerland (where it has 90 per cent of the production capacity), West Germany, the United States, South Africa, Norway, Italy, Ireland and Austria. It mines bauxite in Australia, France, Guinea and Sierra Leone.

By 1976, Alcoa's share of American aluminum production capacity had declined to 30 per cent. Its bauxite now comes from a number of countries, notably Australia, Surinam and Jamaica. Only 6 per cent of its raw material comes from American deposits, but 84 per cent of its aluminum production capacity is in the United States.

During and after the Second World War, Alcan rose to second place in the world aluminum industry and it is currently not far behind its former parent corporation. It was the first company to become multinational, and it enjoys a number of advantages, including very cheap electricity in its Canadian smelters. On the other hand, it has the disadvantage of not exercising leadership in the American aluminum industry, and has not become integrated downstream to the same extent as Alcoa. Alcan's American associate provided it with the essential elements of its technology between 1900 and 1950, but it has since become completely independent of Alcoa. Along with the other majors it avoids granting patents and licences and thus maintains the closed character of the aluminum oligopoly. In 1971, Alcan's main bauxite mine was nationalized by the government of Guyana (formerly British Guiana), but the company had long since diversified its sources of supply to include Guinea, Australia and Jamaica.

In 1972, six large producers — Alcoa, Alcan, Reynolds, Kaiser, PUK and Alussuisse — accounted for 71 per cent of the capitalist world's aluminum output. This represented a slight decrease in concentration since 1936 as well as a major internal change within the oligopoly.[17] Three of the six leading companies are now American, and two of these three are recent entries in the industry. A number of markets that were monopolies in the pre-war period — notably the United States — have become oligopolies. This has come about because of the effects of the war in a number of countries (Germany, Japan, England) and because of direct intervention by the American government aimed at reducing the concentration of the industry in the United States. In countries where the new North American giants have not invested, such as France and Italy, the industry is even more concentrated than it was before. Thus, it can be concluded that there has been no mechanism inherent in the economy of the industry that has led "naturally" to a gradual reduction of concentration.

The industry has become internationalized, especially over the last forty years, because bauxite reserves in France and the United States proved insufficient. Producers' cartels have fixed prices on the basis of the prices charged by the companies with the lowest costs (especially Alcoa and Alcan); these companies have tended to keep prices low and this has not encouraged the entry of new competitors. As the industry has become geographically diversified through the use of new sources of bauxite in the Caribbean, Africa and Australia, there has been a proliferation of joint ventures among the majors. Through these joint ventures, the companies have attempted to meet the very high cost of new installations and put themselves in a better position to resist pressures from host country governments aiming to raise taxes, increase the extent of processing within their borders, or nationalize the subsidiaries of the multinationals outright.

The mining stage of the industry has not been the only one affected by geographical redistribution. In 1936 there were only thirteen countries in the world that produced aluminum, while by 1976 this figure had risen to thirty-six. A number of semi-industrialized countries, such as India, Brazil, Argentina and Mexico, produce small quantities for their domestic markets. Most of the world's production remains concentrated in about ten industrialized countries.

In 1974, the major bauxite exporting countries — Australia, Guinea, Guyana, Jamaica, Sierra Leone, Surinam and Yugoslavia — formed the International Bauxite Association (IBA), and the Dominican Republic, Ghana and Haiti joined the organization soon afterwards. In 1976 the IBA represented about 70 per cent of world bauxite production and 90 per cent of world trade in the mineral. It succeeded in playing a role in determining prices, and some facilities were nationalized in a few producing countries. The IBA has not, however, succeeded in changing the location of aluminum production facilities, which remain close to the major markets. The aluminum companies have resisted the erosion of their bargaining power, which has hardly been reduced at all over three-quarters of a century, and maintained the essential elements of the industry's market concentration. They have managed to do this because of their firm control of technology and consumer markets and because of the high proportion of production costs that occur at the smelting stage.

The World Zinc Industry

Zinc ore has been known to mankind for centuries. In most of the deposits currently being mined it is found along with lead, and it is also sometimes found with copper. In either case, the ore contains some gold, silver and cadmium. Zinc ore also has a high sulfur content, so that sulfuric acid production is a common sideline for zinc mining companies.

Between the turn of the century and the First World War, the United States and Germany were the world's leading zinc producing countries. A number of other European countries, such as Spain, Italy and Sweden, were also major producers during this period. The disarray into which the European industry was thrown by the First World War stimulated production in Mexico and Canada. Because of Canada's abundant hydroelectric resources, the industry's entry into Canada was encouraged by the invention of electrolytic processes and their commercial application in the United States in 1916. Thus, by 1933 Canada was the world's third largest producer of zinc ore, after Australia and Germany (the American producers were the hardest hit by the Depression) and the second largest producer of metallic zinc, after Belgium.[18]

In the nineteenth century zinc refining was concentrated in Germany and Belgium, but in 1909 the United States became the leading producer of metallic zinc. Germany, Belgium and the U.S. together accounted for 55 per cent of mine production and 80 per cent of refinery production in 1913. The leading companies were Beer Sondheimer, Metallgesellschaft, and Aaron Hirsch & Sohn in Germany, the S.A. de la Vieille Montagne in Belgium, and Anaconda and U.S. Steel in the United States. As a result of the war, the American and Canadian industries grew enormously and the European producers declined in relative terms. The first electrolytic refinery in Canada was installed in 1916, the same year that the first such plant opened in the United States.

In the 1920s and 1930s the European industry was reorganized. The Belgian firms merged to form a company that is still the largest in the industry, the Société Générale des Mines, with its head office in Brussels. An Anglo-Australian group, Imperial Smelting, brought the British refineries and the Australian mines together under a single corporate umbrella. The world market outside the United States was controlled by these two companies. The division of pre-war imperial Germany between Germany and Poland brought about the dismemberment of the German companies, and the Polish section of the industry fell into the hands of the large American and Belgian producers, notably Anaconda and Vieille Montagne. Meanwhile, new Canadian and Australian producers appeared on the scene. In Canada, Consolidated Mining and Smelting (now Cominco), a subsidiary of Canadian Pacific, and Hudson Bay Mining and Smelting, then under American control, built modern electrolytic refineries in the 1920s and became an important element in the world industry, even though their combined refining capacity represented only 7 per cent of world capacity in 1930. As a result of Canada's plentiful reserves of ore and electrical energy, the superiority of the new electrolytic technology, the exhaustion of European deposits and the high transportation costs of Australian ore, the Canadian producers had significant advantages over their competitors.

To a small degree, the process of multinationalization began in this period. The European producers used ore from continental sources; the American producers were integrated within the United States and controlled mines in Mexico, Canada, Australia and Poland; and the British producers had subsidiaries in Australia, Mexico and Rhodesia. But because of the presence of large zinc deposits in Europe and the United States, which in 1930 produced about 90 per cent of the world's zinc ore and consumed 92 per cent of the metallic zinc, there was little need for companies to become multinational.

The Second World War threw European zinc production into disarray and led to an increase in Canadian, American and Australian output. In addition, the multinationals took the initiative in making a number of Latin American countries, notably Peru and Mexico, major producers.

The British mining multinational Consolidated Zinc, the successor company to Imperial Smelting, was absorbed by Rio Tinto in 1962, and the London-based company, renamed Rio Tinto-Zinc, gained control of the Broken Hill deposits in Australia. RTZ had 5 per cent of the world's refining capacity in 1976.[19] The Belgian group, comprising Metallurgie Hoboken-Overpelt, the Société Générale des Mines, the S.A. de la Vieille Montagne and the Compagnie Royale Asturienne des Mines and linked to the Société Générale de Belgique, had almost 20 per cent of the world's refining capacity in 1976, but produced ore only in a few European mines. These are the largest European groups. They have recently been joined in the industry by new Japanese producers, notably Mitsui, Mitsubishi, Toho Zinc and Nippon Mining. The seven Japanese producers together accounted for almost 16 per cent of world refining capacity in 1976. Except for two small subsidiaries in Peru, they have virtually all their mines in Japan, and also buy ore on the open market.

The American producers have steadily lost ground as a result of the exhaustion of American deposits and competition from new integrated producers, notably the Canadian companies. Older American refineries were not modernized and have been abandoned. Thus, the United States produced only 6 per cent of the capitalist world's zinc ore in 1979 and its refining capacity was only 8 per cent of the total. On the other hand, Canada produced 25 per cent of the non-communist world's zinc ore and refined 16 per cent of the total.

Electrolytic reduction of zinc in Canada was divided among three producers — Cominco, Canadian Electrolytic Zinc (part of the Noranda group) and Canterra. Canada accounted for about half the zinc ore exports and a quarter of the metallic zinc exports in the capitalist world. Noranda was the world's leading producer of zinc in 1979, with more than 8 per cent of the world total.[20]

The Third World has not benefited from the reduced concentration and changed geographical distribution of the world zinc industry. In 1979, Third World countries (not including Australia and South Africa) produced 25 per cent of the world's zinc ore and refined 7 per cent of the capitalist world's zinc. As a result, there has been hardly any erosion of the multinationals' bargaining power. Peru is the only country that has nationalized a portion of its zinc production, with the expropriation of Cerro de Pasco in 1973. The government-owned corporation that resulted from the takeover, Centromin, produced only 2 per cent of the capitalist world's refined zinc in 1979. Because much of the world's zinc ore is mined in Europe, Canada, the United States and Australia, and because of the location of the world's zinc refineries and their technological complexity and scale of production, the higher stages of zinc production have remained in the industrialized countries. As with other metals, the concentration of consumer markets in Europe and North America has also contributed towards maintaining the multinationals' bargaining power, even though corporate concentration in the industry has been significantly reduced.

The World Lead Industry

The United States has been the world's leading producer, refiner and consumer of lead for a hundred years. To a degree, each of the three stages of lead production — mining, smelting and fabrication — came under the control of different companies. The leading American lead mining company was St. Joseph Lead, which exploited the large Missouri deposits from the 1870s on; at the smelting stage, American Smelting and Refining (Asarco), established in 1899, was the leading company; while the largest company in all aspects of lead fabrication was National Lead, founded in 1891. Four companies controlled 75 per cent of American mine production in 1932, while Asarco had close to an absolute monopoly at the smelting stage. Along with the number two American producer of smelted lead, American Metals, Asarco also controlled Mexican lead production, and with its subsidiaries, the smelting giant accounted for two-thirds of the world's metallic lead output at the beginning of the Depression.[21]

Two groups dominated lead mining and smelting in Europe — the Anglo-American zinc group, whose corporate instrument was Imperial Smelting, and the French Penarroya group, which controlled mines in Spain. During the 1920s and 1930s, the world lead industry was changed by the meteoric rise of Canada. Using pre-First World War methods, it had not been possible for Canada to be more than a marginal lead producer, but with the invention of electrolytic smelting and refining processes, Cominco was able to climb to the ranks of the major companies in the few years following 1916. When the Depression began, five producers — Asarco, American Metals, Penarroya, Imperial Smelting and Cominco — controlled the world lead industry. Cominco had held the number one position in both lead and zinc production for a number of years.[22]

There has been no fundamental change in the geographical distribution of lead production in the last forty years. Spain is no longer a significant factor in the industry as a result of the exhaustion of its mines. Lead refining has become even more heavily concentrated in the industrialized countries. Penetration of the refining stage by Japanese companies has not occurred in lead production to the same extent as in other mining industries. In Canada, only Noranda Mines has managed to chip away at Cominco's monopoly of smelting and refining. As a result of the smelting and refining plant recently built by its subsidiary Brunswick Mining and Smelting, Noranda accounts for one-third of Canadian metallic lead production capacity, while Cominco has the other two-thirds.

There has been some decline in the concentration of the industry, but a large proportion of the world's lead ore is produced in North America, Europe and Australia, so that Third World producers have not been able to reduce the role of the multinationals significantly. Only Peru, with its nationalization of Cerro de Pasco in 1973, and Mexico, with its 1961 mining legislation, have gained control over a portion of their lead resources. Meanwhile, lead refining has become even more heavily concentrated in the major consuming countries.

B: CANADIAN MULTINATIONALS IN THE WORLD MINING INDUSTRY

In the first part of this chapter, we looked at the structural develop-

TABLE 1

Lead Production, 1932 and 1978

(a) Mine Production

Country	1932	Percentage of world production 1978
United States	23	21
Australia	16	16
Canada	10	14
Peru	—	7
Mexico	12	7
Spain	9	—
Total, five leading producers	70	65

(b) Refinery Production

Country	1932	Percentage of world production 1978
United States	22	25
West Germany	8	10
United Kingdom	—	8
Australia	16	8
Japan	—	7
Canada	10	6
Mexico	12	—
Spain	9	—
Total, six leading producers	77	64

Sources: W.Y. Elliott et al., International Control of the Non-Ferrous Metals (New York: Macmillan, 1937), pp. 598, 603; American Bureau of Metal Statistics, Non-Ferrous Metals Data 1979 (New York, 1980).

ment of five non-ferrous metal industries in which Canadian direct investment in foreign countries is significant. In each of these industries we noted a trend away from economic concentration; this trend is slight in the case of the aluminum smelting industry, moderate in the zinc and lead industries, and considerable in nickel and copper. In the remainder of the chapter, we will examine Canadian multinational corporations' response to the structural changes in each industry. Among the adaptations we will see are economic and geographical diversification, changes in the degree of control exercised over the multinationals' subsidiaries, and joint ventures with host-country governments, local private partners and other multinationals.

Based on the observations in this section, a number of hypotheses can be advanced. First, as concentration is reduced and competition becomes more intense in a mining industry, multinationals operating in that industry will have a greater tendency to resort to economic diversification. By pursuing a strategy of diversification, a multinational aims to provide itself with a fallback option in case its share of the market and its worldwide activities are reduced. Thus, nickel and copper producers have diversified their output to a greater extent than aluminum producers, which remain more highly specialized. Similarly, increased competition will also result in greater multinationalization, as companies attempt to control natural resources for which no concessions have yet been granted.

As in the oil industry, the entry of new competitors in the mining sector improves the bargaining position of host-country governments, which become able to insist that the multinationals enter into joint ventures with them or not hold more than 49 per cent of the stock of their local subsidiaries. Thus, host-country governments would enter into joint ventures most frequently with nickel and copper companies, while joint ventures would be less common in the aluminum industry. And finally, the more a country is industrialized, the more its government can impose conditions on the multinationals. Thus, when negotiating the entry of a foreign company into its country, the government of Brazil, Mexico or India would be in a stronger position than other Third World governments.

International Nickel (Inco)

Founded in New Jersey in 1902, International Nickel was the result of a merger between the largest Canadian nickel producer, Canadian Copper, and the American company that refined its ore, Orford

Copper. The new company was formed by J.P. Morgan and American steel interests linked to U.S. Steel, and its creation was the American financiers' response to an attempt by the government of Ontario, the province in which the nickel deposits were located, to ensure that nickel was refined within the province.

As noted above, Sudbury took a definitive lead over New Caledonia in nickel ore production in 1905, and the Ontario deposits gave the new company world supremacy in the industry. Inco totally dominated the North American market, with the arms industry accounting for the largest portion of its sales. It also had a share of the European market, the largest in the first quarter of the twentieth century. During the First World War, Inco produced between 75 and 90 per cent of the world's nickel ore.

It was also a major copper producer. In fact, when the Sudbury deposits were discovered in 1883, they first attracted attention because of their high copper content. It was only later that the value of the nickel ore contained in the matte was recognized. However, nickel production was Inco's primary interest, and its copper production was determined by its nickel output. In the years 1900-1930, its share of the world copper market was less than 5 per cent.[23]

In 1918, under the combined pressure of the provincial government, the war effort and public opinion, Inco moved part of its refining operations to Canada, and in 1926 it opened a Canadian copper refinery. It absorbed its major competitor in Canada, Mond Nickel, in a share exchange in 1928-29, and acquired a Canadian charter at the same time. Its stock was dispersed among shareholders in the United States (where 42 per cent of its shares were held), Canada (22 per cent) and Britain (34 per cent), but control remained in the hands of the American financiers.[24] Through the merger with Mond it increased its European operations, as it inherited Mond's refineries and fabrication plants in Britain. Inco retained its near-monopoly of the world nickel industry without much change from 1930 to 1960. Although concentration began to decline in the 1950s, Inco changed neither its specialization in the nickel industry nor its reliance on the Sudbury deposits as a source of supply. However, its monopoly came apart between 1950 and 1980, when its share of world nickel production fell from 85 to 30 per cent.

In 1960, Inco purchased the Lake Izabal lateritic nickel deposit in Guatemala from the U.S.-based Hanna Mining Company. Mining did not begin until 1977, and in 1979 the mine's output was 7,000 short tons, representing 1 per cent of the world's nickel ore production.[25] This was Inco's first venture into geographical diversification of its sources of ore supply.

In 1968, Inco obtained exploration rights on the island of Sulawesi in Indonesia, and the first stage of the project was completed in 1977. Like the Guatemalan installation, the Indonesian project consists of a mine and smelter, from which Inco ships matte to its refineries in the industrialized countries. The Indonesian facilities have a capacity of 17,500 short tons of ore, and Inco plans a second stage that will raise the capacity to 50,000 tons.

Inco purchased ESB Inc., an American multinational corporation that manufactures batteries, for $234 million in 1974. This conglomerate expansion was Inco's second defensive move in response to the erosion of its market power in the nickel industry.[26] At the same time the company strengthened its vertical integration by increasing its involvement in the metal products industry. As a result of this diversification program, Inco's metals division accounted for 42 per cent of its sales in 1979, its batteries division 34 per cent, and its metal products division 22 per cent.[27] Inco had become a conglomerate, more than half of whose total sales did not come from the mining industry.

However, Inco's international expansion has been subject to several delays. Skyrocketing energy prices reduced the profitability of tropical nickel ores, which consume large quantities of energy at the concentration and smelting stages. In order to come to terms with the difficulties encountered by its Indonesian and Guatemalan operations, Inco has had to postpone its other expansion plans — in New Caledonia, Brazil and elsewhere — indefinitely. In any case, Inco has never been a leader in the multinationalization of the nickel industry. The initiative in international expansion was taken much earlier by its major rivals, notably Falconbridge, whose ore reserves were not nearly as rich as Inco's.

All the nickel multinationals are currently establishing joint ventures to develop the tropical deposits. Le Nickel has joined with Kaiser, Amax and Patino to develop reserves in New Caledonia; Sherritt Gordon Mines has a joint project in Indonesia with U.S. Steel and Newmont Mining; and Falconbridge is associated with Armco Steel in the Dominican Republic. Inco, meanwhile, owns 80 per cent of the shares of Exmibal, its Guatemalan subsidiary, while Hanna Mining has the other 20 per cent. The Guatemalan government has an option on newly-issued shares that could reduce Inco's share to 56 per cent. In Indonesia Inco took up 75 per cent of the shares in the project and a consortium of Japanese refiners took up the other 25 per cent; the Indonesian government retains options but even if they were exercised Inco would still have majority control.[28]

Economic diversification, international expansion, joint ventures — these are Inco's responses to the reduction of its share in the world nickel oligopoly. Our study of Falconbridge, the industry's number two company, will show that these strategies are not unique to Inco.

Reflecting these changes, the company changed its name from the International Nickel Company of Canada to Inco Ltd. in 1976. In addition, with the increasing proportion of its shares held by Canadians, Inco moved most of its head office activities from New York to Toronto. In October 1976, 48 per cent of Inco's shares were held in Canada; 37 per cent were held in the United States and 15 per cent were held elsewhere.

Falconbridge Nickel Mines

Falconbridge was established in 1928 to buy some mining concessions in Sudbury and an electrolytic refinery in Norway, and it built a smelter in Sudbury that began operations in 1930. Inco made no attempt to prevent the establishment of this new competitor. The new producer was small, its market was Europe and not North America, and Inco's monopoly was the subject of intense public and regulatory attention, making it impossible for the giant to conspire against its rival without running into antitrust suits; all these factors contributed towards Inco's tolerant attitude. In addition, Falconbridge was not heavily dependent on the capital markets, since it was funded directly from the financial reserves of several major capitalists, and it was also fully integrated, which gave it further protection against Inco's manoeuvres from the outset.[29]

Falconbridge was founded by a Canadian capitalist raised in the United States, Thayer Lindsley, and a group of partners. Lindsley maintained firm control of Falconbridge until 1957, when it was purchased by a Canadian company, McIntyre Porcupine Mines. During its first decade of existence Falconbridge made a modest profit, selling its output at the high prices dictated by the industry leader. During the Second World War, with Norway under German occupation, Falconbridge's nickel had to be refined by Inco, and after the war Falconbridge continued to grow at an unspectacular pace, although with the European industry in disarray it had risen to second place among the world's nickel companies.

The company's growth accelerated in the 1950s as a result of long-term contracts with the U.S. Defense Material Procurement

Agency in 1951 and 1953. Falconbridge's international expansion also began at this time. In 1955 it bought concessions in the Dominican Republic from Inco, but did not develop them until fifteen years later. It also established a number of subsidiaries in Africa. In 1956 it began producing copper in Uganda, and remained in the country until its interests were nationalized by the Idi Amin regime in 1975. In addition, it entered Southern Rhodesia (now Zimbabwe) to operate three gold mines, one of which is still active. Another African venture was Western Platinum in South Africa, undertaken jointly with Lonrho of London, which holds 51 per cent of the shares. Western Platinum produces nickel, platinum and copper, which are refined in Falconbridge's facilities in Norway.[30]

Falconbridge passed from Canadian to American control between 1965 and 1967 when McIntyre Porcupine was purchased by a Houston company, Superior Oil, owned by the Keck family. But its international expansion did not stop. Falconbridge built its smelters in the Dominican Republic and began to operate them in 1977. This was the first of a new wave of nickel mining projects based on lateritic ores in tropical and semi-tropical regions, and Falconbridge was thus the pioneer in the movement towards multi-nationalization. Inco, Le Nickel, Sherritt Gordon and new companies soon fell into step.[31] In 1971, Falconbridge opened a copper mine in the South African-administered territory of Namibia with the financial participation of the South African government. Falconbridge currently has subsidiaries in a large number of countries, including Argentina, Australia, Brazil, Chile, the Philippines and Zaïre.[32]

A number of the problems that attended Inco's international expansion have affected Falconbridge as well. The entry of American, European, Japanese and even Australian competitors on a massive scale has reduced Falconbridge's share of the world market, from almost 20 per cent in 1974 to less than 10 per cent in 1979. At the same time, the Dominican deposits, like other lateritic ferronickel ores, have proved less profitable than anticipated because of the increase in energy prices. And in addition to the problems it shares with other nickel producers, Falconbridge has encountered some difficulties of its own. It opened a new Ontario refinery using West German technology in 1970, but had to close it permanently in 1972 because of technical problems. And when Falconbridge's subsidiary in Uganda, Kilembe Copper Cobalt, was expropriated in 1975, the company received only what the *Financial Post* described as "modest" compensation for it.[33]

Falconbridge is a less diversified company than Inco. Metal sales accounted for 85 per cent of its income in 1979; half this total came from nickel, and another quarter from copper. Since the Superior Oil group, of which Falconbridge is a part, has diverse interests in the mining field, there has been no need for Falconbridge as such to resort to conglomerate diversification as a defensive measure against the erosion of its market power — which is, in any case, a very recent phenomenon. However, when Falconbridge's expenditures on exploration are analyzed, it becomes clear that the company is making an effort to discover metals other than nickel. In 1979, the company spent 27 per cent of its exploration budget looking for nickel deposits (17 per cent in Canada and 10 per cent elsewhere) and 73 per cent looking for other metals (43 per cent in Canada and 30 per cent elsewhere).[34] This indicates that the company is pursuing a strategy of diversification within the metals sector along with international expansion.

Noranda Mines

Noranda Mines was established in 1922 by a group of American engineers and financiers to explore mining concessions in northwestern Quebec. In 1926, the American financial backers sold their shares to a number of Canadian mining companies, including Hollinger Mines, and individuals. Noranda's first copper smelter, the planning for which was done in New York, was installed in 1927. Four years later, Canadian Copper Refiners, a joint subsidiary of Noranda, Nichols Metals of New York, and an English company, British Metals, opened an electrolytic refinery in the east end of Montreal. The necessary technology was supplied by Nichols Metals. Noranda completed its vertical integration by buying a controlling interest in Canada Wire and Cable in 1930. This company had existing plants in Toronto and Hamilton, and built a new one in the east end of Montreal to process the copper refined by Canadian Copper Refiners. When the Depression struck, Noranda's main product was copper, but it also produced gold. While the price of copper collapsed the price of gold did not, and this made it possible for Noranda to continue expanding.

In 1935 Noranda purchased a major Ontario gold producer, Pamour Porcupine Mines. Two years later it made its first purchase outside Canada, buying the Compania Minera La India, which operated a gold mine in Nicaragua. In 1940 it established a second Nicaraguan mining company (Empresa Minera El Setentrion). At the same time, Noranda extended its holdings in Canada. It gained control of Gaspé Copper Mines in Quebec in 1937 and Kerr Addison Gold Mines in Ontario at the end of the Second World War. With the establishment in 1946 of a new subsidiary, Noranda Copper and Brass, it became involved in the production of brass. At this point, Noranda was a large mining company within Canada, but had only a minor international presence. All through the 1940s and 1950s it continued to diversify its Canadian operations, becoming involved in the production of zinc, lead, silver and other metals. In 1962-63, through its subsidiary Canadian Electrolytic Zinc, it built an electrolytic zinc refinery in Valleyfield, Quebec, and in 1971 it opened a 70,000-ton aluminum smelter in New Madrid, Missouri. Through this latter venture, it aimed to master the technology of a metal that is copper's most direct competitor.

Noranda's international expansion continued when it bought Empresa Minera Fluorspar, a Mexican fluorspar mining company, in 1957. Twelve years later, however, it sold 51 per cent of the shares in this company to Mexicans to meet the requirements of the legislation that Mexicanized the country's mining industry. Noranda also bought Chile Canadian Mines in 1964 to produce copper cement; this company was nationalized by the Chilean government in 1971.[35]

The Noranda division that expanded most widely outside Canada was Canada Wire and Cable, the manufacturing subsidiary that from 1966 on was under the absolute control of the parent company. Entering the 1960s, Canada Wire had been Canada's leading wire and cable manufacturer for half a century, and had followed a strategy based on exports for at least as long a period. These circumstances placed it in a good position to expand internationally in a significant way. At the time, Canada Wire was faced with new tariff barriers in its export markets, and its main goal in deciding to engage in manufacturing outside Canada was to get around these barriers. It began to become multinational in 1961 when it bought an electric wire and cable manufacturer in Colombia. In 1962 it established a subsidiary in Venezuela jointly with local interests, and then expanded into Mexico in 1963, the Dominican Republic in 1965, New Zealand and Spain in 1969, and Brazil and Australia in 1972.[36]

Canada Wire's new interests outside Canada have generally taken the form of joint ventures, in which its minority control has been strengthened by the technological services it provides its subsidiaries.[37] In 1976, it had subsidiaries in twelve countries (the United States not among them), and these subsidiaries represented 35 per cent of its gross income. They used processes patented by the parent company in the relatively traditional wire and cable manufacturing industry. Starting in 1976-77, however, Canada Wire changed its strategy, and decided to expand in high-technology fields, especially fibre optics, in the United States. In 1977, it bought a minority interest in an American electro-optical equipment works.[38]

Noranda, meanwhile, continued its mining exploration both in Canada and elsewhere. During the 1970s it spent about half its exploration budget in Canada. Exploration in the United States accounted for the lion's share of the other half, but Noranda also explored for minerals in Argentina, Australia, Brazil, Britain, Chile, Greece, Ireland, Mexico, the Philippines, South Africa and Spain. Such geographically varied exploration activity is one indication that it is pursuing an international strategy, but not the only one. At the same time, a number of projects are coming to fruition. In Ireland, Noranda is the principal partner in Tara Exploration and Development, which it controls jointly with Cominco and the Irish government. Tara undertook a $150 million lead-zinc project, which was completed in 1977. It produced 205,000 tons of zinc concentrate and 37,000 tons of lead concentrate in 1983. The concentrate is sent to smelters elsewhere in Europe. In Brazil, Noranda is planning to build a copper smelter and refinery in a joint venture with a local company, Eluma SA. Noranda also has four mining projects in the United States, each in the $30 million to $50 million range.

Other Noranda projects, however, were abandoned before reaching the production stage, including the $390 million Andacollo project in Chile, in which Noranda held a 51 per cent interest. The project involved mining reserves of 210 million tons of ore with a copper content of 0.6 per cent starting in January 1983, but it was dropped following a feasibility study. And the company's subsidiary Noranda Australia undertook the development of a uranium mine in Australia's Northern Territory, but Noranda sold its interest before the mine began production. Meanwhile, Placer Development, a Canadian subsidiary of Noranda, controls and operates a copper-gold-silver mine in the Philippines with a capacity of 16,000 tons a day. Placer is also involved in exploration activity in Canada, the United States, Spain, Italy, Mexico, the Philippines, Australia and New Guinea.

Noranda's geographical diversification has gone hand in hand with economic diversification. In 1961, Noranda became involved in the forest industry, buying four sawmills in British Columbia, which it brought together as Northwood Mills. The next year, it formed Northwood Pulp to produce wood pulp for paper manufacture in a joint venture with an American company, Mead Corp. Mead and Noranda gained control of one of Canada's largest forest products companies, British Columbia Forest Products, in 1969. In January 1980, Noranda bought the controlling block of shares in Maclaren Power and Paper, a Quebec paper company with annual sales of about $120 million, from the Maclaren family, and four months later it gained control of Canada's largest forest multinational, MacMillan Bloedel. Meanwhile, Noranda itself was taken over in 1981 by Brascan and the Caisse de Dépôt et Placement du Québec through their subsidiary, Brascade.

Noranda's income in 1979 was $395 million, 86 per cent of which came from Canada. Mining, smelting and refining accounted for 75 per cent of its total income, with the rest divided equally between manufacturing and the forest industry. In that year Noranda produced more than 8 per cent of the world's zinc and about 2 per cent of its copper and lead. In addition, it produced significant quantities of silver, gold, aluminum, molybdenum, potash, phosphates and cadmium.[39]

In October 1980, Canada Wire announced that it was adopting the continuous casting process for fabricating refined copper. A new factory would be built in Montreal to exploit the process patented by Metalurge Hoboken-Overpelt in Belgium with equipment provided by a West German company, Krupp Industrie.[40] With this imported technology, which is being adopted in Europe and the United States, copper tube can be made directly from cathodes supplied by the refinery. Noranda showed its ability to adopt new foreign technologies and master them quickly when it assimilated the electrolytic reduction process for copper and zinc, and it is showing this same ability again with continuous casting. Noranda is not a major technological innovator, but rather an alert follower of American and European developments.

Alcan Aluminium

As noted earlier, Alcan was founded in 1902 as a subsidiary of Alcoa called the Northern Aluminum Company. Its initial purpose was to operate a small electrolytic reduction plant and a wire and cable mill in Shawinigan, Quebec. It grew rapidly, and exported most of its output, as the Canadian domestic market was very limited. Nevertheless, in 1914 it was the smallest of the six aluminum majors. As an exporter, it was a full participant in the two pre-war international aluminum cartels, joining with European producers in 1901-8 and again in 1912-14.

During the 1920s Alcan underwent major changes. It was a participant in the hydroelectric development of the Saguenay River in 1925, built a large refinery on the river and at the same time created the town of Arvida. In 1928, Aluminium Limited (later Alcan Aluminium Limited) was established to run the Canadian and international operations of Alcoa. At that point Alcan and Alcoa had the same controlling shareholders, but Alcan was no longer a subsidiary of an American company, and the two companies became more and more distinct from each other as time went on. Among the foreign assets that Alcan received from its former parent company was Demerara Bauxite, which became its main raw material supplier. Alcan's growth in the 1920s and 1930s made it the world's second largest aluminum producer behind Alcoa, with 14 per cent of world refining capacity in 1936.

The company's production capacity, which stood at 83,000 tons of aluminum a year in 1939, increased fivefold during the Second World War. New facilities were developed at Arvida and Île Maligne on the Saguenay and a new 30,000-ton plant was built near Montreal. The Saguenay facilities were enlarged a number of times in the years immediately following the war. In 1950 Alcan expanded into British Columbia, and four years later it opened its smelter at Kitimat and hydroelectric plant at Kemano. In this period its bauxite came from British Guiana (now Guyana) and Jamaica, alumina was refined in Jamaica and Canada, and aluminum was produced in Canada. In 1955, Alcan lost its monopoly of Canadian aluminum production when British Aluminium began to build a smelter in Baie-Comeau, Quebec, which it opened in 1957. Alcan was an American-controlled company at this point: American residents held 72 per cent of its shares, Canadians 26 per cent and nationals of other countries about 2 per cent.[41]

In the 1950s, Alcan's search for additional bauxite mines and sites for aluminum smelters took it into a number of new countries. By 1960, Alcan obtained its bauxite from Guinea and France in addition to its main deposits in the Caribbean, and produced aluminum in Brazil, India, Italy, Japan, Norway and Sweden. Its production capacity was 750,000 short tons a year in Canada and 200,000 tons a year elsewhere.[42] Sixteen years later, it had added Australia and Spain to the list of countries in which it produced aluminum, and its production capacity outside Canada (866,000 tons) was almost equal to its capacity within Canada (907,000 tons). It had also established aluminum fabrication plants in the United States and expanded its facilities in Britain. [43]

In 1971, Alcan lost its main source of bauxite when Demerara Bauxite was nationalized. This was the first takeover of a subsidiary of one of the six aluminum majors, but no wave of such nationalizations followed. Action by the bauxite producing countries was limited to the formation of the International Bauxite Association, through which they aimed to raise prices and increase taxes on the companies' operations. Alcan easily made up for the loss of its bauxite deposits in Guyana through its new mines in Brazil, Guinea, India and Malaysia as well as its existing ones in Jamaica.

In 1957 the company had begun to establish and acquire subsidiaries to fabricate aluminum products in order to provide markets for its Canadian ingot output. In 1970, it had fabrication subsidiaries in thirty-three countries, spanning all the continents. Alcan retained exclusive or majority control of these subsidiaries. The bauxite mines, on the other hand, were operated as joint ventures, under the control of the majors but sometimes with the participation of host country governments. Thus, the Compagnie des Bauxites de Guinée is 51 per cent owned by Halco Mining, a consortium in which Alcoa and Alcan each own 27 per cent of the shares. The remaining 49 per cent is held by the government of Guinea. Joint ventures of this sort are organized so that the companies can better resist pressure from the producing countries and share the cost of large mining projects.

Alcan's expansion in the United States, Japan and the industrialized countries of Europe and Latin America has been the result of a very different strategy. Two developments in the 1960s threatened its markets, and Alcan was forced to respond to them. The three American aluminum majors were becoming vertically integrated by buying firms that fabricated finished products, and Alcan had to follow suit if it wanted to avoid losing customers. In addition, the formation of the European Common Market in 1960 threatened its export markets. Alcan's twofold international expansion allowed it to preserve its share of the world market — about 10 per cent of the world's aluminum output and 12 per cent of its alumina output.

In 1979 Alcan mined bauxite in seven countries (Australia, Brazil, France, Guinea, India, Jamaica and Malaysia), refined it into alumina in six (Australia, Brazil, Canada, Jamaica, India and Japan), and produced aluminum in nine (Australia, Brazil, Britain, Canada, India, Japan, Norway, Spain and West Germany). Alcan's aluminum smelters, counting its share of smelters operated by subsidiaries it owned jointly with other companies, had a capacity of 1.5 million metric tons, 60 per cent of which was located in Canada. Alcan was the largest manufacturing company in Britain, Brazil, Canada, India and New Zealand.[44] It was a fully integrated producer in Australia and Brazil — in both of which it was expanding rapidly — and in India. And finally, Alcan fabricated aluminum products in thirty-five countries and had marketing subsidiaries in a hundred countries.[45]

The aluminum companies, and Alcan in particular, provide evidence of the role of concentration on a world scale in influencing a firm's diversification strategy. With no substantial erosion of their market shares or bargaining power, Alcan and the other aluminum majors did not undertake a strategy of economic diversification similar to that of other metal mining and refining companies. Instead, Alcan continued to engage in the activities in which it had been involved for eighty years. Its increasingly multinational character in the post-war period was the result of tariff barriers raised by the countries in which it sold its products, a strategy of diversifying its sources of bauxite, and the competition that the newcomers Kaiser and Reynolds introduced into the world oligopoly. This new competition was primarily in the area of downstream vertical integration, which explains why most of Alcan's foreign subsidiaries are fabricators of finished aluminum products.

Cominco

In 1906, a number of Canadian Pacific Railway mining subsidiaries in British Columbia were merged into the Consolidated Mining and Smelting Company. The company, whose name was changed to Cominco in 1966, is still under the majority control of Canadian Pacific Ltd.

British Columbia metal deposits, and especially the lead, zinc and silver of the Sullivan mine that Cominco purchased in 1909, have been the backbone of the company throughout its history. However, vertical integration and economic and geographical diversification began very early. In 1916 Cominco purchased a hydroelectric company, West Kootenay Power and Light, to meet the energy requirements of its electrolytic reduction process. Lead and zinc smelters and reduction plants were built at Trail, B.C. starting in 1916, using American technology. In 1930 the company expanded into fertilizer and chemical production based on the sulfuric acid that separates off from metallic gases during electrolytic reduction. At the same time, Cominco's exploration in the Northwest Territories led to the discovery of gold deposits that would later be mined by its subsidiary, Pine Point Mines. With its complete vertical integration in British Columbia, Cominco became part of the world lead and zinc oligopolies in the early 1930s.

In 1946, Cominco purchased chemical and fertilizer factories built by the Canadian government during the Second World War, and continued its economic diversification within Canada in subsequent years. It expanded into integrated iron and steel production in British Columbia in 1964, and began producing potash in Saskatchewan in 1969. Cominco's international expansion started in 1930 when it began to mine phosphate in Montana, but it did not become genuinely multinational until after the war. During the 1960s and 1970s, multinationalization occurred at a very rapid rate. In 1963 it entered into a joint venture in India to build a plant to smelt and refine zinc and produce sulfuric acid. Cominco Binani Zinc Ltd. of Calcutta, 40 per cent owned by Cominco, was inaugurated in 1967 and accounts for 17 per cent of the zinc reduction capacity in India (where there are only two producers). Also in 1963, Cominco entered into a joint venture in Japan, Mitsubishi Cominco Smelting Co., in which it holds 45 per cent of the shares. Mitsubishi Cominco produces lead from concentrates shipped by the Canadian multinational from its mines in the Northwest Territories, and controls 9 per cent of Japan's lead refining capacity.[46] The Indian and Japanese ventures are aimed at creating markets for Cominco's Canadian ores.

Cominco also established marketing subsidiaries in England and West Germany and later in Holland to sell the ores and metals it produces in Canada. These companies are wholly owned subsidiaries, and thus represent a different market penetration strategy from the policy of undertaking joint ventures with local interests that Cominco has followed in the production field. Cominco's only manufacturing subsidiary in Europe is Mazak, of which it owns 50 per cent. Purchased in 1966, Mazak produces zinc alloys in the United Kingdom.

Cominco has been involved in large-scale mining outside Canada since the late 1960s. In 1968, it began to produce lead and zinc in the United States. Cominco American's Missouri deposits accounted for about 15 per cent of the lead produced in the U.S. in 1979. In 1971, Cominco bought 55 per cent of the shares of Aberfoyle, an Australian company that mines tin, gold and tungsten. The Black Angel lead-zinc mine in Greenland, 62 per cent owned by Cominco, came into production in 1973. Cominco later acquired a 47 per cent share of Exploración Minera Internacional España

(Exminesa), a Spanish lead-zinc mining company that entered into production in 1978. Cominco's Australian subsidiary, in which it has had to reduce its participation to 47 per cent, is currently expanding into lead-zinc production. The company has also become highly diversified in the chemical products and fertilizer industry in the United States, and it owns ammonia and urea plants in Texas and an ammonium nitrate plant in Nebraska.

In 1979, 63 per cent of Cominco's income came from the sale of ores and metals, 24 per cent came from fertilizers and chemical products, and 13 per cent came from other activities. In geographical terms, 70 per cent of its income came from Canada, 22 per cent from the United States and 8 per cent from other countries.[47]

The company appears to have followed a two-pronged diversification strategy. On the one hand, it has become economically diversified in Canada and the United States. This diversification was slow between 1930 and 1960 but has been very rapid since 1960 and has put an end to the company's fifty-year dependence on lead-zinc production. It has involved Cominco in the production of fertilizers, iron and steel, and potash and on a minority basis in companies producing coal and oil. On the other hand, the company has become geographically diversified in the mining and fabrication of the two minerals in which it has the greatest expertise — lead and zinc. Thus, it has acquired new smelting and refining subsidiaries in India and new mines in the United States, Spain, Australia and Greenland.[48] In 1980 Cominco was one of the world's largest producers of lead, with more than 5 per cent of total world production, and zinc, with more than 4 per cent of the total. There has been a slow but sure trend away from concentration in the lead and zinc markets in the last forty years, but Cominco's complete vertical integration and recent international expansion have allowed it to retain a leading position in those markets.

Canadian mining companies with investments in other countries operate in oligopolistic markets and benefit from a high degree of concentration. In the nickel industry, Inco, Falconbridge and Sherritt Gordon Mines are the only three Canadian producers, and Inco has always accounted for more than 50 per cent of Canadian nickel output. In the aluminum field, Alcan enjoyed an outright monopoly from 1902 to 1955 and a near-monopoly in subsequent years. The oligopoly in the copper industry is not as concentrated as in nickel or aluminum. The dominant position of Inco and Noranda Mines has been eroded by the emergence of Canterra in recent years, while Falconbridge and Hudson Bay have remained minor partners in the oligopoly. Canada has only four integrated zinc producers (Noranda, Cominco, Canterra and Hudson Bay), and only two integrated lead producers (Cominco and Noranda). Stephen Hymer's thesis that economic concentration in the country of origin is an initial condition for international expansion is strikingly confirmed in the case of the Canadian mining sector.

On the other hand, the model of the obsolescing bargain does not fit Canadian mining companies as neatly as it did the utility sector. All five of the industries we examined have undergone a reduction in concentration — limited in the aluminum industry, moderate in lead and zinc, and substantial in copper and nickel. However, this reduced concentration has come about much more as the result of the entry of new Japanese, American, European, Canadian, or Australian competitors than of the nationalization of multinationals' subsidiaries in the Third World. Only in the copper industry has nationalization been more than a marginal phenomenon, and competition from Third World companies, whether publicly or privately owned, has been almost nonexistent. Because access to financial markets has been difficult for companies based in peripheral countries, because the multinationals continue to control technology and commercial networks, and because consumer markets are concentrated in a small number of countries, the wave of nationalizations that took place between 1967 and 1974 has not continued.

Thus, the theory of the erosion of the multinationals' bargaining power appears to be only partially applicable to the mining sector. The change in the balance of forces that takes place when concentration in an industry is reduced is not in itself sufficient to make it possible for host country governments to take over the subsidiaries of multinational corporations. On the other hand, reduced concentration has resulted in a proliferation of regulations concerning the degree of control that a parent corporation can exercise over its subsidiary, the repatriation of profits, the ways in which a company can reinvest its profits or reduce its investment, and similar matters. In other words, the multinationals' obsolescing bargain has tended to result in joint ventures rather than publicly-owned corporations in the peripheral countries. The governments of Spain, Mexico, India and Brazil have become especially skilled at enacting regulations of this sort.[49]

The effects on Canadian companies of this reduction in concentration have been varied. In the nickel and copper industries, Canadian multinationals' share of the world market has been reduced, and they have resorted to economic and geographical diversification, expanding into new industries and increasing their international operations throughout the post-war period. At the opposite extreme, in the lead and zinc industries, it has been Canadian companies — notably Cominco and Noranda — that have helped lead the movement away from concentration by becoming multinational and increasing their market shares. In the aluminum smelting industry, meanwhile, Alcan has maintained its share of the world market, and as a result has not resorted to economic diversification; at the same time, it has sought to accelerate its international expansion to meet world demand.

Canadian multinationals are masters of existing know-how, but they are not major originators of technology except in the nickel industry. With the exception of Sherritt Gordon's nickel refining process, the various electrolytic refining processes used for the five metals under examination were all imported from outside Canada. Most of the smelting technology used by Canadian companies has also been imported, except in the copper industry where three Canadian companies — Inco, Noranda and Sherritt — have their own patented processes. The new continuous casting technology for copper fabrication was imported in 1980 by Noranda, which acquired it from the leading Belgian copper producer. On the other hand, Canadian companies may introduce changes and technical improvements into these imported processes, and eventually export these changes. On the whole, if Louis T. Wells, Jr. is correct in arguing for the existence of an international pecking order, Canada's place in that order is a little behind the innovating countries and far ahead of the countries of the Third World. Because of the size of Canada's corporations and market, its geographical and cultural proximity to the United States and Europe, and its high standard of living, Canada is able to adopt the innovations produced by American and European companies very quickly. It is ahead of Australia in acquiring these technological advantages, and far ahead of the most highly industrialized countries in Latin America such as Argentina, Brazil and Mexico.

Thus, it appears that innovation is not a necessary condition for international expansion. A mining company does not necessarily have to be innovative to be transnational. It must only be part of an oligopoly, be of sufficient size, and have the know-how and the means to buy technology from innovative firms before that technology becomes too widely disseminated. The advantage held by Canadian multinationals lies not in their innovative character but in their economic, geographical and cultural proximity to innovative companies in the United States and Europe. While Vernon's model of an innovative oligopoly may apply to the "typical" cases of American or western European multinationals, it is less valid for countries in which industrialization took place later, such as Canada and perhaps Australia.

There have been a number of factors operating against the multinationalization of Canadian mining companies — Canada has large ore deposits of its own, the American market is very close, and there is little political risk in Canada. However, the major Canadian mining companies finally opted for international expansion after the Second World War to meet the new international competition and maintain their share of the world market. Because they came so late and had little to offer in the way of technological innovation, Canadian companies had to offer the host countries a better deal, so that their expansion most often took the form of joint ventures with host country governments or local private interests. But despite their weaknesses, Canadian companies are a growing force in the world mining industry.

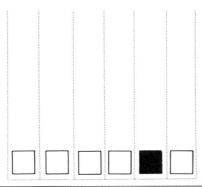

5 Multinationals and the Manufacturing Sector

As noted in Chapter 2, manufacturing investment represents about half of Canadian direct investment in foreign countries. Table 1 shows that the beverage, non-ferrous metals, wood and paper, iron and iron products, and chemical industries account for 92 per cent of Canadian manufacturing investment. One of these industries, non-ferrous metals, is made up of integrated mining companies (such as Alcan or Cominco) and was thus covered in the previous chapter.

Official statistics present some obstacles to an in-depth study of multinationalization in the major manufacturing industries. Statistics Canada has one set of designations for industrial branches (these are the designations used in Table 1), and a different set for economic activities. In addition, because of the need to maintain confidentiality, each of its categories encompasses a number of very different industries, and these categories are thus too broad in scope.

For example, the beverage industry (number 109 in the classification of economic activities) comprises four different industries — soft-drink manufacturing and bottling, distilling, brewing, and winemaking. Canadian companies had foreign investments in each of these industries in 1977; Crush International in the soft-drink industry, Carling-O'Keefe in brewing, and Seagram in distilling and winemaking are examples in each category. But these industries are not all of equal interest in terms of their degree of multinationalization. As a comparative examination of Canadian and foreign multinational corporations in these industries shows, distil-

TABLE 1

Distribution of Canadian Manufacturing Investment in Foreign Countries by Industry, Leading Host Countries, 1980 (%)

Industry	U.S.	U.K.	Other	Total
Beverages	21	22	12	19
Non-ferrous metals	31	39	50	37
Wood and paper products	21	16	14	19
Iron and products	8	21	13	11
Chemical and allied products	9	1	4	6
Other manufacturing	10	1	6	8
Total (%)	100	100	100	100
Total (C$ million)	6,568	1,528	2,698	10,794

Source: Statistics Canada, Cat. 67-202 (Ottawa, 1983).

ling is the most multinational of the four Canadian beverage industries. In fact, the largest and the third largest distilling corporation in the world have their head offices in Canada and are controlled by Canadian interests, and each of these firms has a large number of subsidiaries spread over many countries. On the other hand, while Canadian breweries constitute a very tight oligopoly in the domestic market, they are much smaller and less transnational than the distilleries.

In each of the major Statistics Canada categories, we will look at one representative industry. Thus, among the beverage industries, we will focus on distilling; in wood, paper and related industries, we will look at paper manufacturing; in iron and iron products, we will concentrate on farm machinery manufacturing; among the chemical industries, we will examine synthetic rubber; and in the category of other manufacturing we will study the telecommunications equipment industry. In each of these industries, there is at least one world-scale Canadian transnational corporation — Seagram and Hiram Walker in distilling, MacMillan Bloedel and Domtar in the paper industry, Massey-Ferguson in farm machinery, Polysar in synthetic rubber, and Northern Telecom in telecommunications equipment.

In the first section of this chapter, the five industries under study will be examined one by one. In the second section, we will take a more detailed look at six Canadian multinationals operating in these industries. We will focus on their strategies for international expansion, their responses to changes in the worldwide structure of the industries in which they operate, and their place in the Canadian and world markets.

A: THE MAJOR MANUFACTURING INDUSTRIES

One conclusion can be drawn immediately — the industries we are looking at run the gamut from the most traditional (distilling) to the most modern (synthetic rubber and telecommunications equipment). Like their American and European counterparts, Canadian transnational corporations are not concentrated in the most traditional industries but cover the whole manufacturing spectrum.

Another look at Table 1 leads to a second conclusion. Canadian manufacturing investment is concentrated primarily in advanced industrialized countries and not in the underdeveloped countries of the Third World. In this respect, Canadian multinationals are more like those based in the advanced countries than like multinationals based in semi-industrialized countries.

The Distilled Liquor Industry

The distilled liquor industry comprises the manufacture of a number of different alcoholic products, intended for non-industrial use and distilled from grain (whisky), wine (brandy and cognac), molasses (rum), fruit and other substances. Whisky has consistently been the most significant of these products in terms of both volume and aggregate value. Whisky originated in the United Kingdom and has been manufactured in North America since the eighteenth century. The United States became the largest consumer market in the late nineteenth century. In 1960, the United States accounted for 83 per cent of world consumption of whisky in all its varieties, Canada 6 per cent, the United Kingdom 5 per cent and the rest of the world 5 per cent.[1] Before the Second World War, whisky represented more than 90 per cent by volume of the distilled liquor sold in the United States, but throughout the post-war period white goods (vodka, rum, gin, etc.) cut into whisky's share of the market so that it stood at only 45 per cent in 1978. At the same time, distilled liquor has represented a steadily decreasing proportion of the whole alcoholic beverage market. While distilled liquor had 25 per cent of the market in 1971, this figure had been reduced to 20 per cent by 1978. Wine had 13 per cent of the market in 1978 and beer almost two-thirds.[2]

The industry has always been characterized by a high degree of corporate concentration in the principal producing and consuming countries. In the United States, the industry went through two major stages. In the late nineteenth century, an American whisky producers' pool was formed; this "whisky trust" became a national monopoly, the Distilling Company, in 1890. However, since scale of production and know-how are not insurmountable barriers to entry in this industry, independents periodically succeeded in getting into the market. The national near-monopoly was broken by prohibition, imposed in 1918. When it was lifted in 1933 four companies, two American (National Distillers and Schenley) and two Canadian (Seagram and Hiram Walker), took the largest share of the market. After the Second World War, however, the concentration of whisky production was steadily reduced, as Table 2 shows.

In Canada, corporate concentration in the distilled liquor industry has always been very high, and there is no indication that it has lessened in recent decades. Two companies, Seagram and Hiram Walker, stand out. Hiram Walker was founded in 1858 and led the industry for many years. In 1927, during a merger wave in which Canadian industry was reorganized from top to bottom, it absorbed Gooderham and Worts. Distillers Corp., founded in 1924, grew to countrywide and international scale when it purchased J.E. Seagram four years later. Because of prohibition in the United States, Canadian distilling companies were spared from American competition, both in Canada and elsewhere in the world. Canadian companies also grew rich from sales of bootlegged whisky in the United States throughout the prohibition period. After the Second World War there was no reduction in concentration in Canada. In 1948, the three largest distilling firms accounted for 84 per cent of the jobs in the industry;[3] in 1970, the four largest firms represented 86 per cent of the value added in the industry in Canada.[4]

In Britain, the dominant company was Distillers Co. Ltd. (DCL), formed in 1877. In 1936 it was a holding company controlling some twenty-six companies and two-thirds of British whisky production.[5] As they expanded internationally, Canadian companies absorbed a substantial portion of Britain's independent whisky producers but did not threaten DCL's dominant position in the British market.

TABLE 2

Concentration in the American Distilled Liquor Industry: Output of the Four Largest Firms as a Percentage of the Industry Total, 1947-72

Year	Blair data	Morton data
1947	75%	—
1954	64%	63%
1958	60%	60%
1963	58%	56%
1967	—	52%
1972	—	50%

Sources: John M. Blair, *Economic Concentration* (New York: Harcourt Brace Jovanovich, 1972), p. 324; Morton Research Co., *The U.S. Distilled Liquor Industry* (New York, 1979), p. 81.

The Canadian, American and British industries all adopted different strategies towards domestic and export markets. Canadian companies had to become involved in international operations to continue their expansion. Part of the reason for this was the limited size of the Canadian domestic market. In addition, the distilled liquor industry is one of the most heavily regulated in the world, so that the Canadian companies could be threatened by government intervention in their export markets. Hence, the two largest Canadian companies began their international expansion at a very early date (1933) and this made it possible for them to become world leaders in the industry by the end of the Second World War. The imposition of prohibition in the United States and the traditional strategy followed by the dominant British company left the field open to the Canadian multinationals and allowed them to invade the world industry. In the second part of this chapter, we will study the world-wide expansion of the two Canadian distilling giants.

The American companies, which had to reorganize thoroughly after prohibition, adopted a very different policy, preferring to grant licences rather than extend their operations to foreign countries. Faced with Canadian competition in their own home market, they had to consolidate their domestic position instead of expanding internationally.

The British giant chose exports as its primary means of penetrating foreign markets before the Second World War. DCL's international expansion occurred later and was more limited than that of the Canadian companies. Its subsidiary in the United States is only a medium-rank company in that country. It is less diversified than the Canadian companies both geographically and economically and has not been able to keep up with the changes in the alcoholic beverage market that have occurred since the Second World War.

With their greater international diversification, the Canadian companies were in a better position to alter their output in line with changing demand. Seagram has interests in many countries, and can produce Scotch in Britain, bourbon in the United States, rye in Canada and the United States, cognac in France, rum in Jamaica and Puerto Rico, and so forth. Thus, it can respond to structural changes in alcohol consumption while retaining its leading position in the industry.

Meanwhile, other countries have become major distilled liquor producers. In the early 1970s, Japan became the second largest producing country, displacing the United Kingdom. At the same time a Japanese company, Suntory, has passed Hiram Walker to become the world's second largest liquor distilling firm, even though it has not yet penetrated the major western markets. The gains made by Japanese, European and South Korean producers have helped reduce concentration and reopen competition in the industry. Declining concentration has been felt both in the United States — which leads the world in the production and consumption of distilled liquor — and elsewhere, and the Canadian companies have been subject to its effects. They have also been forced to respond to the other major change in market structure: the decline of whisky relative to other distilled liquors combined with the overall reduction of the share of distilled liquor in the alcoholic beverages market.[6]

In this industry, economies of scale and existing companies' monopoly of know-how are not as great an obstacle to competition as in other areas of the economy. The main barrier to entry is consumers' loyalty to established brands, and this barrier is far from insurmountable. Declining concentration and the absence of barriers to entry help explain the recent transformation of Canadian distilling companies into conglomerates.

The Paper Industry

The figures in Table 1 show that Canadian direct investment in foreign countries in wood, paper and allied industries is substantial. This heading comprises four major industrial groups — the wood, furniture, paper, and printing industries. There is no Canadian-based multinational corporation in the furniture industry. There is a highly significant multinational in the printing industry — Moore Corporation, the world's largest manufacturer of business forms, with subsidiaries in more than thirty countries and a market share of 25 per cent in the United States and 10 per cent worldwide. Nevertheless, the scale of Canada's forest industries (wood and paper), the size of the companies involved in this industry, and the current development and future potential of Canadian paper companies all make it worthwhile to concentrate on the forest industries as such and especially on the paper industry, which is the larger of the two. The forest industries encompass a wide variety of activities. The paper industry covers pulp and paper mills and cardboard box and paper bag manufacturers, while the wood industry includes sawmills, veneer and plywood makers, door and sash manufacturers, and similar operations. Today, large North American forest companies are active in both the paper and the wood industry.

As well as being the larger of the two industries, the paper industry is also the more highly concentrated. In 1972, Canada's pulp and paper mills constituted the country's second largest manufacturing activity after the automobile industry. The shipments of the seventy-five Canadian paper companies had a total value of $3.1 billion, and the four leading firms accounted for 35 per cent of this total. Sawn lumber production, the dominant activity within the wood industry, placed seventh among Canadian manufacturing activities. The sawn lumber industry comprised 1,463 companies, with total shipments worth $1.9 billion, of which the four leading firms accounted for 18 per cent.[7] There are many more wood products companies than paper companies, and they are much smaller and more specialized. As a general rule, while only the largest wood products companies have been able to break into the paper industry, all the major paper companies are involved in several aspects of the wood industry. The paper companies' diversification into the wood industry has been a postwar phenomenon. It has occurred prior to, and sometimes simultaneously with, their international expansion.

A series of nineteenth-century technological developments is at the root of the modern paper industry. The Fourdrinier brothers built the first papermaking machine — which still bears their name — in England in 1807. Wood pulp was first made by machine in Germany in 1840; sulfite pulp was invented in the United States in 1867; and sulfate pulp was first manufactured in 1884, again in Germany. The first Fourdrinier machine to arrive in the United States was imported from England in 1827, and two years later paper machines were being built in the U.S. by copying the English models. The machine was introduced into Canada in the late 1850s.

Paper companies grew up in the United States throughout the nineteenth century, first in New England and later on the Pacific Coast. As the result of a merger wave at the end of the century, International Paper, founded in 1898, emerged as the American and world leader in the industry. The other American paper giant was Crown Zellerbach, which operated on the Pacific Coast. The Canadian paper industry was still in its infancy at this time. The American tariff was an obstacle to the development of Canadian paper companies, and they had to face competition from European (especially Scandinavian) and American producers for export markets. Output in Canada, divided among some twenty-six companies, was much smaller than in the United States.

Just after the turn of the century, Canadian provincial governments (which owned 80 per cent of the country's forest reserves), aiming to increase processing within their territory, began to take measures to prevent American paper companies from exporting pulpwood south of the border. Ontario imposed an embargo on the export of pulpwood cut on public lands in 1902, and Quebec followed suit in 1910. In 1913, the U.S. government lifted its tariff on newsprint. This led to the establishment of a number of Canadian paper companies and the expansion of several others, and American companies — notably International Paper in 1921 — crossed the border to establish subsidiaries in Canada. Canadian newsprint production passed that of the United States in 1926, and Canada became, and remains, the world's leading producer and exporter of newsprint.

A number of independent paper companies were absorbed during the unprecedented Canadian merger wave of 1924-31, and five dominant companies emerged from this concentration movement.[8] The largest of these was Canada Power and Paper, which was reorganized under the name of Consolidated Paper in 1931 and renamed Consolidated-Bathurst in 1967. This Canadian-controlled company accounted for 20 per cent of Canadian newsprint production in 1930. In second place was Abitibi Power and Paper, under joint Canadian-American control, which represented 17 per cent of Canadian capacity. Canadian International Paper, a wholly-owned subsidiary of the American industry leader, was third with 15 per cent. Price Brothers, controlled by the Price family of Quebec, followed with 10 per cent, and then came St. Lawrence Corp. with 8 per cent. These five companies, representing 70 per cent of Canadian capacity, constituted the country's paper oligopoly. There were also ten or so smaller independent companies.[9]

The paper companies were followed into Canada by the American manufacturers of papermaking machinery. The American industry leader was Beloit Iron Works (now Beloit Corp.), founded in 1885, and it established a plant in Sorel, Quebec in partnership with Charles Walmsley and Co., the leading British paper machine manufacturer. The second largest American producer, Black Clawson, established a subsidiary in Ontario. Dominion Engineering Works, founded by Canadians in 1920 to manufacture electric and papermaking machinery under licence, was bought out by the American giant General Electric soon afterwards. In sum, the belated creation of the Canadian paper machinery manufacturing industry in the twentieth century occurred wholly under American control.

The North American paper industry was very seriously affected by the Depression of the 1930s. The series of mergers and reorganizations that took place in the 1920s was combined with a wave of overcapitalization, which was followed by a catastrophic decline in production and prices from which the industry did not recover until the Second World War. After the war, the large North American paper companies underwent a twofold process: integration with the wood industry, and international expansion. The most significant merger between a lumber company and a paper company in Canada was the marriage of MacMillan Bloedel with Powell River in 1959, which resulted in the largest forest products concern in the country. In the United States, the most spectacular takeover was the purchase of the second largest lumber company, Long Bell Lumber Corp., by the leading paper firm, International Paper.[10]

The other part of the process has been the international expansion of Canadian and American paper companies. Consolidated Paper began to operate in the United States in the early 1950s and in

West Germany in 1967. Abitibi entered the United States in 1963. Domtar expanded first to England, in 1966, and then to the United States in 1973. Similarly, American paper companies, after establishing their first foreign operations in Canada between 1900 and 1930, have conducted a new international thrust in the last twenty years. Among the more notable moves have been the purchase by International Paper of an Italian subsidiary in 1974 and a Japanese one in 1976, and the entry of Crown Zellerbach into Switzerland in 1962 and the Netherlands ten years later.

There has been a slight reduction in concentration in both Canada and the United States in the last forty years, primarily because of the entry of lumber companies into the paper industry. While the five leading companies represented 70 per cent of Canadian newsprint production capacity in 1930, their share was less than two-thirds in 1978. Nor were the same five companies involved. There were two new firms, MacMillan Bloedel and Ontario Paper, while two others, Abitibi and Price, merged in 1974. Consolidated-Bathurst and Canadian International Paper, which had formed part of the oligopoly in 1930, were still among the five dominant firms in 1978. These are all large corporations, each with sales of more than a billion dollars in 1979. Outside this concentrated oligopoly there are some sixty independent firms.

The Canadian paper industry is an example of an industry characterized by a late-blooming oligopoly. The development of the industry occurred fifty years later than in Europe and the United States, and the concentration stage was reached thirty years later. In these conditions, it is not surprising that the technology used in the industry has been either imported or made in Canada by subsidiaries of American or European equipment manufacturers. The Depression of the 1930s was a serious setback for the industry and helped delay its growth in the international arena. The worldwide expansion of the last twenty years has been based on American and European technology, and Canadian multinationals buy equipment for their American and European subsidiaries in the host countries.

The Canadian paper industry demonstrates that an industrial branch does not have to be innovative to become international. It only has to be organized as an oligopoly and consist of large corporations that are able to buy technology and equipment in the countries that produce them. The geographical expansion of the Canadian paper industry is based on an oligopoly, but it does not fit the model of the "innovative oligopoly" that Raymond Vernon has suggested is at the root of multinational corporations.

Technological development has been very slow in the paper

industry. All the major elements of papermaking technology were known in both North America and Europe by the end of the nineteenth century. Since then, only minor improvements have been made such as increases in the capacity or the speed of papermaking machines. Papermaking technology is accessible to companies that are not extremely large. In these conditions, the stability of the Canadian paper oligopoly has not been due to control of technology. Instead, control of pulpwood supplies has played a strategic role. In some cases, especially in the United States where most public lands have long since been sold to private business interests, the paper companies own huge tracts of land. In Canada, control has been based primarily on long-term concessions to cut pulpwood on crown lands. With the best timberlands already in the hands of the large companies, it is difficult for new competitors to enter the industry.

This is an important asset for the large companies, and has helped make possible their international expansion and diversification into other forest industries. This twofold movement, while late in developing, has been a vigorous one. For the Canadian companies, it has followed a pattern that is likely to continue — expansion first to the United States, then to Europe, and then to other regions. In the second part of this chapter, we will look at the case of MacMillan Bloedel, which has gone through all these stages.

The Farm Machinery Industry

The farm machinery industry comprises the manufacture of a very wide variety of products. The most important of these are farm tractors and harvesting combines, followed by ploughs, binders, mowers and other implements and machines. The leading North American producers of farm machinery are International Harvester, Deere and Co., and Allis-Chalmers in the United States, and Massey-Ferguson in Canada.

The industry in the United States became concentrated very quickly in the early twentieth century during a merger wave that produced International Harvester, the American and world leader in the industry. At the time of its creation, International Harvester represented more than 50 per cent of the American farm machinery industry. In Canada, a similar market structure was established with the merger of the Massey Manufacturing Co. and A. Harris, Son and Co. in 1891 to form Massey-Harris, the leading Canadian firm in the field.[11]

Soon after they were organized, these two dominant firms

invaded each other's markets and expanded into Europe. International Harvester established a subsidiary in Canada in 1903 and by the late 1920s was the leading firm in the Canadian market as well with about a third of total sales.[12] By this time it also had interests in Europe. Massey-Harris purchased its first American subsidiary in 1910 and established subsidiaries in France and Germany between 1925 and 1928. Meanwhile, a North American common market in farm machinery was being established. The United States lifted its tariff on farm machinery in 1913 while Canada lowered its tariff steadily between 1892 and 1944, except for a brief period during the Depression when tariffs were raised. Other large American companies also crossed the border into Canada. Deere purchased a Canadian subsidiary in 1911, while White Motor Corp. took over the second largest Canadian producer, Cockshutt Plow, in 1962.

There was a steady reduction in corporate concentration between the early part of the century and the Second World War, but the situation has stabilized since then. Only six large farm machinery companies manufacturing a full range of products remained in North America in 1984 — International Harvester, Deere, Massey-Ferguson (the result of the merger of Massey-Harris with H. Ferguson in 1953), Allis-Chalmers, White Motors, and Case. The first four of these companies accounted for 44 per cent of the American market in 1958 and 46 per cent in 1972.[13]

The level of concentration has also stabilized in Canada. In 1948 the three leading firms — Massey-Harris, International Harvester and Cockshutt — accounted for 63 per cent of the jobs in the industry.[14] Seven years later, the Royal Commission on Canada's Economic Prospects attributed about 50 per cent of Canadian production to Massey-Ferguson, 25 per cent to International Harvester and 15 per cent to Cockshutt.[15] Another royal commission in 1971 attributed 51 per cent of farm machinery sales to the four largest firms.[16] And for the year 1976, Statistics Canada calculated that the four largest firms accounted for 65 per cent of the total value of products shipped by farm machinery manufacturers.[17] While these measures are not directly comparable, they show that in Canada as in the United States there has been little change in the farm machinery oligopoly, even if there has been some reduction in the level of concentration since the early part of the century.

The firms that make up the North American oligopoly are also leaders on a world scale. In 1968 a writer estimated that the three largest firms — International Harvester, Deere and Massey-Ferguson — each represented between 15 and 20 per cent of the capitalist world's production.[18] These three companies control a large proportion of the industry in Europe, Australia and Latin America.[19]

In becoming multinationals, however, the large companies have followed very different strategies. The American producers were the first to consolidate their position in North America and undertake international expansion. By 1911, International Harvester had plants in Canada, France, Germany, Sweden and Russia, and its foreign subsidiaries accounted for 40 per cent of its sales.[20] Meanwhile, Massey-Harris had a large number of marketing agencies outside Canada but only one foreign plant, in the United States. The Canadian company's international expansion remained slow in the 1920s and 1930s but became very rapid in the 1950s, and becoming more heavily multinational than its American rivals.

TABLE 3

Distribution by Region of the Assets and Sales of the World's Three Leading Farm Machinery Firms, 1976

Company	Assets (%)			Sales (%)		
	North America	Europe	Other	North America	Europe	Other
International Harvester	75	17	8	72	17	11
Massey-Ferguson	38	38	24	31	32	37
Deere	90	7	3	77	10	13

Source: Morton Research Co., *The U.S. Farm Machinery Industry* (New York, 1977), pp. 165-77.

The reason Massey had to adopt a different strategy was that it was chronically weak in the market for farm tractors, the most complex — and the most important — product in the industry. To obtain the technology of tractor production, Massey had to take over an American manufacturer in 1928 and several British ones in the 1950s. The British companies, with their international networks of subsidiaries, affiliated companies and foreign licensees, gave Massey a world stature it had not had before. Most important, they gave it the technological advantages it needed for international expansion. In particular, Massey obtained the technology of tractor production from Ferguson, absorbed in 1953, and diesel engine technology from Perkins, acquired in 1959.

As in other manufacturing industries, the Canadian farm machinery companies have relied heavily on foreign technology. Their specific advantage has been based on their size and their oligopoly control of the Canadian market, not on innovation. Furthermore, their multinationalization has followed a different pattern from that of their American competitors. Unlike the American firms — but like the Canadian distilling multinationals — they have gained a large part of their know-how through the process of international expansion itself.

The Synthetic Rubber Industry

The Canadian chemical industry has substantial investments in foreign countries. Among the major foreign investors within the industry is one of the world's leading manufacturers of synthetic rubber, latex and resins — Polysar Corporation, owned by the federal government with its head office and main production facilities in Sarnia, Ontario. To place Polysar in context, let us first look at the world synthetic rubber and related products industry.

Natural and synthetic rubber are basic to modern industry. The primary market for rubber is the tire industry, which accounts for about 70 per cent of demand. Among the other leading markets are the wire and cable, construction, footwear and aircraft industries. The two kinds of rubber result from two very different industrial processes. Natural rubber is made by coagulating the milky sap of the Hevea tree, a plant native to Brazil. In the early twentieth century, the Hevea was transplanted to Southeast Asia, which within a few years replaced Brazil as the world's major producing region. The industrial use of natural rubber began during the nineteenth century, with the invention of the vulcanization process by Charles Goodyear in the United States in 1839 and the development of rubber tires in England by John Dunlop.[21]

Synthetic rubber, a petroleum derivative, is a much more recent invention. It was first developed in the Soviet Union, Germany and the United States during the first third of the twentieth century, but before the Second World War its price was too high relative to that of natural rubber for large-scale commercial use to be feasible. Significant quantities were produced only in the Soviet Union and Germany. However, the Japanese occupation of Malaya, the Dutch East Indies (Indonesia) and a number of other far eastern countries in 1941 cut off the capitalist industrial economies' source of natural rubber supply. The United States and Canada imposed rationing, and steps were taken to increase Latin American production, but the supply still did not meet demand.

It was necessary to resort to the use of synthetic rubber. Between 1942 and 1944, synthetic rubber factories with a total capacity of 880,000 short tons were designed and built in North America. About 50,000 tons of this capacity was in Canada. In the United States, Standard Oil of New Jersey (now Exxon), which held the patents for synthetic rubber production, was required to share its know-how without royalties for the duration of the war. Starting in 1941, synthetic rubber factories were built with U.S. government financing and then operated by the Goodyear, Firestone and U.S. Rubber companies.[22] In Canada, the federal government established a crown corporation, Polymer Corporation, which acquired the American technology in 1942 and began producing synthetic rubber the next year.

After the war natural rubber regained most of the ground it had lost (See Table 4). A number of American synthetic rubber factories were closed, but Polymer continued its operations. Natural rubber prices rose again during the Korean War, and the synthetic rubber plants were reactivated. Since then, synthetic rubber has steadily increased its market share at the expense of the natural product.

TABLE 4

World Consumption of Natural and Synthetic Rubber, 1935-80

Rubber	1935	1940	1945	1950	1960	1970	1980*
Natural(%)	99	97	23	71	45	34	31
Synthetic(%)	1	3	77	29	55	66	69

* Projected.
Source: Fortune, April 24, 1978, p. 81.

As a result of its uninterrupted production, its permanent absorption of American and German technology, and its own research activity, within a few years of the end of the war Polymer had become one of the world's leading manufacturers of synthetic rubber, in terms of both overall output and the quality and variety of rubbers it produced. For a long time, Polymer had an absolute monopoly of Canadian production.

Meanwhile, synthetic rubber production in the United States took the form of upstream vertical integration by the tire manufacturers during the Second World War. The oil majors also entered the market, starting with Standard Oil of New Jersey, which held the patents. In 1955, the world synthetic rubber industry was still organized as an oligopoly concentrated in North America. Polymer was part of this oligopoly and accounted for 10 per cent of world output.

The late 1950s saw the entry of a number of new European and Japanese producers. These included the International Synthetic Rubber Co. (ISR) in England, jointly owned by a number of European and American tire manufacturers, including Dunlop, Michelin, Firestone, Pirelli and Uniroyal; Buna Werke Huls GmbH in West Germany, jointly owned by Bayer (part of the I.G. Farben group which manufactured synthetic rubber under the Nazi regime) and Veba; the Société de Caoutchouc Butyl in France, jointly owned by Standard Oil of New Jersey and the Compagnie Française des Résines; Italy's government-owned oil company, ENI; and the Mitsubishi and Furakawa groups in Japan.[23]

During the 1960s and 1970s there was an explosion of new producers in Europe and Japan. In Europe, Shell replaced ISR as the leading producer. Local companies such as Montedison and Società Italiana Resina in Italy and Michelin in France compete with subsidiaries of American multinationals such as Firestone, Goodyear, Standard Brands and Du Pont. Polymer (renamed Polysar in 1972) began operating in France and Belgium in the early 1960s in an effort to keep its markets. In 1973, there were close to thirty synthetic rubber producers in the European Economic Community, with the ten largest (seven European companies, two American ones, and Polysar) accounting for almost 80 per cent of output.[24] Production has also increased rapidly in Japan. Here too new competitors entered the market in the 1960s, and Japan has become the world's second-largest producing country behind the United States.

Thus, synthetic rubber production is a new industry that had its beginnings between the two world wars and has experienced a rapid decline in concentration in the last twenty years. During the 1930s, the industry's technology was controlled by a tight cartel of two producers, I.G. Farben in Germany and Standard Oil of New Jersey in the United States. Know-how was disseminated during the Second World War at the impetus of the U.S. government, and a Canadian company, with a monopoly in its own country, became one of the world's leading producers at that time. In the postwar period this company retained its market share as a result of a policy of active expansion both in Canada and elsewhere, which it continues to follow.

Synthetic rubber is another example of an industry in which corporate concentration has been reduced on a world scale as a result of the entry of new producers, especially in Europe and Japan. While technology has been disseminated, production has remained geographically concentrated close to consumer markets — in North America, western Europe and Japan. It is an industry well endowed with capital and technology, and most of its leading companies are controlled either by synthetic rubber users (the tire manufacturers) or by raw material suppliers (the oil companies). In this respect Polysar, which is not integrated either upstream or downstream, is unique. This circumstance has arisen because Polysar is a publicly-owned company in a country where both the upstream and the downstream industries are foreign-controlled. On the other hand, Polysar does resemble many other Canadian multinationals in that it enjoyed an absolute monopoly position for a long time (it now produces only two-thirds of Canada's synthetic rubber) and uses imported technology.

The Telecommunications Equipment Industry

The telecommunications equipment industry, which had its origins in the United States towards the end of the nineteenth century, was for a long time one of the smallest and tightest oligopolies in the world economy. The main component of the industry is the production of telephone equipment for large telephone utilities. Its leading protagonists were — and remain — two American companies, one of which, Western Electric, operates primarily in the United States, while the other, International Telephone and Telegraph (ITT), operates mostly outside the country. However, a Canadian telecommunications equipment manufacturer has succeeded in penetrating this oligopolistic structure.

On the basis of Alexander Graham Bell's American patent, granted in 1876, Bell Telephone grew to become the largest corporation in the United States and the largest telephone company in the world. In 1881, Bell purchased a controlling interest in Western Electric Manufacturing, an electric equipment producer that became its telephone equipment manufacturing arm.

Soon after they were founded in the United States, Bell Telephone and Western Electric established subsidiaries in Canada, the Bell Telephone Company of Canada (1880) and the Northern

Electric and Manufacturing Company. In the United States, Bell — which after 1899 operated under the umbrella of the holding company American Telephone and Telegraph (AT&T) — captured a near-monopoly position within a short space of time. In 1981, AT&T owned more than 85 per cent of the telephones in service in the United States, while some 1,800 "independent" companies shared the remaining 15 per cent. Since then, as a result of antitrust suits against AT&T, the company has had to divest itself of its subsidiaries that provide local telephone service to subscribers.

Bell attained a similar position in Canada, establishing itself in Quebec, Ontario, the maritimes and the Northwest Territories. AT&T gradually sold off its shares in Bell Canada, which has become a wholly Canadian corporation as a result. In addition, in 1906 Bell Canada bought a majority interest in Northern Electric, the manufacturing subsidiary established by Western Electric. However, Northern Electric continued to produce equipment under licence from the American manufacturer, so that what were called Canadian innovations in the telephone equipment field were really only copies. In 1949, the U.S. government undertook judicial proceedings against AT&T and Western Electric with the primary aim of breaking the ownership ties between the two companies. This did not happen, but in the wake of the suit Western Electric divested itself of its shares in Northern Electric in 1956, and Northern Electric was released from its technological dependence on the American company. Northern became a wholly-owned subsidiary of Bell Canada. In 1958, Bell Canada and Northern established Bell-Northern Research Laboratories, and have since then produced a growing number of innovations in telecommunications equipment technology.

Thus, the main structural characteristic of the telecommunications equipment market is vertical integration between the telephone utilities and their manufacturing suppliers. This constitutes a formidable barrier to entry for new competitors, since the two large utility companies, AT&T (at least before the divestiture of its operating companies) and Bell Canada, buy almost all their equipment from their own manufacturing subsidiaries. In addition, the near-monopoly control of the telephone service industry made it impossible for new competitors to enter the market. This explains why there have been only two large telecommunications equipment producers in North America, Western Electric in the United States and Northern Telecom (as Northern Electric has been known since 1976) in Canada. The situation is changing in both the United

States and Canada, however, following deregulation of the industry and antitrust action against AT&T.

Elsewhere in the world, the picture is very different. The only other country where a telephone utility and its equipment supplier are integrated on the North American model is Sweden. The Swedish telecommunications equipment manufacturer, L.M. Ericsson Telephone Co., with its parent company as a captive market, enjoys a virtual monopoly in its home country. Founded in 1876, Ericsson is the fourth largest producer of telecommunications equipment in the world and one of the leading multinational firms in the industry.

Europe's other industrialized countries, however, have followed a different course. First of all, telephone service did not develop as quickly as in North America. At the beginning of the twentieth century, there was one telephone for every 60 people in North America, one for every 115 in Sweden, one for every 139 in Switzerland, one for every 397 in Germany, one for every 1,216 in France and one for every 2,629 in Italy.[25] Second, governments took charge of telephone service in Europe fairly early on. In Germany, Italy and Switzerland, telephone service was organized as a government monopoly from the beginning, while the French government took over the service in 1889 and it gradually became a public enterprise in Britain between 1895 and 1912. Third, the telephone equipment manufacturing industry quickly came under at least partial American control. Beginning in the late nineteenth century, Western Electric established subsidiaries in London, Paris, Antwerp, Milan and Barcelona, as well as affiliated companies in Argentina, Australia, Canada, China and Japan.

After an inquiry by the Federal Trade Commission at the end of the First World War, Western Electric sold its foreign subsidiaries — except its Canadian one — and what might have become a world telecommunications equipment monopoly was thus dismantled. The foreign assets of Western Electric were purchased by International Telephone and Telegraph, which had been formed in 1920 and was rapidly expanding. ITT had just bought telephone companies in Cuba and Puerto Rico, and in 1924 it obtained a telephone service monopoly in Spain. It bought International Western Electric Co. in 1925, renaming it International Standard Electric Co.; ITT manufacturing subsidiaries are still known by this name throughout the world.

Around 1929, ITT had telephone service subsidiaries in Argentina, Brazil, Cuba, Mexico, Puerto Rico, Spain and Uruguay, and telecommunications equipment manufacturing plants throughout

Europe and in a number of Latin American and Asian countries. Its total of 95,000 employees worldwide (except in the United States and Canada) was the largest of any American multinational corporation, and its utility interests alone made it the second largest American utility multinational after American & Foreign Power.[26]

Western Electric and ITT had worked out a territorial division of the world. ITT did not manufacture telecommunications equipment in the United States, while Western Electric now refrained from establishing subsidiaries outside the U.S. Along with this territorial agreeement went a matching division of markets, the essential elements of which are still in effect today.

European competitors were left with the scraps of the telecommunications equipment market. In Germany, Siemens was an early entrant in the industry but its operations were confined to the domestic market, and it had to face competition from ITT, which established a German subsidiary in 1930. Local producers in Britain were fragmented, and this circumstance prevented them from seriously competing with ITT until the three leading companies merged in 1968. The company resulting from this merger, General Electric Co. Ltd., was the first British company that could compete with ITT in the British market. In France, ITT had a virtual monopoly of telecommunications equipment manufacturing before the Second World War. After the war, the French government encouraged local producers, notably the Compagnie Générale d'Electricité and Thomson-CSF, to compete with ITT subsidiaries; its efforts met with limited success. The Spanish government purchased ITT's utility subsidiary in 1945, but the American multinational retained its supremacy in the equipment manufacturing field.

In the telecommunications equipment industry as in other fields, the entry of Japanese producers has upset established market structures. Nippon Electric Co., the leading Japanese manufacturer, was founded in 1899 as a joint venture of Western Electric and Japanese investors. From 1925 on, Nippon was part of the ITT group, but gradually became independent from it during the 1930s. After the Second World War, Nippon became the largest telecommunications equipment manufacturer in Japan and a major multinational firm that now occupies fifth place in the world industry along with Northern Telecom. Hitachi Ltd., which entered the market in the mid-1950s, is the second largest Japanese producer. Govenment control of telephone service in Japan has made it possible for a number of Japanese manufacturing firms to emerge in the postwar period. Through both exports and the international operations of their subsidiaries, the Japanese firms have brought a degree of competition back to an industry that had been dominated by a handful of transnational corporations.[27]

In 1978, telecommunications equipment manufacturing in the capitalist world was, in essence, controlled by ten large companies. Except for Western Electric and CGE, all these companies were transnational in scope.

TABLE 5

Sales of the Leading Telecommunications Equipment Manufacturers, 1978

Company	Country	Sales (US$ million)
Western Electric	U.S.A.	9,522
ITT	U.S.A.	4,656
Siemens	West Germany	2,576
L.M. Ericsson	Sweden	2,098
Northern Telecom	Canada	1,505
Nippon Electric	Japan	1,501
Hitachi*	Japan	3,347
General Electric Co. Ltd.*	U.K.	2,206
CGE*	France	1,390
Plessey	U.K.	633

* Includes sales in the electronics industry.
Source: J.M. Stopford et al., *The World Directory of Multinational Enterprises* (New York: Facts-on-File, 1980).

Northern Telecom and the Japanese companies are among the few newcomers in this tightly controlled industry. There has been no competition from firms in the developing countries. Telecommunications equipment multinationals have been establishing subsidiaries in the Third World since the early twentieth century, and there is no indication that they are in the process of losing control over those interests.

B: THE MAJOR CANADIAN MULTINATIONALS IN THE MANUFACTURING SECTOR

In the previous section, we reviewed some of the manufacturing industries in which Canadian direct investment in foreign countries has been especially significant. We will now look at some of the major Canadian multinationals operating in these industries. We will concentrate on these companies' strategies for dealing with the decline in concentration that has been taking place on a world scale since the end of the Second World War, the origins of their technology, and their place in the Canadian market.

Seagram

Founded in 1924 by the Bronfman brothers, Distillers Corp. established a distillery near Montreal. In 1926, as the plant was being brought into service, the Bronfmans signed an agreement with Distillers Co. Ltd. of London, through which they obtained the British firm's whisky distilling know-how and exclusive rights to market some of its brands. In exchange the Bronfmans yielded 50 per cent of the shares of their company, but the contract contained a clause under which the Canadian partners could buy back the shares held by DCL at a price determined by the two parties.[28]

In 1928 Distillers Corp. bought one of Canada's largest distilleries, J.E. Seagram and Sons, and merged the two companies to form Distillers Corp.-Seagram Ltd. (DC-SL), the name under which the firm operated until 1975. J.E. Seagram was a miller who had established a distillery in Waterloo, Ontario in the nineteenth century, and his children had run the distillery for ten years before selling a controlling interest to the Montreal concern.[29] When the two companies merged, Distillers Corp. stockholders received 75 per cent of the shares of the new firm, while the owners of J.E. Seagram received the other 25 per cent.

When prohibition in the United States was repealed in 1933, DC-SL set out to conquer the American market. The surreptitious entry of its products into the United States had made the Montreal company rich, and now it aimed to establish itself south of the border. Since the British partners were opposed to the firm's having subsidiaries in the United States, the Bronfmans bought back DCL's shares of Distillers Corp.-Seagram and began to acquire American distilleries, first Rossville Union Corp. in Indiana in 1933 and then Maryland Distillery the next year. DC-SL bought a third distillery in the United States in 1937, three more in 1940, and a number of others during the Second World War, consolidating its position as the leading producer of whisky not only in Canada but in North America as a whole.

When the American and Canadian governments banned the manufacture of alcohol for non-military use for the duration of the war, Seagram turned the situation to its advantage by importing rum from Jamaica and then buying a Jamaican sugar estate and distillery, Long Pond Estates. Seagram's Jamaican output was directed towards the Canadian market, and soon afterwards it established another distillery in Puerto Rico — which later became its subsidiary Puerto Rico Distillers — for the American market.

Throughout the 1940s and 1950s, Seagram continued to expand in Canada and the United States by buying up competitors and increasing its production capacity. But in the early 1960s the company changed course. Its revised strategy, which it has followed for the last twenty years, contained three new elements: entry into the production and sale of wines and liqueurs, expansion outside North America and the Caribbean, and conglomerate diversification.

The first of these elements began to take shape in 1961, when Seagram acquired a major American importer of wines and liqueurs. Subsequently it bought Barton & Guestier, a leading Bordeaux wine shipper; Hudson, Ciovini & Cia, Argentina's leading wine exporter (in 1967-68); wineries in France, Italy, Austria, Germany, Spain, Australia and New Zealand; and two of California's largest wine producers, Paul Masson and Christian Brothers. At the same time, it bought a large champagne producer, G.H. Mumm & Cie, and a large cognac producer, Angier Frères & Cie, in France. With all these acquisitions, and other more recent ones, Seagram has moved on from whisky to become a major wine producer and shipper in all the major exporting countries.

This diversification within the alcoholic beverages industry has been one part of Seagram's international expansion. At the same time, it has also begun to produce whisky in a number of different countries. It purchased distilleries in Argentina in 1963 and 1967-68; bought Glenlivet Distilleries Ltd. in Scotland in 1978; and became involved in a joint venture in 1974 with the aim of producing Scotch whisky in Japan.

Conglomerate diversification began in 1963, when Seagram purchased Texas Pacific Oil, an independent American oil company, for $250 million. After contributing to Seagram's profits for seventeen years, Texas Pacific was sold to another American company, Sun Co., in April 1980 for $2.3 billion. When it was sold, Texas Pacific was the fifth largest independent oil producer in the United States, and had subsidiaries in Canada, Spain, Saudi Arabia, Britain (where it had North Sea concessions) and elsewhere. Seagram retained Texas Pacific's Canadian subsidiary and has been considering buying a Canadian oil company. Meanwhile, in March

1981, Seagram tried to obtain control of St. Joe Minerals in the United States, but its attempt failed. Soon afterwards, it became involved in a battle for control of another American oil company, Conoco, and emerged from it with minority control of Du Pont.

In 1979, Seagram was the world's largest producer and seller of alcoholic beverages. It had sales of $2.6 billion (not counting its oil subsidiary), a net profit of $107 million, and assets valued — too conservatively — at $2.4 billion. It produced whisky in nine countries (the United States, Canada, Scotland, Argentina, Brazil, Italy, Japan, Mexico and Venezuela); white goods in Jamaica, Puerto Rico and elsewhere; and wine in France, Italy, Spain, Portugal, Argentina, West Germany, Austria, Australia and elsewhere. It was the largest producer of distilled liquor in both Canada and the United States. It had marketing subsidiaries in more than a hundred countries.[30] North America was its leading market, representing 72 per cent of sales; another 18 per cent of sales were in Europe, and the rest of the world accounted for 10 per cent. This sales distribution reflects the company's commercial strategy, which involves producing wines, liqueurs and white goods all over the world and selling them in North America. Seagram's major whisky distilleries are located in Canada and the United States.

The company is controlled by Samuel Bronfman's four children through their holding company, Cemp Investments. Having recently bought back some shares, Cemp owned more than 40 per cent of Seagram in 1981.[31]

The postwar period has been characterized by renewed competition, reduced concentration in the distilled liquor industry both in the largest market, the United States, and on a world scale, and the decline of distilled liquors within the alcoholic beverages market as a whole. These developments forced Seagram — along with other major distillers such as DCL in Britain and National Distillers in the United States — to diversify both economically and geographically. Unlike its American and British rivals, however, Seagram appears to have made a complete success of its diversification, and as a result has been able to retain its number one position in the world distilling industry.[32]

Hiram Walker Resources

Hiram Walker was founded in 1858 by an American immigrant to Canada and within a few years had become the largest distillery in the country. In 1926, the founder's descendants sold the company to Harry C. Hatch and his partners. Hatch was a Canadian who three years earlier had bought Gooderham and Worts, a Toronto distillery that had been founded in 1832. He merged the two companies to form Hiram Walker-Gooderham and Worts.[33]

Like Seagram, Hiram Walker began its international expansion in 1933 in the United States, as it moved to fill the void left by nearly two decades of Prohibition. It built a distillery in Peoria, Illinois that was the largest in the world at the time. Soon afterwards, in 1936, Hiram Walker bought one of Scotland's major distilleries, George Ballantyne and Son. It acquired two more distilleries in Scotland in 1937 and built another one near Glasgow the next year.

The company's expansion in the United States continued in 1941 when it bought the Frank L. Wight Distilling Co. of Laurel, Maryland. In 1943, it established a subsidiary in Argentina to buy that country's largest distillery, Mattaldi-Simon Ltda. Hiram Walker expanded in Canada as well, gaining control of Colby Distilleries and Canadian Industrial Alcohol Ltd. in 1946.

After the Second World War, Hiram Walker bought six more companies in Scotland to strengthen its position in the Scotch whisky industry. It entered the wine business — much later than Seagram — when it bought a New York wine importer in 1971. It began buying and selling white goods at the same time, and later expanded its interests in this branch of the industry to include the manufacturing stage when it bought a block of shares of Bacardi, an American-based company that is the world's largest producer of rum.

In April 1980, Hiram Walker merged with Consumers Home, a Canadian company whose major activities are the distribution of natural gas in Ontario and oil and gas production and exploration, and changed its name to Hiram Walker Resources. This was seventeen years after Seagram had undertaken its first conglomerate merger. In 1979, Hiram Walker was the third largest distilling company in the world in terms of both assets and net profit, behind Seagram and Suntory but ahead of Heublein Inc. of the United States. The United States accounted for 58 per cent of its sales and Canada for another 16 per cent, with the remainder in Europe and elsewhere. Of its identifiable assets, 55 per cent were located in North America and the rest mostly in Europe.[34]

As with Seagram, Hiram Walker's distilling know-how comes from two sources. One is the experience accumulated by its predecessor companies in the manufacture of Canadian rye whisky. The other is the knowledge acquired through the purchase of distilling companies in Scotland, the United States and elsewhere. It would be difficult to quantify the contribution each of these sources has made to the company's know-how.

In 1979, Hiram Walker had interests in five countries — Canada, the United States, Scotland, Argentina and France. The factors leading to its entry into the four countries outside Canada were different in each case. When it expanded into the United States in 1933, it aimed to capture a major portion of the world's largest market for distilled liquor by taking advantage of the technical knowledge the company already had in Canada. In addition, the American producers had been weakened by prohibition, and there was a gap that the two leaders of the Canadian industry were able to fill. The purchase of whisky producers in Scotland starting in 1936 gave Hiram Walker access to new technical knowledge and control of prestigious companies that could export to the North American market. In entering Argentina in 1943, its goal was to penetrate the largest market in Latin America and control distilleries in one of the world's leading grain producing countries. And the company's entry into France was undertaken at a time when it was seeking to diversify its products, and was interested in wine as well as whisky.

Hiram Walker is smaller, more profitable and less multinational than Seagram. It has concentrated more on whisky, which as a high-priced product has attracted a wealthier clientele, and thus did not get involved in the wine and liqueur trade as early or as heavily as its Montreal-based rival. Looking at the industry in terms of Fred Knickerbocker's theory of the oligopolistic reaction, it can be said that Hiram Walker has followed Seagram's lead, but only after a long delay. It entered the wine business ten years after Seagram, and in the case of its conglomerate diversification the delay was seventeen years. Only once was Hiram Walker ahead of its rival — it entered Argentina twenty years ahead of Seagram — while in the case of expansion into the United States the two companies acted simultaneously in 1933. Since 1980, Hiram Walker has expanded in the oil and gas sector, turning itself into a small petroleum multinational.

MacMillan Bloedel

MacMillan Bloedel is the product of a series of mergers in the 1950s involving Canadian companies operating in the forest industry, primarily in British Columbia.

The oldest of these companies was Powell River, founded in B.C. in 1911 as a subsidiary of Brooks Scanlon Lumber of Minneapolis, Minnesota. Powell River began with a daily newsprint capacity of less than 300 tons, but grew during the 1920s to reach a capacity of 650 tons at the onset of the Depression, which made it Canada's sixth largest paper company at the time.[35] By the time it merged with MacMillan & Bloedel in 1959, a majority of its shares were owned in Canada. The controlling shareholders were a Canadian family, the Foleys, and the original American owners, the Brooks family, who retained a minority interest.

H.R. MacMillan Export was founded as a trading company in 1919 and reorganized in 1930 to undertake the production first of sawn lumber and then of pulp and paper. In 1951 it took over another company, Bloedel & Stewart & Welch, in a share exchange, and adopted the name of MacMillan & Bloedel Ltd. Finally, Mac-Millan & Bloedel merged with Powell River in July 1959 to form MacMillan Bloedel & Powell River. By merging, the two companies aimed to regain export markets, compete with larger companies remain under Canadian control and become diversified. The Foley, MacMillan, and Bloedel families retained control of the new company. The positions of the two companies at the time they merged is compared in Table 6.

TABLE 6

MacMillan Bloedel and Powell River in 1959

	MacMillan Bloedel	Powell River
Sales (C$ million)	160.5	55.6
Total assets (C$ million)	192.2	93.7
% of shares held in Canada	85	65
Annual production capacity (tons)		
Newsprint	215,000	525,000
Kraft paper and cardboard	60,000	—
1958 output		
Kraft pulp	332,549	—
Wood (millions of cords)	525	83

Source: Financial Post, July 4, 1959, p. 3.

The new company represented 10 per cent of Canada's newsprint production capacity, and it was not far behind the leaders — Abitibi, CIP and Consolidated Paper. It also became, and remains, the leading Canadian forest products company in terms of sales and the eleventh largest forest products company in North America.

During the 1960s and 1970s, MacMillan Bloedel climbed to second place among Canadian newsprint producers, behind Abitibi-Price, the largest newsprint producer in the world. Meanwhile, it expanded vigorously outside Canada, acquiring interests in the United States, Europe and elsewhere. In 1964, it bought two British container manufacturers and merged them into MacMillan Bloedel Containers. In 1969, it opened a huge $90 million forest complex in Pine Hill, Alabama, comprising a sawmill, a plywood factory and a pulp and cardboard mill. The equipment for this endeavour — which became MacMillan Bloedel's largest subsidiary — was provided entirely by American suppliers. Black Clawson supplied a Fourdrinier machine and a pulp mill, while other American manufacturers supplied the rest of the facilities.[36] In 1973, MacMillan Bloedel bought Canadian Gulf Lines of Houston, an ocean shipping firm specializing in paper transport. The next year, it began building a used paper treatment plant in California and bought a minority interest in Industrial America Corp. of Jacksonville, Florida, a manufacturer of forest products treatment systems. It announced a $274 million expansion of its Pine Hill facilities in 1980.

In Europe, MacMillan Bloedel granted a licence to a French company, the Groupement Européen de la Cellulose (GEC), to make kraft paper in 1973. The next year it bought 40 per cent of the shares of Cellulose d'Aquitaine, GEC's parent company. In Scotland, it took control of Scotpack in 1974, giving its British subsidiary two more container factories. It also acquired a subsidiary in the Netherlands, Royal Dutch Paper, one of Europe's leading paper producers.[37]

Meanwhile, MacMillan Bloedel also expanded into Asia and Latin America. It announced that it was undertaking forest operations in Malaysia in 1972, and plans for a pine and eucalyptus plantation in Brazil in collaboration with Brascan were made public two years later.

It has also expanded continuously in Canada over the last twenty years, and through this expansion has retained its rank in the North American forest products industry and its leading position in Canada. To carry out the successive enlargements of its Canadian plants, it has turned to a number of American equipment manufacturers in Scandinavia and elsewhere.[38]

In 1979, MacMillan Bloedel was the largest forest products company and the second largest newsprint producer in Canada. In terms of sales, it was the thirteenth largest paper company in North America. The United States accounted for 47 per cent of its sales, Canada for 19 per cent, Europe for 20 per cent, and the rest of the world for 14 per cent. Its assets were located in Canada (68 per cent), the United States (23 per cent), Europe (8 per cent) and elsewhere. The company had nineteen active subsidiaries in the United States, eight in the United Kingdom and eleven in other countries.[39]

The company's interests were heavily concentrated in the forest products sector. Lumber accounted for 34 per cent of its sales, newsprint for 20 per cent, cardboard and containers for 19 per cent, and wood panelling for 11 per cent. This failure to diversify outside the forest products sector reflects MacMillan Bloedel's stable position in an industry in which the level of concentration has remained constant for the last fifty years.

MacMillan Bloedel is a striking example of international expansion based on foreign technology. The technology of the forest products industry is widely known and accessible. Multinational corporations acquire advantages primarily by achieving economies of scale and by controlling a sufficiently large quantity of high-quality forest resources.

Throughout this period of rapid expansion, MacMillan Bloedel has remained under Canadian control. Canadian Pacific bought a minority block of shares in the company in stages between 1964 and 1973. In 1978, CP tendered an offer to buy 51 per cent of MacMillan Bloedel's shares, but had to withdraw it in January 1979 as a result of opposition from the Social Credit government of British Columbia. Soon afterwards, Canadian Pacific sold its minority interest to the British Columbia Resources Investment Corporation, B.C.'s joint public-private holding company. Finally, in March 1981, Noranda Mines gained control of the Canadian forest products giant.

Massey-Ferguson

Massey-Harris, as the company was known until 1953, was the result of an 1891 merger between Canada's two largest farm machinery and implement manufacturers — Massey, founded in 1847, and Harris, founded in 1857. These two companies had followed a similar course. They manufactured equipment under licence from American producers and exported part of their output to Europe, Australia and elsewhere. The American market, however, was closed to them as a result of customs duties and the strength of local competition, and probably also as a result of restrictive clauses in the licences they had acquired.

The new company produced almost half of Canada's farm implements and machinery. In 1910, a year before the Laurier government's attempt to bring about a Canada-U.S. reciprocity treaty ended in failure, Massey-Harris purchased its first foreign manufacturing subsidiary, a company in Batavia, New York that produced harvesters for the export market. During the First World War, the Ford Motor Company introduced tractors to the North American market, and this new machine quickly became the industry's leading product. Between 1919 and 1923, Massey-Harris sought unsuccessfully to manufacture tractors under licence in Canada. To get around the technological obstacle that was preventing it from penetrating this market, the company purchased an American tractor manufacturer, J.L. Case Plow Works of Racine, Wisconsin. As the company's historian, E.P. Neufeld, has written, it was access to foreign technology more than innovation as such that contributed to Massey-Harris's success in the early part of the century.[40]

While it was consolidating its position in the United States, Massey-Harris opened plants in France in 1925-27 and in Germany in 1927-28 to manufacture simple farm machines. These two subsidiaries remained marginal operations. In 1930, when the government of Australia erected new tariff barriers in an effort to deal with the Depression, Massey-Harris bought a minority interest in H.V. McKay Pty, an Australian farm implement manufacturer.

When farm income fell during the 1930s, Massey-Harris was very seriously affected, and its output declined catastrophically. Its share of the Canadian market, which had been 50 per cent at the end of the nineteenth century, was only 19 per cent in 1935. Competition from International Harvester, whose Canadian subsidiary had been producing farm machinery in Ontario since 1903, had reduced Massey-Harris to a secondary position in its main market. In the United States, Massey-Harris was the seventh largest producer. It did not offer a high-quality model in the tractor market, and in the market for harvesters and other machines and implements competition was very intense.

In 1936-37, Massey-Harris brought a self-propelled harvesting combine, which had already been tested in Australia and Argentina by an Australian technician, to the stage of commercial production. The machine was a spectacular success, and on the basis of this triumph Massey-Harris climbed to third place in the world farm machinery industry. The Second World War brought more good times for the company, which converted some of its facilities to military production.

From 1945 on, Massey-Harris began to produce farm machinery in Britain and consolidated its shaky German and French subsidiaries. The company made enormous profits during the postwar boom, but starting in 1951 its income began to fall. In 1953, 83 per cent of Massey-Harris's production and 66 per cent of its sales were in North America. It had not overcome its traditional weakness in tractor production, where competition from International Harvester, Deere and Ford left it with only a small portion of the market. Massey-Harris's major asset was its harvesting combine, but its leading competitors were beginning to penetrate that market as well.

In 1953, Massey-Harris absorbed H. Ferguson, Britain's leading tractor exporter. Ferguson was a company that engineered and sold tractors, while the actual manufacturing was done by Standard Motor in England and Continental Motors in the United States. Ferguson was one of the most innovative tractor designers of its time, and by acquiring it Massey-Harris (now Massey-Ferguson) broadened its range in the tractor market. Not long afterwards, in 1959, Massey-Ferguson purchased Standard Motor and F. Perkins. Perkins was one of the pioneers in the manufacture of diesel engines, and the engines it made included the ones used in Ferguson tractors. With the purchase of the three British companies, Massey acquired the know-how it needed to expand internationally at a very rapid pace.

It extended its activities in France and Germany to include the production of farm tractors, harvesting combines and diesel engines. In 1961 it entered a joint venture in India to manufacture tractors with Perkins engines. A Spanish subsidiary that in 1958 had produced harvesting combines with SEAT engines began making Perkins engines in 1963. It expanded its Spanish operations in 1965 by buying a minority interest in Motor Iberica, which had been manufacturing tractors under licence from Ford and was converted to produce Massey-Ferguson tractors. In 1966, the company began to make Ferguson tractors in Mexico, while in 1960 it bought all the shares of Landini s.p.a., an Italian company that held 10 per cent of Italy's tractor market.

In Australia, it took over McKay in 1956 and diversified its operations to include harvesters and sugar cane reapers. It took a majority interest in an associated company in South Africa and had

40 per cent of the South African tractor market by 1965. It began to manufacture farm machinery in Argentina around the same time and in 1973 became involved in a joint venture with Volvo, Perkins and the Peruvian government to make tractors in Trujillo in northern Peru.[41] Along with its geographical extension, Massey-Ferguson also began to diversify economically in the late 1960s, expanding into the production of construction machinery. In 1974 it bought the construction machines division of a West German company, Hanomag, and soon afterwards took over Akron Industrial Machinery in Ohio. It also began to make construction machinery in Brazil, Argentina and other countries.

At the height of its growth in 1976, Massey-Ferguson produced 20 per cent of the tractors, 20 per cent of the harvesting combines and 14 per cent of the diesel engines in the capitalist world.[42] It was the largest producer of farm machinery in Canada and the third largest in North America and the world. It was also the leading farm machinery manufacturer in Mexico, Brazil, Argentina and the United Kingdom and one of the leaders in continental Europe.

Then, in the next four years, the company collapsed, and by late 1980 it was on the verge of bankruptcy. This disaster was the result of a number of independent factors. The first was Massey-Ferguson's strategy of expanding on the basis of bank loans rather than stock issues. Argus Corp., the Toronto holding company that controlled Massey-Ferguson between 1945 and 1980, held only 16 per cent of its shares, and refused to authorize the sale of new stock because it did not want its own percentage of the company to fall too low. When North American interest rates rose in the late 1970s, Massey-Ferguson's bank repayments increased drastically and the company was left in a poor position. Second, farm machinery markets were seriously affected by the world recession. Massey-Ferguson's sales stagnated just as the demands of its creditors were becoming more and more urgent.

Third, the company's tractor production was concentrated in the area of small and middle-sized units, while with the growth of average farm size, demand was moving in the direction of large tractors. Thus, in 1979, Massey-Ferguson had 20 per cent of the North American market for small tractors and harvesting combines, but it had only 4 per cent of the market for large tractors — and this was the only market that had not declined.[43] Fourth, the company's diversification into construction machinery had gone sour as a result of the recession in the construction industry. And finally, the value of the pound sterling rose, preventing the export sales of Massey-

Ferguson's British subsidiaries from continuing at their usual levels.

In 1978, the management of Massey-Ferguson agreed to a program of reducing the company's investment. The next year it sold M-F Mexico, which had sales of $64 million and 45 per cent of the Mexican tractor market in 1978. The purchaser was one of Mexico's largest privately-owned conglomerates, the Alfa industrial group, which signed an agreement with Massey to continue production under licence.[44] Massey-Ferguson also sold its American industrial machinery subsidiary in 1979. In 1980, it liquidated Hanomag in West Germany and sold its stock in Motor Iberica to Nissan Motor of Japan.[45] It sold off some of its stock in its Australian and South African subsidiaries (leaving its share of the South African company at 25 per cent) and sold its construction machinery factories in Australia. Its Argentinian subsidiary was closed late in 1980 and it stopped making construction machinery in Brazil.

In October 1980, Argus Corp. turned over its block of Massey-Ferguson shares to the company's employee pension fund in an effort to obtain aid from either the Canadian or the Ontario government. At the time, the company was carrying a debt of $1.5 billion on sales of $3 billion.[46] Finally, between December 1980 and February 1981, the company was saved from bankruptcy when its creditors — banks in Canada, Britain, the United States, France, West Germany, Italy, Switzerland, Brazil and Australia — agreed to exchange their debt instruments for preferred shares. A sale of shares to the public completed the company's refinancing. The company's senior management personnel remained the same throughout these changes.[47]

In 1976 Massey-Ferguson was the most multinational of the farm machinery majors. While North American operations accounted for 76 per cent of International Harvester's operations and 80 per cent of Deere's, the figure for Massey-Ferguson was only 38 per cent. Another 38 per cent of Massey's assets were in Europe, 17 per cent were in Latin America, 4 per cent in Australia and 3 per cent in Africa.[48] As for sales, 31 per cent were in North America and 32 per cent in Europe in 1976. Three years later, with the company in the midst of its reorganization, 36 per cent of its sales were in North America. This increase was a revealing indication of Massey's strategic retreat.[49] The product composition of its sales also changed. Construction, industrial and other machinery, which had constituted 21 per cent of sales in 1975, represented only 12 per cent in 1979. Thus the company was retrenching both geographically and economically, once again becoming concentrated in North America and Europe and the farm machinery market.

Massey-Ferguson has used foreign technology in a variety of ways. We have already mentioned its purchase of American patents on a massive scale in the nineteenth and early twentieth centuries, its use of models developed by its foreign subsidiaries and associated companies in the 1930s, its purchase of an American tractor producer in 1928 and British ones in 1953 and 1959, and its takeover of Perkins in 1959 to acquire diesel engine technology. In addition, the company does by far the largest part of its research and development in its American laboratories. Thus, in 1979, only $6 million of Massey-Ferguson's $44 million R&D budget was spent in Canada.[50] This was not a new policy. According to the Royal Commission on Farm Machinery, in 1967 Massey-Ferguson spent $2.6 million on R&D in Canada as compared with $16.2 million in the United States.[51] In this way, the company is able to use the personnel and the research coming out of the universities in the Detroit area. Massey-Ferguson is another example of international expansion based on foreign technology. The company's major advantage is not innovation, but rather its size and its position as the leader of the Canadian farm machinery oligopoly, as a result of which it is able to get its hands on innovations originating elsewhere.

Polysar

During the Second World War, natural rubber supplies from Southeast Asia were interrupted, and the supply of rubber was insufficient to meet military needs. As a result, Canada built a large-scale industrial complex to produce synthetic rubber. Late in 1941 the Canadian government established a consultative committee on rubber substitutes, and early the next year rubber rationing began.

The Minister of Munitions and Supply, C.D. Howe, obtained the American patents and specifications for the production of two kinds of synthetic rubber, Buna S (a widely-used rubber known today as styrene-butadiene, or SBR) and butyl. In March 1942, Ottawa established Polymer Corp., a federal crown corporation, to produce synthetic rubber for war needs. Construction began in August 1942, and by December 1943 the Polymer plant in Sarnia, Ontario was in operation. It had an annual capacity of 34,000 tons of Buna S and 4,000 tons of butyl. All the technology was imported from the United States and the technical side of the operation was run by senior personnel from a number of American corporations.[52] Polymer became the only Canadian producer of synthetic rubber and retained its monopoly for almost thirty years. As with the other companies we have examined, a highly concentrated market structure in Canada gave rise to international expansion.

Polymer's growth was stimulated by demand from the automobile industry, the major consumer of its product, and occurred at a very rapid pace. By the 1950s, Polymer had 10 per cent of the world synthetic rubber market and exported rubber to a number of countries. In 1960, it decided to establish — at a cost of $40 million — two manufacturing subsidiaries in Europe, one to make Buna S and nitrile near Strasbourg, France and the other to make butyl near Antwerp, Belgium, to protect its markets in the embryonic European Economic Community. At the same time, Polymer established a network of sales subsidiaries in Europe, headquartered in Switzerland, to market the output of its European factories.[53]

Polymer's international expansion, which began in this fashion in 1960, has gathered speed since then. In 1962, Polymer helped South Africa build its own synthetic rubber factory by providing design, engineering and technical management; in exchange, it took up a minority of the share capital of the new company.[54] Soon afterwards, it initiated a joint venture in Mexico to manufacture synthetic rubber and related products, Hules Mexicanos S.A., and retained 40 per cent of its shares. In 1972 it granted licences to the Rio Tinto group in Spain, and in 1973 it signed an agreement with Indian Petro-chemical Corp. to provide technological assistance in the design, construction and management of a synthetic rubber plant in the Indian state of Gujarat.[55]

Along with the growth of its international operations, Polymer also diversified economically. This process began in 1966, when Polymer expanded into plastics production in Canada by buying an independent manufacturer. In 1970 it bought a major American polystyrene producer, Solar Chemical Corp., along with its two subsidiaries, in a move aimed at expanding its position in the plastics industry.[56] The same year it purchased a minority interest in another American company, Stressed Structures, and bought the Canadian rights for this company's new and innovative reinforced concrete technology. Also in 1970 Polymer bought Comshare (Canada) Ltd., a manufacturer of computer time-sharing devices, which until then had been a subsidiary of an American company with the same name. Polymer continued to expand in the United States, beginning construction of a latex plant in Tennessee and buying two more American plastic products manufacturers in 1971.

As Polymer's 1971 annual report explained, the company's economic diversification strategy was the result of growing competition in the rubber market: "Polymer recognized that it was in a vulnerable position and that it would be unwise to rely over the long term on opportunities for growth and earnings in the single industry represented by synthetic rubber. The Company, therefore, moved to widen its base through diversification."[57]

Polymer's American holdings grew year by year. In 1972 it bought a solid rubber factory, which until then had belonged to Standard Brands Chemical Industries. The company (by now known as Polysar) bought another American firm in 1973, and purchased one of Europe's leading plastics producers, Bellaplast, a multinational corporation with its head office in Wiesbaden, West Germany, that same year. The German company's avant-garde technology was transferred to Polysar's North American subsidiaries and later sold to local companies in various countries. Finally, in 1978, Polysar bought Comshare Corp. in the United States and became a multinational in the data processing field.

Another significant chapter in the company's history has been its upstream vertical integration. This was accomplished with the establishment in 1973 of Petrosar, a joint subsidiary of Polysar (which holds the controlling interest), Du Pont of Canada and Dow Chemical of Canada. At Petrosar's Sarnia plant, which opened in 1977, Alberta oil is refined into ethylene, propylene and other olefins; benzene, gasoline, synthetic gas and other substances are also produced there. Further processing of the refinery's various chemical products is carried out by the three partners, and the largest part of its output goes to Polysar. Meanwhile, in 1972, control of Polysar was transferred to the Canada Development Corporation, which is controlled by the federal government but has private minority shareholders.

In 1979 Polysar produced about 10 per cent of the world's synthetic rubber in its plants in Canada, France, Belgium and Mexico. It was also a major producer of plastics and latex in the United States and Europe. Rubber represented 58 per cent of the company's sales, plastics 28 per cent and latex 13 per cent.[58] By region, the United States accounted for 27 per cent of its sales, Canada for 21 per cent, Europe for 43 per cent and the rest of the world for 9 per cent.

Having grown rapidly and diversified its production both geographically and economically, Polysar has been able to maintain its share of the world synthetic rubber market and become a major producer of plastics and latex as well. It is a profitable and dynamic company, and a virtually unique example of a government-owned multinational corporation in the manufacturing sector. Its expansion has been based essentially on foreign technology, which it assimilated and improved. Its main advantages have been its size, which was substantial from the beginning of its operations, and its monopoly of the Canadian market.

Northern Telecom

The coming of Bell, the American telephone holding company, to Canada in 1880 was followed by the arrival of its manufacturing subsidiary. Northern Electric and Manufacturing Co., a subsidiary of Western Electric, was founded in Canada in 1882. In 1906, Bell Canada, at the time controlled by American Telephone and Telegraph (as the Bell holding company had become known), purchased a majority of Northern Electric's shares, while Western Electric retained a minority interest.

As we have seen, AT&T gradually allowed Bell Canada to become a Canadian company. However, the two companies had identical equipment, since Northern Electric used Western Electric's technology under licence. During the 1950s, as a result of the U.S. government's antitrust suit against Western Electric, the American manufacturer divested itself of its shares in Northern Electric, which were taken up by Bell Canada. In 1958, Bell Canada and Northern Electric jointly organized a research laboratory with the aim of making the Canadian manufacturer self-sufficient in design and technology. Within a few years, the laboratory was the largest research centre in Canada, and Northern Electric had become completely autonomous in the technical sphere.

In the early 1970s, Northern introduced some significant innovations in the telecommunications equipment field, including a number of avant-garde digital exchanges and a complete range of digital switching and transmission equipment. Northern was still Bell Canada's regular supplier — giving it 80 per cent of the Canadian market — but in the late 1960s it also began to export substantial quantities of equipment to Africa, the Caribbean, Greece, Turkey and other areas. In 1969 it opened its first plant outside Canada, the result of a joint venture with the Turkish government in which Northern held 51 per cent of the shares.

In 1971, Northern established a subsidiary in the United States, Northern Telecom, Inc., and built its first American plant in Port Huron, Michigan, aiming to sell telecommunications equipment to the portion of the American telephone system outside the AT&T/Western Electric network. This portion constituted 15 per cent of the American market. Northern penetrated the American market very quickly, and had four factories in the United States in 1973, twelve in 1976, and twenty-two in 1979.

Northern's entry into the European market has taken a number of forms. In 1973, Northern opened an equipment factory in Ireland. The operation was a success, but it faced stiff competition from the telecommunications equipment oligopoly in the European Common Market, consisting of the many local subsidiaries of the ITT group as well as a number of indigenous companies such as General Electric Co. Ltd. and Plessey in England, the Compagnie Générale d'Electricité and Thomson-CSF in France, Siemens in West Germany, and Philips in Holland. In these circumstances, Northern adopted a strategy of granting licences to the national companies. Thus, it granted licences to Plessey in 1974; licensed the SL-1 exchange to Thomson-CSF in France, Ericsson in Sweden, and General Electric in the U.K. in 1977; and granted another licence to Thomson-CSF for the Contempra phone that same year.

Northern has not penetrated markets elsewhere in the world to the same degree. In 1973, it established a pilot plant in Malaysia to build electronic equipment. Three years later, it bought Cook Electric, a company with seven factories in the United States and subsidiaries in Canada and Brazil. With this purchase, Northern acquired a plant in Latin America's largest market. And early in 1981, Northern announced the establishment with the Alfa industrial group of a joint venture in Mexico to assemble telephone equipment under licence. In conformity with Mexican law, the new company, Telco, was to be under Mexican majority control.

Since the early 1970s, the ties between Bell Canada and Northern Electric — renamed Northern Telecom in 1976 — have loosened slightly. Up until 1973, Northern was a wholly-owned subsidiary of Bell, but in that year the parent company sold off 10 per cent of its stock, and since then its share of Northern gradually diminished, until it stood at 55 per cent in 1980. The commercial links between the two companies have also become looser. In the early 1960s, practically all of Northern's output was sold to Bell Canada and its subsidiaries and affiliated companies, but by 1979 Bell's orders represented only 34 per cent of Northern's sales.[59] In that year, 50 per cent of Northern's total sales were in Canada, 40 per cent were in the United States and 10 per cent were overseas.

While Northern's entry into the American market was a great success in the area of telecommunications equipment, it has had more difficulty penetrating the American electronics market. With the use of digital equipment, the new technologies in telecommunications and in electronics tend to converge, and this circumstance led Northern to buy up a number of American electronic equipment manufacturers between 1975 and 1979. However, these acquisitions proved very costly for Northern, and in 1980 the company reported a substantial loss, the first in its history. The loss was attributable to the electronics sector, which by 1979 represented 20 per cent of Northern's sales (telecommunications equipment accounted for 79 per cent).

Since the Second World War, Northern Telecom and a few Japanese and French companies have been the only new competitors to enter the tight oligopoly prevailing in the telecommunications equipment industry. As a result of a sustained research and development effort, Northern reached a position in the avant garde of the industry's technology within twenty-five years of gaining its technological independence from Western Electric. Some observers have maintained that its diversification into electronics was premature. The company, however, has argued that the rapid convergence of the data processing and telecommunications industries was inevitable and left it no choice.[60]

Among our six case studies of multinationals in the manufacturing sector, Northern Telecom is the only one whose expansion has been based on its own innovations. But innovation has not been Northern's only asset. The initial condition that made it possible for Northern to become a large company with a capacity for innovation was the presence of a captive market — the Bell Canada system. The ties between Bell and Northern were the source of substantial sales for the manufacturer, and Bell also co-financed the laboratories that produced the innovations. Thus, innovation in this case was a result of the near-monopoly situation that Bell and Northern have enjoyed.

* * *

As would be expected from the writings of both Hymer and Vernon, the major manufacturing industries in which Canadain multinational corporations operate have experienced a steady reduction in concentration on a world scale. This reduction has been moderate in the telecommunications equipment and farm machinery industries, more substantial in the distilled liquor and paper industries, and highly pronounced in the synthetic rubber industry.

The Canadian transnational corporations we have looked at have followed different courses since the Second World War. Canadian distilling companies have declined somewhat, although they have retained the number one and number three positions in the world industry. In the synthetic rubber industry, Polysar has maintained its market share for the last quarter of a century, despite the entry of new competitors in Europe, North America and Japan. In the paper, farm machinery and telecommunications equipment industries, Canadian companies are among the new giants in the international arena.

None of the companies except Northern Telcom is a major innovator in the technological sphere. In the distilling and farm machinery industries, Canadian companies obtained much of their know-how through takeovers of British and American firms or through licences. In the synthetic rubber and related products industry, technology was acquired largely by importing American patents during the Second World War and later by absorbing American and German companies. The international expansion of the Canadian paper industry has been based primarily on American machinery and engineering. In addition, many large Canadian multinational corporations concentrate all of their R&D in the United States (as in the case of Moore Corp.) or at least most of it (Massey-Ferguson), so as to have greater access to the human resources and university-based research that are available there. Technological innovation has not been the main advantage enjoyed by Canadian multinationals, with the exception of Northern Telecom.

The main characteristic of the industries in Canada that have given rise to multinational corporations in the manufacturing sector is their high degree of corporate concentration. In the same manner as Alcan or Inco, manufacturing companies that have become multinationals either had an absolute monopoly in their respective industries over a long period of time (Polysar, Northern Telecom) or else were part of an oligopoly that remained stable for many years (Seagram, Hiram Walker, MacMillan Bloedel, Massey-Ferguson). Thus, these companies are leaders in their respective industries. The Canadian market is not large enough to have room for more than a small number of world-scale companies — often only one such company — in each industry. Because of this characteristic of Canadian industry, Fred Knickerbocker's theory of the oligopolistic reaction and Christian Palloix's thesis of the internationalization of industrial branches do not really apply to the Canadian situation. In Canada, it is not industrial branches that become international, but rather the leaders in each industry. Only two of Canada's eight distilling companies are multinational corporations. Out of 400 companies in the slaughtering and meat packing industry, only the leader — Canada Packers, which has half the Canadian market — is a multinational firm. There are more than 200 companies listed as telecommunications equipment manufacturers in Canada, but only one, Northern Telecom (which controls 85 per cent of the Canadian market), is a multinational.

How do large Canadian companies differ from large companies based in other late-blooming industrialized countries? An initial

TABLE 7

Assets, Sales and Control of the Leading Canadian Multinational Corporations in the Industrial Sector, 1981

Company	Assets (C$ million)	Sales (C$ million)	Control
Alcan Aluminium	7,517	5,969	internal
Bata Shoes*	1,500	2,500	Bata family (100%)
Canada Packers	523	2,943	internal
Cominco	2,028	1,417	CP Enterprises (54%)
Hiram Walker Resources	4,918	2,945	internal
Inco	4,476	2,261	internal
MacMillan Bloedel	2,172	2,210	Noranda Mines (49%)
Massey-Ferguson	3,012	3,175	Employee pension funds (16%)
Moore Corp.	1,291	2,253	internal
Noranda Mines	5,248	3,030	Brascade (37%); Zinor (16%)
Northern Telecom	2,147	2,571	Bell Canada (55%)
Polysar	1,042	1,347	CDC (100%)
Seagram	7,245	2,127	Bronfman family (39%)

* Estimates. Bata is a private company and publishes no financial statements.
Source: Annual reports, 1981; *Financial Post Survey of Industrials,* 1982.

difference is the size of the leading Canadian companies. On *Fortune*'s 1981 list of the 500 largest industrial corporations outside the United States, one company was based in Argentina, seven in Australia, seven in Brazil, six in Mexico, ten in South Korea, seven in South Africa and two in India, but thirty-three were based in Canada. In other words, there were almost as many large industrial corporations in Canada as in all the most advanced semi-industrialized countries combined.

But the highly concentrated structure of Canadian industry and the large size of Canadian corporations are not the only reasons for Canada's lead over the semi-industrialized countries. Canada's geographical, cultural and commercial closeness to the United States and Britain allows Canadian companies to absorb technology a short time after it is introduced in these highly advanced industrialized countries. It is hard to imagine an Argentinian or Australian company establishing its research laboratories in Boston, New York or Detroit. But for a company based in Montreal or Toronto — only a short flight away — such a move is entirely appropriate. A Montreal- or Toronto-based company is also in a good position to purchase and control dynamic, innovative American subsidiaries. In fact, it can supervise an American subsidiary more easily than a subsidiary in Vancouver or Halifax. And even Britain is not that far away; for a Montreal-based firm, London and Edmonton are the same distance from head office.

Although concentration has been reduced on a world scale in the industries we have looked at, this reduction has not resulted in the establishment of large companies controlled by local public or private interests in the Third World. Instead, the reduction in concentration has been the result of the "non-American challenge" issued by the industrialized countries that were rebuilt after the Second World War and by Canada. Even in such long-established industries as distilling and papermaking, it has been new Japanese, European or Canadian competitors rather than Third World producers that have entered the market. There is hardly any sign here of Raymond Vernon's product cycle.

Canadian transnational corporations have adopted a variety of strategies to deal with worldwide structural changes in their industries. Northern Telecom has emphasized innovation and expansion outside Canada rather than economic diversification. At the opposite extreme, the Canadian distilleries have become conglomerates with interests in mining and oil and gas production. Concentration in the distilling industry has declined and the major consumer markets have been stagnant, and the distilleries have resorted to diversification in an effort to compensate for the resulting instability in their income.

In the other three industries under study, Canadian multinationals have diversified their operations to a degree by undertaking the manufacture of related products. For Polysar and the paper companies this strategy has been a complete success. Massey-Ferguson, however, ran into difficulties in implementing this strategy and has had to come back to its main activity, farm machinery production. We saw earlier in connection with Canadian mining corporations that when concentration in an industry is reduced, the industry's leading companies become diversified. The evidence in this chapter shows that, generally speaking, this rule is valid for Canadian manufacturing companies as well.

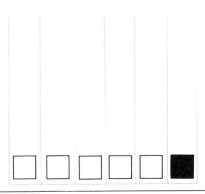

6 Conclusion

Canada is one of the world's major capital-exporting countries. On a per capita basis, Canadians invest almost as much outside their country as Americans do. Moreover, the breakdown of Canadian investment, both by broad sector of activity and by type of host country, is similar to the breakdown of American investment. More than four-fifths of Canadian capital invested outside Canada is invested in developed countries and less than one fifth in underdeveloped countries — similar proportions as for American capital invested outside the United States.

However, Canada and the United States have very different industrial histories. Industrialization in Canada occurred much later than it did in the United States, and — even more significantly — it occurred largely under American control. While Canada is one of the world's leading importers of technology, the United States remains the world's leading technology producer.

This brief comparison between Canada and the United States contradicts a large number of studies of transnational corporations. In the view of many writers, multinational firms arise either as members of innovative oligopolies in the industrialized countries, or else as local companies in semi-industrialized countries that purchase and improve innovations originating elsewhere and then use them in still less developed countries. However, our analysis of the leading Canadian multinationals has shown that, on the one hand, they are not very innovative, and on the other hand, they invest primarily in other industrialized countries. How can we explain this apparent contradiction?

Giant Companies and Domestic Oligopolies

The first characteristic of Canadian multinationals that commands our attention is their size. As we noted in Chapter 2, large Canadian companies are comparable, in terms of both sales and total assets, with the leading European or Japanese companies. And as Hymer and other writers have shown, the size of a firm is one of the main factors determining whether or not it will invest outside its home market.[1] When a company is very large, it has the financial and technological resources to establish subsidiaries that are themselves substantial in size, and thus it is able to set up administrative structures that are better adapted to international operations. We saw in Chapter 2 that 86 per cent of Canadian investment in foreign countries was accounted for by sixty-five companies, each with more than $25 million invested outside Canada (65 per cent of the total was accounted for by only sixteen companies, each with more than $100 million invested in foreign countries). Only very large companies can afford foreign investment on this scale.

Second, it is worth noting that most large Canadian multinational corporations are leaders in highly concentrated domestic oligopolies.[2] Some Canadian multinationals exercised near-absolute monopolies in their respective industries (aluminum, nickel, synthetic rubber) for many years. In other industries — copper, zinc, lead, paper, distilled liquors, farm machinery — Canadian multinationals are members of small, stable oligopolies. It is well known that oligopoly leads to increased profits, and that companies can use these profits to expand internationally. Once again, Canadian multinationals provide a striking validation of Stephen Hymer's explanations.[3]

Technological Imitators

Canadian multinationals have produced few major innovations, and as a group they can be characterized as technological imitators — even technological predators. Except for Northern Telecom, Sherritt Gordon Mines and a few others, they use foreign technology. They have acquired this technology in four major ways:
a) By purchasing patents, licences, technical services and equipment in foreign countries. This method has been used by Canadian utility multinationals throughout the twentieth century; by Poly-

mer in 1942; by Cominco, Noranda and Canterra to acquire electrolytic reduction technology for non-ferrous metals; and by Canada Wire and Cable to acquire the new continuous casting technology for copper in Europe. When innovations appear, Canadian companies are in a position to buy them very quickly, master them and improve them. Thus, starting with a licence for basic styrene-butadiene production in 1942, Polysar has produced numerous varieties of this kind of rubber, while MacMillan Bloedel has improved the process for making kraft paper.

b) By purchasing innovative producers in foreign countries. Examples of the use of this method, which could be called predatory acquisition of technology, include Massey-Harris's purchase of a number of American and British producers to acquire the technology of tractor production; Northern Telecom's purchase of American electronics firms; Polysar's acquisition of a highly innovative West German plastics producer; and Falconbridge's acquisition of electrolytic nickel reduction technology by buying a Norwegian company. With their large size and considerable resources, Canadian companies are often able to absorb foreign companies that are themselves multinational in scope. Canadian multinationals do not have to innovate themselves to enter more technically complex fields, but only need to have the financial and administrative resources to absorb innovative companies in foreign countries. Recent demonstrations of this fact include the purchase by Molson, the Canadian brewing concern, of an American chemicals multinational, Diversey Corp., in 1978; and the takeover by Inco of the international battery producer, ESB, in 1974.

c) By using technology inherited from a former parent corporation. This method has been used by Canadian companies that were once subsidiaries of foreign firms, operating in industries where technological change is slow. In these cases, when Canadians acquire the company, the most effective technology in the industry comes along with it as a package. Alcan and Inco are examples of Canadian multinationals of this sort.

d) By establishing laboratories or research centres in foreign countries. Some Canadian multinationals have concentrated all or most of their research and development facilities outside Canada. Moore Corp. has done all its R&D in Grand Island, New York since 1977[4]; Massey-Ferguson does most of its research near Detroit; and even though Northern Telecom maintains the largest R&D centre in Canada, a growing proportion of its innovation is done in the United States. Technology markets are highly imperfect, some innovation takes place in government and university research centres, and a firm's capacity for innovation depends in part on hiring qualified personnel. In moving their research centres to countries that are more advanced industrially, some Canadian multinationals take advantage of these countries' innovations, qualified personnel and tax write-offs for R&D.

Thus, while Canadian multinationals are big-league oligopolists, they are not major innovators. In this respect, they do not correspond to Raymond Vernon's characterization of the multinational firm, in which innovation constitutes the multinational's primary advantage. Nor do they fit Louis T. Wells, Jr.'s model of multinationals based in the semi-industrialized countries of the Third World. The multinationals described by Wells acquire technology quite late, simplify it and re-export it to less developed countries. Canada, on the other hand, invests primarily in the United States and Europe. What advantages, then do Canadian multinationals hold in these industrially more advanced countries?

This phenomenon can be explained by a combination of factors. First, Canadian companies acquire technology before it has become too widely disseminated. There are fewer impediments in technology markets among Canada, Britain and the United States than among any other comparable group of countries. Second, in some industries, Canadian multinationals can assimilate and improve technology quickly and thus obtain certain advantages over their rivals. Third, these multinationals are in a position to use the advantages they have acquired in third markets. Thus, Canadian multinationals, which earlier in the century generated electricity in Brazil and Venezuela using American equipment and engineers, now sell German plastics technology to the United States and make British tractors and American synthetic rubber on the European continent, Scotch whisky in Argentina, and French and Japanese subway cars in the United States.

In other words, because technology markets are highly imperfect, because Canada is so close geographically, culturally and commercially to the United States and Britain, and because Canadian multinationals enjoy the advantages of large size, considerable resources and oligopoly control of a substantial market, these multinationals are probably among the world's fastest "followers." As soon as innovations are in commercial use elsewhere, Canadian multinationals can get their hands on these innovations through one of the four channels described above.

Third World multinationals, on the other hand, obtain information about innovations much later; cannot buy it until it is widely disseminated and standardized, and are incapable of taking over innovative companies or establishing research centres in advanced industrial countries. Their principal means of absorbing technology is the purchase of patents, technical services and equipment, and in many cases this takes place only after the original discovery has been in commercial application for a number of years. And apart from these structural differences between Canada and other technology-importing countries, Canadian companies may have an additional advantage in technology markets. According to some observers, notably J.M. Katz, innovators behave as discriminatory monopolies in establishing conditions for the sale of technology. Thus, Argentina obtains patents from American and European companies under more advantageous conditions than the countries of the Andean Group (Venezuela, Colombia, Ecuador, Peru, Bolivia). It is not hard to imagine that large Canadian companies would obtain them on even easier terms than the Argentinians. In other words, if market conditions for the flow of technology depend primarily on the relative bargaining power of the buyer and seller, Canadians would have to be among the least disadvantaged buyers of technology in the world.[5]

Declining and Expanding Multinationals

Canadian multinationals in the utility sector have gone through a complete cycle, starting with their establishment in Brazil, Mexico, the Caribbean and elsewhere in the late nineteenth century and ending gradually between the 1940s and the 1970s with the liquidation or sale of the foreign subsidiaries of the Canadian holding companies. During this cycle, the Canadian companies took advantage of their easy access to major financial markets and foreign — especially American — technology. Starting in the 1940s, however, as the host countries finally mastered the industry's know-how and new national and international financial institutions emerged, these initial advantages disappeared.

In the mining sector, different processes have taken place and they have led to different results. Here too, technological innovations have been produced in the industrialized countries, but the industrialized countries are also the principal markets for mineral products and access to international financing is not as easy as in the utility sector. Thus, in most mining industries, the multinationals' bargaining power, based on control of technology, consumer markets and financing, remains greater than that of the host countries. Hence, even though the concentration of world mining oligopolies has clearly been reduced, it is not inevitable that mining multinationals' subsidiaries in Third World producing countries (some rich countries, such as Canada, the United States and Australia, are also major mineral producers) will be expropriated.

The obsolescing bargain is clearly evident only in the petroleum industry, where returns are so high and markets in so little doubt that the producing countries have been able to take control. The producing countries' bargaining power in the copper and bauxite industries is much weaker, and in other mining industries it is almost nonexistent. Rather than the nationalization of subsidiaries of multinationals in the Third World, the most widespread result of the reduction in concentration of the world mining industry has been joint ventures. Canadian companies, meanwhile, have been only slightly affected by nationalizations in the mining sector.

Finally, in the manufacturing sector, the product cycle has lasted longer than the theory would lead us to expect. Some Third World countries — Brazil, South Korea, India, Mexico — have achieved substantial industrial development in the last twenty years, and these countries have passed the stiffest laws regulating foreign capital. At the same time, manufacturing in other countries, such as Argentina and Chile, has been in decline, and economic policy in these countries has been aimed at wholesale deindustrialization. Canadian multinationals have adapted to conditions in these different host countries. As a group, they are in a safe position in all of these countries, and even safer in the industrially less advanced countries of Asia and Africa. They are also gaining control of a growing portion of some traditional industries in the Third World, such as the manufacture of alcoholic beverages and shoes. In the manufacturing sector, the evidence supports Hymer's thesis that companies are not necessarily destined to grow old and die, but can apparently go on indefinitely. This is reflected in their international operations, where signs that they are declining are not conspicuous.[6]

The cycle followed by manufacturing multinationals seems to be somewhere between Raymond Vernon's product cycle and Constantine Vaitsos's monopoly cycle, and no evidence that this cycle is entering a decline phase has yet appeared.

The Internalization of Markets

Looking at some of Peter J. Buckley and Marc Casson's theses, we find that these too are only partly applicable to Canadian multinationals. Their theory, based on the internalization of markets in technology, machinery and intermediate goods, predicts that the most R&D-intensive firms will be the most highly multinational and will have higher rates of growth and profitability than other companies. However, Buckley and Casson themselves remarked that Canadian multinationals were not found in R&D-intensive industries with the same frequency as multinationals based in other countries.[7] And Table 1 shows that while high-technology Canadian multinationals grew more quickly than low-technology firms, their rate of return was lower, primarily as a result of the poor performance of Massey-Ferguson in the late 1970s.

TABLE 1

Increase in Total Assets and Net Profit of Major Canadian Industrial Multinational Corporations Between 1970 and 1979

Company	No. of host countries*	Percentage increase	
		total assets	net profit
High-technology			
Northern Telecom	7	419	2,160
Polysar	10	306	722
Massey-Ferguson	18	171	-190
Weighted Average	12	246	82
Low-technology			
Alcan Aluminium	31	33	472
Bata Shoes	102	n.d.	n.d.
Canada Packers	6	155	100
Cominco	9	193	750
Hiram Walker	5	113	152
Inco	10	137	-32
MacMillan Bloedel	5	103	812
Moore	13	281	166
Noranda	13	281	3
Seagram	26	97	194
Weighted average	25	98	96

*Number of countries in which the company has manufacturing subsidiaries and affiliated companies.

In addition, the least R&D-intensive firms 'are the most highly multinational ones. To be sure, these are also the oldest companies (Bata Shoes and Moore Corp. were founded in the nineteenth century, and Alcan in 1902), but a large part of their international expansion has taken place since the Second World War, as they have taken a leaf from the book of the new multinationals such as Polysar or Northern Telecom. These data tend to show that multinational corporations are not declining even in the most traditional manufacturing industries. It is true, however, that one of the secrets of resisting erosion for companies such as Bata Shoes (with subsidiaries in 102 countries) or Moore Corp. (37 countries) lies in the fact that they make their own equipment and allow only their subsidiaries to have access to it.[8] Thus, internalization of technology markets does appear to be a factor contributing to the staying power of multinational corporations, even in the most traditional industries.

The Non-American Challenge and the Reaction of Canadian Multinationals

In the industries under study, concentration has been reduced since the Second World War primarily by the entry of Japanese and European multinationals and to a lesser extent by the entry of Canadian ones. Despite the new competition, Canadian multinationals have not lost a significant part of their world market share except in the nickel and distilled liquor industries. In no case have Canadian mining or manufacturing multinationals been seriously threatened by companies in Third World host countries. The new competition has come from industrialized countries that have been rebuilt since the Second World War. These sources of the non-American challenge and the reduced concentration of world oligopolies were correctly identified by Stephen Hymer and Robert Rowthorn.

Canadian multinationals have followed a strategy of diversifying their operations economically, and the extent of this diversification has been a function of intensity of world competition. In industries such as nickel and distilled liquor in which Canadian multinationals have lost considerable ground, these companies have become conglomerates, expanding into industries that are completely unrelated to their traditional activities. In other industries, where world concentration has been reduced more slowly or Canadian multinationals have maintained their market shares (paper, rubber, copper, zinc, lead), the Canadian firms have diversified into

176

related industries. And in industries where barriers to entry have remained very high (aluminum, telecommunications equipment) Canadian firms have become vertically integrated but that has more or less been the limit of their diversification. Meanwhile, Canadian multinationals in all industries have expanded geographically to protect export markets.

The Multinationalization of Industrial Branches and the Oligopolistic Reaction

The models proposed by Fred Knickerbocker and Christian Palloix do not fit the Canadian case very well, since in general only one Canadian firm in each industrial branch has become multinational. Furthermore, in the two cases in which two Canadian companies in the same industrial branch have become multinational (nickel and distilled liquor), there has been a long interval between the leader's international expansion and that of the second company, while in Knickerbocker's model, firms in the same industrial branch become multinational within a few years of one another. As for Palloix's model, it would be better to speak of the multinationalization of the leading firm in each branch than the multinationalization of the branch itself. The Canadian market is fairly small and highly concentrated, so that the oligopoly in each industry is made up of only a very few firms, and the marginal companies within these oligopolies do not become multinational.

Imperialism and Dependency

As we noted in Chapter 1, classical Marxist theories of imperialism do not explain Canadian multinational corporations. Canada has no colonies and no investment banks, and invests mainly in more advanced industrialized countries. In these respects, it is completely different from the European metropolitan powers that Hilferding and Lenin studied in the early twentieth century. Contemporary dependency theories, such as those of Cardoso, Evans and Vaitsos, are somewhat complementary to the approach, in terms of national and international oligopolies, that has been followed in this work. However, the dependency perspective emphasizes the economic and social structure of the host countries; here, following Hymer and Rowthorn, the emphasis has been placed on the structure of the investing countries and the world market.

Canadian Multinational Corporations: A Unique Case

We have called on a number of the major theories of multinational corporations in our analysis of large Canadian companies. Stephen Hymer's theories have been largely confirmed by our findings, especially in the areas of the relationship between size and multinational expansion, the oligopolistic character of multinational corporations, and the identification of the new competition in world markets as being of Japanese, European and Canadian origin.

Our examination of the theses of Raymond Vernon and Louis T. Wells, Jr. has led to mixed results. The Vernon-Wells theory is the only one that correctly predicts the decline of multinational corporations in the utility sector, which has reached its final stage in recent years. In the mining sector, however, it appears necessary to reformulate the thesis of the obsolescing bargain. The relative decline in the multinationals' bargaining power and the reduction in world concentration lead to a proliferation of joint ventures among the multinationals themselves or between the multinationals and the host countries. In the manufacturing sector, Canadian multinationals have not been subject to any erosion as a result of competition from Third World companies, even in the most traditional industries (shoes, business forms, alcoholic beverages, paper). Wells's thesis of the international pecking order, meanwhile, predicts that companies that produce little or no technology of their own will invest in less advanced countries. However, while Canadian firms have show little inclination towards innovation, the pattern of international development and incorporation of technology followed by these firms does not correspond to Wells's model. Finally, no definite conclusion can be drawn about Buckley and Casson's theses — no doubt partly because of the kind of information that would be needed to test them. And Knickerbocker and Palloix's theses are completely contradicted by the data. In countries such as Canada, Sweden, Switzerland, Belgium or Holland, only the leader in each industry attains multinational status.

We have described Canada as a case of international expansion based on foreign technology. It would appear to be the only such case. The country that most resembles Canada in terms of its industrial structure is Australia. However, Canada's direct investment in foreign countries was greater than Australia's by a factor of 7.5 in 1974, or a factor of 5 on a per capita basis.[9] In addition, most Australian capital was invested in the less developed countries of Southeast Asia and the Pacific. And finally, companies owned outside Australia accounted for a very large part of Australian direct investment in foreign countries. Thus, the Australian case appears to come much closer to the model of Third World multinationals. To this writer's knowledge, no Australian multinational has purchased a company in the industrialized countries that is on the same scale as the firms absorbed by Canadian multinationals. The small size of the Australian market and the distance between Australia and the English-speaking industrialized countries make it impossible for Australia to follow the same course as Canada.

On the basis of the available information, Canada must also be classed apart from such industrialized European countries as Switzerland, Sweden, Belgium and Holland. Unlike Canada, these countries have multinational corporations based on indigenous technology. In the area of the internationalization of capital, the Canadian model appears to be one with no imitators.

Footnotes

Preface

[1] Isaiah A. Litvak and Christopher J. Maule, "Canadian Multinationals in the Western Hemisphere", *Business Quarterly*, Autumn 1975, pp. 30-42. A collection of articles by Litvak and Maule has been published under the title *The Canadian Multinationals* (Toronto: Butterworths, 1981). G. Garnier, "Les investissements directs du Canada à l'étranger", *L'Actualité économique*, April-June 1973, pp. 211-36.

[2] E.P. Neufeld, *A Global Corporation: A History of the International Development of Massey-Ferguson* (Toronto: University of Toronto Press, 1969); John Deverall et al., *Falconbridge: Portrait of a Canadian Mining Multinational* (Toronto: James Lorimer and Co., 1975); Jamie Swift et al., *The Big Nickel: Inco at Home and Abroad* (Kitchener: Between the Lines, 1977).

[3] Tamir Agmon and Charles P. Kindleberger, eds., *Multinationals from Small Countries* (Cambridge, Mass.: MIT Press, 1977).

[4] United Nations, *Multinational Corporations in World Development* (New York, 1973).

[5] J.N.H. Britton and J.M. Gilmour, *The Weakest Link: A Technological Perspective on Canadian Industrial Underdevelopment*, Science Council of Canada Background Study No. 43 (Ottawa: Supply and Services Canada, 1978). Britton and Gilmour write that "one or two [Canadian] firms may have subsudiaries in the United States" (p. 94), while in fact, there are more than 300 Canadian manufacturing companies operating in the United States, and Canada is the third largest foreign investing country in the U.S.

Chapter 1: Theoretical Considerations

[1] Stephen Hymer, *The International Operations of National Firms* (Cambridge, Mass.: MIT Press, 1976).

[2] Stephen Hymer, *The Multinational Corporation: A Radical Approach*, edited by R.B. Cohen (Cambridge: At the University Press, 1979).

[3] Peter J. Buckley and Marc Casson, *The Future of the Multinational Enterprise* (New York: Holmes and Meier, 1976).

[4] Raymond Vernon, *Sovereignty at Bay* (New York: Basic Books, 1971); Raymond Vernon, *Storm Over the Multinationals* (Cambridge, Mass.: Har-

vard University Press, 1977). See also Vernon's original formulation of the product cycle theory in "International Investment and International Trade in the Product Cycle", *Quarterly Journal of Economics*, May 1966, pp. 190-207.

[5] Ian H. Giddy, "The Demise of the Product Cycle Model in International Business Theory," *Columbia Journal of World Business*, Spring 1978, pp. 90-97.

[6] Raymond Vernon, "The Product Cycle Hypothesis in a New International Environment," roneograph (Harvard University, 1979).

[7] Constantine Vaitsos, *Intercountry Income Distribution and Transnational Enterprise* (Oxford: At the University Press, 1974).

[8] Frederick T. Knickerbocker, *Oligopolistic Reaction and Multinational Enterprise* (Cambridge, Mass.: Harvard University Press, 1973).

[9] Buckley and Casson, *Future of the Multinational Enterprise*, pp. 79-80.

[10] Tamir Agmon and Charles P. Kindleberger, eds., *Multinationals from Small Countries* (Cambridge, Mass.: MIT Press, 1977).

[11] Louis T. Wells, Jr., "The Internationalization of Firms from Developing Countries," in Agmon and Kindleberger, eds., *Multinationals from Small Countries*, pp. 133-56. See also Louis T. Wells, Jr., "Third World Multinationals," *Multinational Business* (London), no. 1 (1980).

[12] Buckley and Casson, *Future of the Multinational Enterprise*.

[13] Notable among such theories is R.Z. Aliber's explanation of foreign direct investment as a flow of capital from strong currency areas to weak currency areas. Aliber's theory does not predict foreign direct investment within the same currency area, such as Canadian direct investment in the United States or American direct investment in Canada. Nor does it predict differences in behaviour in foreign direct investment originating in the same currency area — for example, between American and Canadian direct investment. See R.Z. Aliber, "A Theory of Direct Investment", in Charles P. Kindleberger, ed., *The International Corporation* (Cambridge, Mass.: MIT Press, 1970), pp. 17-34.

[14] Rosa Luxembourg, *The Accumulation of Capital* (1913; new edition with an introduction by Joan Robinson, London: Routledge and Kegan Paul, 1963); Arghiri Emmanuel, *Unequal Exchange: A Study of the Imperialism of Trade* (New York, Monthly Review Press, 1972). Emmanuel strongly attacks theories of imperialism based on foreign direct investment; see his article "Le mythe de l'impérialisme d'investissement," *L'Homme et la société* no. 22, Oct.-Dec. 1971, pp. 67-96.

[15] V.I. Lenin, *Imperialism, the Highest Stage of Capitalism* (1916; Moscow: Progress Publishers, 1970).

[16] Catherine Coquery-Vidrovitch, "De l'impérialisme ancien à l'impérialisme moderne — l'avatar colonial," *L'Homme et la société*, no. 18, Oct.-Dec. 1970, pp. 61-90.

[17] On the control of large American corporations, see A.J. Chandler, Jr., *The Visible Hand* (Cambridge, Mass.: Harvard University Press, 1978). For Canada, see the author's *The Economy of Canada: A Study of Ownership and Control* (Montreal: Black Rose Books, 1978).

[18] Kari Levitt, *Silent Surrender: The Multinational Corporation in Canada* (Toronto: Macmillan of Canada, 1970).

[19] Paul Baran, *The Political Economy of Growth* (New York: Monthly Review Press, 1957); André Gunder Frank, *Capitalism and Underdevelopment in Latin America* (New York: Monthly Review Press, 1967); Meir Merhav, *Technological Dependence, Monopoly and Growth* (London: Pergamon Press, 1969); Samir Amin, *Accumulation on a World Scale: A Critique of the Theory of Underdevelopment* (New York: Monthly Review Press, 1974); Charles Bettelheim, *Planification et croissance accélérée* (Paris: Maspéro, 1963).

[20] Baran, *Political Economy of Growth*, p. 200.

[21] Paul Baran and Paul Sweezy, *Monopoly Capital: An Essay on the American Economic and Social Order* (New York: Monthly Review Press, 1966).

[22] Merhav, *Technological Dependence*.

[23] Harry Magdoff, "The Multinational Corporation and Development — A Contradiction," in D.E. Apter and L.W. Goodman, eds., *The Multinational Corporation and Social Change* (New York: Praeger, 1976), pp. 208-9. See also Harry Magdoff, *The Age of Imperialism* (New York: Monthly Review Press, 1969).

[24] Fernando H. Cardoso, "Dependent Capitalist Development in Latin America," *New Left Review*, no. 74, July-Aug. 1972, pp. 83-95.

[25] Bill Warren, "Imperialism and Capitalist Industrialization," *New Left Review*, no. 81, Sept.-Oct. 1973, pp. 3-45.

[26] Bill Warren, *Imperialism, Pioneer of Capitalism* (London: NL Books, 1980).

[27] Christian Palloix, *L'économie mondiale capitaliste*, 2 vols. (Paris: Maspéro, 1971).

[28] Charles-Albert Michelet, *Le capitalisme mondial* (Paris: Presses Universitaires de France, 1976).

[29] *Ibid.*, p. 101.

[30] *Ibid.*, p. 29.

Chapter 2: The International Expansion of the Canadian Economy

[1] Mira Wilkins, *The Emergence of Multinational Enterprise: American Business Abroad from the Colonial Era to 1914* (Cambridge, Mass.: Harvard University Press, 1970), chapter 7; Tom Naylor, *The History of Canadian Business*, 2 vols. (Toronto: James Lorimer and Co., 1975).

[2] Herbert Marshall et al., *Canadian-American Industry* (1936; reprint ed., Toronto: McClelland and Stewart, 1976), p. 141.

[3] Canada, Statistics Canada, Cat. no. 61-210 (annual), *Corporations and Labour Unions Reporting Act, 1977 Report, Part I: Corporations* (Ottawa: Supply and Services Canada, 1980).

[4] Wilkins, *Emergence of Multinational Enterprise*, p. 110.

[5] Marshall et al., *Canadian-American Industry*, p. 63.

[6] *Ibid.*, p. 29.

[7] Naylor, *Canadian Business,* 2:39.

[8] *Ibid.*, 2:46.

[9] O.J. Firestone, *Economic Implications of Patents* (Ottawa: Éditions de l'Université d'Ottawa, 1971), p. 38.

[10] *Ibid.*, p. 377.

[11] Pierre L. Bourgault, *Innovation and the Structure of Canadian Industry,* Science Council of Canada Background Study No. 23 (Ottawa: Information Canada, 1972).

[12] Along with Spain, Greece, Iceland and Portugal (1967 data). Bourgault, *Innovation.*

[13] Canada, Science of Council of Canada, *Innovation in a Cold Climate: The Dilemma of Canadian Manufacturing,* Report No. 15 (Ottawa: Information Canada, 1971).

[14] E.P. Neufeld, *The Financial System of Canada* (Toronto: Macmillan of Canada, 1972), p. 99. The banks in question are the Bank of Montreal, the Royal Bank of Canada, the Canadian Imperial Bank of Canada, the Bank of Nova Scotia and the Toronto-Dominion Bank.

[15] Joe S. Bain, *International Differences in Industrial Structure* (New Haven: Yale University Press, 1966); Canada, Royal Commission on Corporate Concentration, *Report* (Ottawa: Supply and Services Canada, 1978).

[16] William Woodruff, *Impact of Western Man: A Study of Europe's Role in the World Economy 1750-1960* (London: Macmillan, 1966), p. 150.

[17] Stefan H. Robock and Kenneth Simmonds, "How Big It Is — The Missing Measurement," *Columbia Journal of World Business,* May-June 1970.

[18] Calculated from Canada, Statistics Canada, Cat. no. 67-202, 1980, p. 54.

[19] J.S. Arpan and D.A. Ricks, *Directory of Foreign Manufacturers in the U.S.* (Atlanta: Georgia State University, 1979).

[20] Canada, Export Development Corporation, *Annual Report,* 1979, p. 16.

[21] *Financial Post,* April 29, 1978, EDC supplement, p. 3.

[22] *Financial Post,* November 5, 1977, p. 11.

[23] Canada, Canadian International Development Agency, *Annual Report,* 1972-73, pp. 53, 58.

[24] Organization for Economic Co-operation and Development, *Investing in Developing Countries* (Paris, 1979).

[25] International Finance Corporation, *Annual Report,* 1980.

[26] *Le Devoir,* September 17, 1980, p. 17.

[27] Y. Tsurumi, *The Japanese Are Coming* (Cambridge, Mass.: Ballinger, 1976), p. 34.

[28] "Japanese Multinationals," *Business Week,* June 16, 1980, pp. 92-102.

[29] Louis T. Wells, Jr., "Third World Multinationals," *Multinational Business* (London), no. 1 (1980), pp. 12-19.

[30] Peter J. Buckley and Marc Casson, *The Future of the Multinational Enterprise* (New York: Holmes and Meier, 1976), p. 29.

[31] *International Management* (London), August 1964; *Realidad Economica*

(Buenos Aires), January-February 1974, pp. 18-19; *Mercado* (Buenos Aires), August 27, 1981; p. 23; J.C. Casas, *Las multinacionales y el comercio latino americano* (Mexico City: CEMLA, 1973 qy), pp. 39-49; *Wall Street Journal,* February 5, 1975, p. 9; *Wall Street Journal,* July 22, 1975, p. 4; *Wall Street Journal,* February 8, 1978, p. 24; *Wall Street Journal,* February 11, 1978, p. 3; *Wall Street Journal,* August 19, 1980, p. 18; Dan Morgan, *Merchants of Grain* (New York: Viking Press, 1979).

[32] Casas, *Las multinacionales: Mercado* (Buenos Aires), August 27, 1981; *Business Latin America* (New York), January 30, 1980, p. 39; *Business Latin America,* November 25, 1981, p. 375.

[33] Casas, *Las multinacionales; Business Latin America* (New York), February 27, 1969; *Business Latin America,* June 26, 1969, p. 206.

Chapter 3: The Rise and Fall of the Utility Multinationals

[1] Ralph G.M. Sultan, *Pricing in the Electrical Oligopoly,* 2 vols. (Cambridge, Mass.: Harvard University Press, 1974), 1:10 and 1:21. For the beginnings of the oligopoly in the electrical industry, see H.C. Passer, *The Electrical Manufacturers 1875-1900* (Cambridge, Mass.: Harvard University Press, 1953).

[2] Mira Wilkins, *The Emergence of Multinational Enterprise: American Business Abroad from the Colonial Era to 1914* (Cambridge, Mass.: Harvard University Press, 1970), p. 158.

[3] Sultan, *Electrical Oligopoly,* pp. 22-23.

[4] J.C. Bonbright and Gardiner C. Means, *The Holding Company* (1932; New York, Kelley Publishers, 1969), p. 126.

[5] On instances of inflation of capital by utility holding companies, see Bonbright and Means, *Holding Company,* pp. 159 et seq. On the acquisition of wealth by Canadian promoters, see J.C.M. Oglesby, *Gringos from the Far North* (Toronto: Macmillan of Canada, 1976), pp. 129-30; A.J.P. Taylor, *Beaverbrook* (London: Hamish Hamilton, 1972); and, on the fortune of the promoter James Ross, *Monetary Times,* December 27, 1918, p. 961.

[6] Wilkins, *Emergence of Multinational Enterprise,* p. 110; Mira Wilkins, *The Maturing of Multinational Enterprise: American Business Abroad from 1914 to 1970* (Cambridge, Mass.: Harvard University Press, 1974), p. 57.

[7] Wilkins, *Maturing of Multinational Enterprise,* p. 330. For 1977, see United States, Department of Commerce, *Survey of Current Business,* August 1978, p. 28.

[8] J.F. Rippy, *Latin America and the Industrial Age* (New York: Putnam, 1944), chapters 3, 10, 11 and 14.

[9] H. Quigley, "The World Market for Electrical Goods," in *World Power* (London) 3, no. 17 (May 1925), 240-48; "The Postwar Foreign Market for Electrical Goods," *Beama Journal* (London), April 1944, pp. 24 et

seq.; "Role of the United States in Brazil Electrical Trade," *Electrical World* 74, no. 2 (July 12, 1919), p. 98.

[10] "American Control of Foreign Utilities," *Electrical World* 92, no. 25 (December 22, 1928), p. 1249.

[11] *Monetary Times,* February 22, 1913, p. 429.

[12] *Monetary Times,* June 29, 1912, pp. 2619-20.

[13] *Canadian Electrical News* (Toronto) 15, no. 5 (May 1905), pp. 83-88.

[14] *Canadian Electrical News* (Toronto), 16, no. 4 (October 1905), p. 223 et seq.

[15] *Canadian Electrical News* (Toronto) 7, no. 5 (May 1905) p. 79 et seq.

[16] *Annual Financial Review* (Toronto), 1903 (West India Electric), 1904 (São Paulo Tramway), etc.

[17] *Financial Post.* June 21, 1952, p. 16.

[18] J.S. Carson, "The Power Industry," in L.J. Hughlett, comp., *Industrialization in Latin America* (New York: McGraw-Hill, 1946), pp. 329, 341.

[19] Miguel S. Wionczek, *El nacionalismo mexicano y la inversión extranjera* (Mexico City: Siglo XXI, 1967), Part 1.

[20] *Public Utilities Fortnightly.* May 13, 1965, p. 90; *Financial Post.* January 6, 1979, p. 11.

[21] For the initial stage of São Paulo Tramway and Rio de Janeiro Tramway, see F.J. Mulqueen, "A Canadian Enterprise Abroad," *Canadian Banker* 59, no. 1 (Winter 1952), pp. 34-55; *Annual Financial Review* (Toronto), 1901-12. For the Canadian interests of the companies' Toronto founders, see H.V. Nelles, *The Politics of Development: Forests, Mines and Hydro-Electric Power in Ontario 1849-1941* (Toronto: Macmillan of Canada, 1974).

[22] *Monetary Times* (Toronto), February 1, 1913, p. 291; *Annual Financial Review* (Toronto), 1909, p. 548.

[23] Oglesby, *Gringos from the Far North,* p. 133.

[24] *Financial Post.* May 5, 1951, p. 42; *Financial Post.* February 23, 1952, p. 15; *Financial Post,* June 21, 1952, p. 16.

[25] *Financial Post.* June 21, 1952, p. 16.

[26] *Wall Street Journal.* October 13, 1965, p. 9.

[27] Judith Tendler, *Electric Power in Brazil* (Cambridge, Mass.: Harvard University Press, 1968), pp. 7-17.

[28] *Ibid.,* chapter 2. See also Catullo Branco, *Energia eletrica e capital estrangeiro no Brasil* (São Paulo: Alfa-Omega, 1975).

[29] *Business Latin America.* October 31, 1973, pp. 350-51.

[30] Jorge Niosi, *The Economy of Canada: A Study of Ownership and Control* (Montreal: Black Rose Books, 1978), chapter 2; E. Roy Birkett, *Brascan Ltd.: A Corporate Background Report for the Royal Commission on Corporate Concentration.* RCCC Study No. 2 (Toronto, January 1976).

[31] *Financial Post.* January 6, 1979, p. 11; *Financial Post.* January 13, 1979, p. 9.

[32] Taylor, *Beaverbrook.* p. 37.

[33] *Annual Financial Review* (Toronto), 1926-30.

34 *Financial Post,* July 1, 1978, p. 10.
35 *Public Utilities Fortnightly,* April 25, 1968, p. 42.
36 Canadian International Power, *Annual Report,* 1977.
37 *Business Latin America,* July 23, 1980, p. 235.
38 Monenco Ltd., *Annual Report,* 1977.

Chapter 4: Multinationals in the Mining Sector

1 For the history of nickel up to 1950, see A. Skelton, "Nickel," in W.Y. Elliott et al., *International Control of the Non-Ferrous Metals* (New York: Macmillan, 1937), pp. 109-209; O.W. Main, *The Canadian Nickel Industry* (Toronto: University of Toronto Press, 1955).
2 A.F.W. Liversidge, "The Beguiling New Economics of Nickel," *Fortune,* March 1970, pp. 100 et seq.; "Big Gamble for Nickel Markets," *Financial Post,* March 20, 1971, pp. 1-2.
3 American Bureau of Metal Statistics, *Non-Ferrous Metals Data 1979* (New York, 1980), p. 122.
4 "Inco Gears Expansion to Both Long, Short Terms," *Financial Post,* October 10, 1970, p. 37; "Big Gamble for Nickel Markets," *Financial Post,* March 20, 1971, pp. 1-2.
5 A. Skelton, "Copper," in Elliott et al., *International Control,* p. 459.
6 T.R. Navin, *Copper Mining and Management* (Tucson: University of Arizona Press, 1978), Part 3.
7 Skelton, "Copper," p. 406.
8 Martin S. Brown and John Butler, *The Production, Marketing and Consumption of Copper and Aluminum* (New York: Praeger, 1968), pp. 56-58.
9 Michael Tanzer, *The Race for Resources* (New York: Monthly Review Press, 1960), p. 128.
10 American Bureau of Metal Statistics, *Non-Ferrous Metals Data 1979,* pp. 22-24; company annual reports.
11 Dorothea Mezger, *Copper in the World Economy* (New York: Monthly Review Press, 1980).
12 *Ibid.,* p. 68.
13 Herbert Marshall et al., *Canadian-American Industry* (1936; reprint ed., Toronto: McClelland and Stewart, 1976), pp. 94, 101.
14 *Financial Post,* January 13, 1979, p. 7.
15 Joe S. Bain, *Barriers to New Competition* (Cambridge, Mass.: Harvard University Press, 1956).
16 Donald H. Wallace, *Market Control in the Aluminum Industry* (Cambridge, Mass.: Harvard University Press, 1937); Louis Marlio, *The Aluminum Cartel* (Washington: The Brookings Institution, 1947), chapters 3-4.
17 Organization for Economic Co-operation and Development, *Industrial Adaptation in the Primary Aluminium Industry* (Paris, 1976).
18 A. Skelton, "Zinc," in Elliott et al., *International Control,* p. 693.
19 American Bureau of Metal Statistics, *Non-Ferrous Metals Data 1979,* pp. 77-78.

[20] Energy, Mines and Resources Canada, *Zinc* (Ottawa: Supply and Services Canada, 1976).

[21] Skelton, "Zinc," p. 615.

[22] *Ibid.,* p. 623.

[23] Skelton, "Copper," chapter 8.

[24] Skelton, "Nickel," p. 174.

[25] Jamie Swift et al., *The Big Nickel: Inco at Home and Abroad* (Kitchener: Between The Lines, 1977), pp. 63-80.

[26] "It is in the setting of the collapse of Inco's dominance in the world nickel market that the company's decision to move into the laterite ores in Indonesia and Guatemala and to acquire ESB Ltd. should be interpreted. Both constitute attempts to protect corporate strength" (*Financial Post,* November 19, 1977, p. 22). See also L. Lamont, "Inco: A Giant Learns How to Compete," *Fortune,* January 1975, pp. 104 et seq.

[27] Inco Ltd., *Annual Report,* 1979, p. 1.

[28] "Inco in Depth," *Financial Post,* October 2, 1976, p. 40; "Big Gamble for Nickel Markets," *Financial Post,* March 20, 1971, pp. 1-2.

[29] *Financial Post,* October 2, 1976, p. 43.

[30] John Deverell et al., *Falconbridge: Portrait of a Canadian Mining Multinational* (Toronto: James Lorimer and Co., 1975), chapters 7-8.

[31] "Falconbridge Opens New Dominican Nickel Mine," *Financial Post,* July 1, 1972, p. 17.

[32] "The Founder's Son," *Forbes,* September 15, 1976, pp. 81-86.

[33] "One Setback after Another for Falconbridge Nickel," *Financial Post,* March 15, 1975, p. 20.

[34] Falconbridge Nickel Mines, *Annual Report* 1979, p. 9.

[35] *Northern Miner* (Toronto), Magazine Supplement, July 6, 1972. This issue is a much better source of data than the company's official history: Leslie Roberts, *Noranda* (Toronto: Clarke Irwin, 1956).

[36] "Three men who built a multinational firm with a difference," *Financial Post,* May 13, 1972, p. 33.

[37] J.H. Stevens, "Joint Ventures in Latin America: Corporate Philosophy and Practice," *Business Quarterly,* Winter 1974, pp. 66-71.

[38] *Financial Post,* April 17, 1976, p. 15; *Financial Post,* February 26, 1977, p. 25; *Financial Post,* March 19, 1977, p. 29.

[39] Noranda Mines, *Annual Report 1979,* pp. 2-3.

[40] "Cables Canada investit $25 millions à Montréal-Est," *La Presse,* October 11, 1980, p. A-17.

[41] John David, *Mining and Mineral Processing in Canada,* a study prepared for the Royal Commission on Canada's Economic Prospects (Ottawa: Queen's Printer, 1957).

[42] *Moody's Industrial Manual* (New York: Moody's Investors' Service, 1961), p. 1534.

[43] *World Aluminium Survey* (London, 1977).

[44] Alcan, *Alcan Today* (Montreal, 1979), p. 5.

[45] C. Davies, "Alcan's Power Plays Off," *Canadian Business,* November 1980, pp. 86-94.

[46] "Cominco," *Canadian Mining Journal*. May 1954; *Moody's Industrial Manual*. 1960-80; American Bureau of Metal Statistics, Non-Ferrous Metals Data 1979.
[47] Cominco, Annual Report, 1979, pp. 14-15.
[48] "Cominco Strives to Get Past Its Lead-Zinc Dependence," *Financial Post*. September 5, 1970, p. 31; "Cominco is Pledged to Keeping Diversified," *Financial Post*. May 3, 1975, p. 17.
[49] P.E. Sigmund, *Multinationals in Latin America* (New York: The 20th Century Fund, 1980).

Chapter 5: Multinationals in the Manufacturing Sector

[1] J.R. Petrie, *Some Economic Facts About the Beverage Distilling Industry in Canada* (Montreal: Association of Canadian Distillers, 1961).
[2] Morton Research Co., *The U.S. Distilled Liquor Industy* (New York, 1979), pp. 7 et seq.
[3] Gideon Rosenbluth, *Concentration in Canadian Manufacturing Industries* (Princeton, N.J.: Princeton University Press, 1957), p. 111.
[4] Canada, Statistics Canada, Cat. no. 31-402, *Industrial Organization and Concentration in Manufacturing, Mining and Logging Industries* (Ottawa: Information Canada, 1975), p. 57.
[5] M.R. Rosenbloom, *The Liquor Industry* (Braddock, Pa.: Ruffsdale, 1937), p. 61.
[6] "Changing Habits in American Drinking," *Fortune*. October 1976, pp. 156-66; "The Whisky Distillers Put Up Their Dukes," *Fortune*. September 1977, pp. 155-68.
[7] Canada, Statistics Canada, *Canada Year Book 1976-77* (Ottawa: Supply and Services Canada, 1977), p. 855.
[8] Jack Weldon, "Consolidations in Canadian Industry, 1900-1948," in L.A. Skeoch, ed., *Restrictive Trade Practices in Canada* (Toronto: McClelland and Stewart, 1966), pp. 226-80.
[9] John A. Guthrie, *The Newsprint Paper Industry: An Economic Analysis* (Cambridge, Mass.: Harvard University Press, 1941), p. 65.
[10] John M. Blair, *Economic Concentration* (New York: Harcourt Brace Jovanovich, 1972), p. 271.
[11] E.P. Neufeld, *A Global Corporation: A History of the International Development of Massey-Ferguson* (Toronto: University of Toronto Press, 1979), chapter 1.
[12] Canada, Royal Commission on Farm Machinery, *Report* (Ottawa: Information Canada, 1971), p. 49.
[13] Morton Research Co., *The U.S. Farm Machinery Industry* (New York, 1977), p. 127.
[14] Rosenbluth, *Concentration*. p. 112.
[15] J.D. Woods & Gordon Ltd., *The Canadian Agricultural Machinery Industry*. a study prepared for the Royal Commission on Canada's Eco-

nomic Prospects (Ottawa: Queen's Printer, 1956), p. 15.

[16] Canada, Royal Commission on Farm Machinery, *Report.*

[17] Canada, Statistics Canada, Cat. no. 11-001E, *Statistics Canada Daily,* September 21, 1979, p. 4.

[18] "Massey-Ferguson's Global Strategy," *International Management,* September 1968, pp. 44-49.

[19] On control of the world farm tractor industry, see R.T. Kurdle, *Agricultural Tractors: A World Industry Study* (Cambridge, Mass.: Ballinger, 1975).

[20] Mira Wilkins, *The Emergence of Multinational Enterprise: American Business Abroad from the Colonial Era to 1914* (Cambridge, Mass.: Harvard University Press, 1970), p. 103.

[21] Philip Schidrowitz and T.R. Dawson, *History of the Rubber Industry* (Cambridge: W. Heffer & Sons, 1952).

[22] Mira Wilkins, *The Maturing of Multinationals Enterprise: American Business Abroad from 1914 to 1970* (Cambridge, Mass.: Harvard University Press, 1974), pp. 255, 269-70.

[23] John Davis, *The Canadian Chemical Industry,* a study prepared for the Royal Commission on Canada's Economic Prospects (Ottawa: Queen's Printer, 1957).

[24] DAFSA, *Les caoutchoucs synthétiques et naturels* (Paris, 1974), p. 66.

[25] John Brooks, *Telephone: The First Hundred Years* (New York: Harper and Row, 1975), p. 94.

[26] Wilkins, *Maturing of Multinational Enterprise,* p. 130.

[27] Early in 1981, the government of Argentina had to decide which bidder would be awarded a big contract to extend the country's telephone system. Standard Electric, Siemens, Ericsson and Philips all submitted bids, but a Japanese group led by Nippon Electric offered to fulfill the contract at 50 per cent under its competitors' prices. See *Latin America Regional Report* (Southern Cone, London), January 30, 1981, pp. 2-3.

[28] Amy Booth, "The Bronfmans," *Financial Post,* Part 1: November 13, 1976, pp. 10-11, 20, and Part 2: November 20, 1976, pp. 11-13; Peter C. Newman, *Bronfman Dynasty: The Rothschilds of the New World* (Toronto: McClelland and Stewart, 1978), pp. 104-6.

[29] W.F. Rannie, *Canadian Whisky: The Product and the Industry* (Lincoln, Ont., 1976), pp. 111-113.

[30] The Seagram Co., *Annual Report,* 1979, especially p. 34.

[31] Booth, "The Bronfmans."

[34] Hiram Walker — Gooderham and Worts, *Annual Report,* 1979, pp. 17, 20.

[35] Guthrie, *Newsprint Paper Industry,* pp. 57-75.

[36] *Paper Trade Journal,* May 5, 1969, pp. 38-48.

[37] "B.C. Multinational Giant Moves in New Direction," *Financial Post,* October 2, 1971, p. 13; "MacMillan Bloedel Concentrates on Worldwide Expansion Program," *Financial Post,* September 15, 1973, p. 40.

[38] See *Paper Trade Journal,* especially the issues of April 20, 1970, p. 13; August 10, 1970, pp. 41, 43; and February 28, 1981, p. 17.

[39] MacMillan Bloedel, *Annual Report,* 1979, pp. 6, 41.
[40] Neufeld, *A Global Corporation,* p. 17.
[41] *Business Latin America,* August 23, 1973 and December 5, 1973.
[42] *Financial Post,* February 14, 1976, p. 26.
[43] *Financial Post,* December 1, 1975, p. 22.
[44] *Financial Post,* September 15, 1979, p. 33; *Financial Post,* September 22, 1980, p. 10.
[45] *Financial Post,* February 2, 1980, p. 18.
[46] *La Presse,* April 4, 1980, p. B-1.
[47] *Le Devoir,* December 13, 1980, p. 11; *La Presse,* February 9, 1981, p. C-1.
[48] Morton Research, *U.S. Farm Machinery.*
[49] Massey-Ferguson, *Annual Report,* 1979, p. 40.
[50] *Ibid.,* p. 28; *Financial Post,* October 25, 1980, p. S-1.
[51] Canada, Royal Commission on Farm Machinery, *Report.*
[52] *Monetary Times,* March 1944, pp. 32-35. Notable among the American companies that licensed their technology were Standard Oil of New Jersey, Dow Chemical, Goodyear Tire and Rubber, Firestone Tire, U.S. Rubber and B.F. Goodrich Tire and Rubber.
[53] *Monetary Times,* December 1960, p. 26; *Monetary Times,* December 1961, p. 24.
[54] *Monetary Times,* August 1962, p. 73.
[55] *Financial Post,* January 8, 1972, p. 11; *Financial Post,* March 24, 1973, p. 4.
[56] *Financial Post,* September 12, 1970, p. 3.
[57] *Polymer,* Annual Report, 1971, p. 2.
[58] *Polysar,* Annual Report, 1979, p. 4.
[59] Northern Telecom, *Annual Report* 1979, p. 3.
[60] *Le Devoir,* September 11, 1980, p. 11; *Le Devoir,* October 16, 1980, p. 24.

Conclusion

[1] Stephen Hymer and R. Rowthorn, "Multinational Corporation and International Oligopoly: The Non-American Challenge," in Charles P. Kindleberger, ed., *The International Corporation* (Cambridge, Mass.: MIT Press, 1970), pp. 74-75. In the case of Sweden, twenty-one companies account for 80 per cent of the sales of all foreign subsidiaries of Swedish multinationals. See S.E. Rolfe, *The International Corporation* (New York: The International Chamber of Commerce, 1969), p. 175.
[2] The exception to this rule is Bata Shoes, which was Czechoslovakia's leading shoe company and a large multinational when its head office was transferred to Canada during the Second World War.
[3] Stephen Hymer, *The International Operations of National Firms* (1960; Cambridge, Mass.: MIT Press, 1976); chapters 2-3.
[4] *Financial Post,* July 3, 1976, p. 21.

[5] J.M Katz, *Importación de tecnología, aprendizaje a industrialización dependiente* (Mexico City: Fondo de cultura economica, 1976), pp. 34-35, 70.

[6] Stephen Hymer, "U.S. Investment Abroad," in *The Multinational Corporation: A Radical Approach,* edited by R.B. Cohen (Cambridge: At the University Press, 1979), pp. 209-10.

[7] Peter J. Buckley and Marc Casson, *The Future of the Multinational Enterprise* (New York: Holmes and Meier, 1976), pp. 29, 35.

[8] K. Atkinson, "Tom Bata's Empire," *Financial Post Magazine,* February 10, 1977, p. 4; P. Anderson, "Moore Corp. in Form for Tough Era," *Financial Post,* March 20, 1976, p. 21.

[9] Helen Hughes, "The Australian Experience," in Tamir Agmon and Charles P. Kindleberger, eds., *Multinationals from Small Countries* (Cambridge, Mass.: MIT Press, 1977), pp. 117 et seq.

Bibliography

1. Theoretical, General and Comparative Works

1.1 Books

Agmon, Tamir A., and Kindleberger, Charles P. *Multinationals from Small Countries.* Cambridge, Mass.: MIT Press, 1977.

Amin, Samir. *Accumulation on a World Scale: A Critique of the Theory of Underdevelopment.* New York: Monthly Review Press, 1974.

Apter, D.E., and Goodman, L.W. *The Multinational Corporation and Social Change.* New York: Praeger, 1976.

Bain, Joe S. *Barriers to New Competition.* Cambridge, Mass.: Harvard University Press, 1956.

―――. *Industrial Organization.* New York: J. Wiley and Sons, 1968.

―――. *International Differences in Industrial Structure.* New Haven: Yale University Press, 1966.

Baran, Paul A. *The Political Economy of Growth.* New York: Monthly Review Press, 1957.

―――, and Sweezy, Paul M. *Monopoly Capital: An Essay on the American Economic and Social Order.* New York: Monthly Review Press, 1966.

Bettelheim, Charles. *Planification et croissance accélérée.* Paris: Maspero, 1963.

Blair, John M. *Economic Concentration.* New York: Harcourt Brace Jovanovich, 1972.

Buckley, Peter J., and Casson, Marc. *The Future of the Multinational Corporation.* New York: Holmes and Meier, 1976.

Chandler, A.J. *Strategy and Structure.* Cambridge, Mass.: MIT Press, 1962.

―――. *The Visible Hand.* Cambridge, Mass.: Harvard University Press, 1978.

Channon, D.F. *The Strategy and Structure of British Enterprise.* London: Macmillan, 1972.

Emmanuel, Arghiri. *Unequal Exchange: A Study of the Imperialism of Trade.* New York: Monthly Review Press, 1972.

Frank, André Gunder. *Capitalism and Underdevelopment in Latin America.* New York: Monthly Review Press, 1967.

Franko, L. *The European Multinationals.* London: Harper and Row, 1976.

Girvan, Norman. *Corporate Imperialism — Conflict and Expropriation.* New York: Monthly Review Press, 1976.

Hymer, Stephen H. *The International Operations of National Firms.* 1960. Cambridge, Mass.: MIT Press, 1976.

———. *The Multinational Corporation: A Radical Approach.* Papers by S.H. Hymer. Edited by R.B. Cohen. Cambridge: At the University Press, 1979.

Katz, J.M. *Importación de tecnología, aprendizaje e industrialización dependiente.* Mexico City: Fondo de cultura economica, 1976.

Kindleberger, Charles P. *American Business Abroad.* New Haven: Yale University Press, 1969.

———, ed. *The International Corporation.* Cambridge, Mass.: MIT Press, 1970.

Knickerbocker, Frederick T. *Oligopolistic Reaction and Multinational Enterprise.* Cambridge, Mass.: Harvard University Press, 1973.

Lenin, V.I. *Imperialism, the Highest Stage of Capitalism.* 1916. Moscow: Progress Publishers, 1970.

Luxembourg, Rosa. *The Accumulation of Capital.* 1913. London: Routledge and Kegan Paul, 1963.

Magdoff, Harry. *The Age of Imperialism.* New York: Monthly Review Press, 1969.

Merhav, Meir. *Technological Dependence, Monopoly and Growth.* London: Pergamon Press, 1969.

Michalet, Charles-Albert. Le capitalisme mondial. Paris: Presses Universitaires de France, 1976.

———. *La multinationalisation des entreprises françaises.* Paris: Gauthier-Villars, 1973.

Ozawa, T. *Multinationalism, Japanese Style: The Political Economy of Outward Dependency.* Princeton, N.J.: Princeton University Press, 1979.

Palloix, Christian. *L'économie mondiale capitaliste.* 2 vols. Paris: Maspero, 1971.

————. *Les firmes multinationales et le processus d'internationalisation.* Paris: Maspero, 1973.

Paquet, Gilles, ed. *Multinational Firm and the Nation State.* Don Mills, Ont.: Collier-Macmillan, 1972.

Tsurumi, Y. *The Japanese are Coming.* Cambridge, Mass.: Ballinger, 1976.

United Nations. *Multinational Corporations in World Development.* New York, 1973.

Vaitsos, Constantine. *Intercountry Income Distribution and Transnational Enterprises.* Oxford: At the University Press, 1974.

Vaupel, J.W., and Curhan, J.P. *The World's Multinational Enterprise.* Cambridge, Mass.: Harvard University Press, 1977.

Vernon, Raymond. *Sovereignty at Bay.* New York: Basic Books, 1971.

————. *Storm over the Multinationals.* Cambridge, Mass.: Harvard University Press, 1977.

Warren, Bill. *Imperialism, Pioneer of Capitalism.* London, NL Books, 1980.

Wilkins, Mira. *The Emergence of Multinational Enterprise: American Business Abroad from the Colonial Era to 1914.* Cambridge, Mass.: Harvard University Press, 1970.

————. *The Maturing of Multinational Enterprise: American Business Abroad from 1914 to 1970.* Cambridge, Mass.: Harvard University Press, 1974.

Woodruff, William. *Impact of Western Man: A Study of Europe's Role in the World Economy 1750-1960.* London: Macmillan, 1966.

Yoshino, M.Y. *Japan's Multinational Enterprises.* Cambridge, Mass.: Harvard University Press, 1976.

1.2 Articles

Cardoso, Fernando H. "Dependent Capitalist Development in Latin America." *New Left Review* no. 74 (July-August 1972), pp. 83-95.

Coquery-Vidrovitch, Catherine. "De l'impérialisme ancien à l'impérialisme moderne — l'avatar colonial." *L'homme et la société* no. 18 (Oct.-Dec. 1970), pp. 61-90.

Emmanuel, Arghiri . "Le mythe de l'impérialisme d'investissement." *L'homme et la société* no. 22 (Oct.-Dec. 1971), pp. 67-96.

Giddy, Ian H. "The Demise of the Product Cycle Model in International Business Theory." *Columbia Journal of World Business.* Spring 1978, pp. 90-97.

Robock, Stefan H., and Simmonds, Kenneth. "How Big It Is — The Missing Measurement." *Columbia Journal of World Business,* May-June 1970, pp. 6-19.

Vernon, Raymond. "International Investment and International Trade in the Product Cycle." *Quarterly Journal of Economics,* May 1966, pp. 190-207.

————. "The Product Cycle Hypothesis in a New International Environment." Roneograph. Harvard University, 1979.

Warren, Bill. "Imperialism and Capitalist Industrialisation." *New Left Review* no. 81 (Sept.-Oct. 1973), pp. 3-45.

Wells, Louis T., Jr. "Third World Multinationals." *Multinational Business* no. 1 (1980), pp. 12-19.

2. Works About Specific Industries

Bonbright, J.C. *The Holding Company.* 1932. New York: Kelley, 1969.

Branco, Catullo. *Energia eletrica e capital estrangeiro no Brasil.* São Paulo: Alfa-Omega, 1975.

Brooks, John. *Telephone: The First Hundred Years.* New York: Harper and Row, 1975.

Brown, Martin S., and Butler, John. *The Production, Marketing and Consumption of Copper and Aluminum.* New York: Praeger, 1968.

DAFSA. *Les caoutchoucs synthétiques et naturels.* Paris, 1974.

Elliott, W.Y. *International Control of the Non-Ferrous Metals.* New York: Macmillan, 1937.

Gouldon, J.C. *Monopoly.* New York: Putnam, 1968.

Guthrie, John A. *The Newsprint Paper Industry: An Economic Analysis.* Cambridge, Mass.: Harvard University Press, 1941.

Hyghlett, L.J. *Industrialization in Latin America.* New York: McGraw-Hill, 1946.

Kurdle, R.T. *Agricultural Tractors: A World Industry Study.* Cambridge. Mass.: Ballinger, 1975.

Marlio, Louis. *The Aluminum Cartel.* Washington: The Brookings Institution, 1947.

Mezger, Dorothea. *Copper in the World Economy.* New York: Monthly Review Press, 1980.

Navin, T.R. *Copper Mining and Management.* Tucson: University of Arizona Press, 1978.

Organization for Economic Co-operation and Development. *Indus-*

trial Adaptation in the Primary Aluminium Industry. Paris, 1976.

Passer, H.C. *The Electrical Manufacturers 1875-1900*. Cambridge, Mass.: Harvard University Press, 1953.

Rippy, J.F. *Latin America and the Industrial Age*. New York: Putnam, 1944.

Rosenbloom, M.R. *The Liquor Industry*. Braddock, Pa.: Ruffsdale, 1937.

Schidrowitz, Philip, and Dawson, T.R. *History of the Rubber Industry*. Cambridge: W. Heffer & Sons, 1952.

Sigmund, P.E. *Multinationals in Latin America*. New York: The 20th Century Fund, 1980.

Sultan, Ralph G.M. *Pricing in the Electrical Oligopoly*. 2 vols. Cambridge, Mass.: Harvard University Press, 1974.

Tanzer, Michael. *The Race for Resources*. New York: Monthly Review Press, 1980.

Tendler, Judith. *Electric Power in Brazil*. Cambridge, Mass.: Harvard University Press, 1968.

Wallace, Donald H. *Market Control in the Aluminum Industry*. Cambridge, Mass.: Harvard University Press, 1937.

Wionczek, Miguel S. *El nacionalismo mexicano y la inversion extrajera*. Mexico City: Siglo XXI, 1967.

———. "Electric Power: The Uneasy Partnership." In *Public Policy and Private Enterprise in Mexico,* edited by Raymond Vernon, pp. 21-110. Cambridge, Mass.: Harvard University Press, 1964.

3. Works About Canada

3.1 Books and Theses

Bourgault, Pierre L. *Innovation and the Structure of Canadian Industry*. Science Council of Canada Background Study No. 23. Ottawa: Information Canada, 1972.

Britton, J.N.H., and Gilmour, J.M. *The Weakest Link: A Technological Perspective on Canadian Industrial Underdevelopment*. Science Council of Canada Background Study No. 43. Ottawa: Supply and Services Canada, 1978.

Canada. Science Council of Canada. *Innovation in a Cold Climate: The Dilemma of Canadian Manufacturing*. Report no. 15. Ottawa: Information Canada, 1971.

Clement, Wallace. *Continental Corporate Power*. Toronto: McClelland and Stewart, 1977.

Deverell, John, et al. *Falconbridge: Portrait of a Canadian Mining Multinational.* Toronto: James Lorimer and Co., 1975.

Di Sanza, E. *Canadian Relations with the Caribbean and Latin America: Perspectives on Canada's Role in the World System.* MA thesis, McMaster University, Hamilton, 1978.

Firestone, O.J. *Economic Implications of Patents.* Ottawa: Éditions de l'Université d'Ottawa, 1971.

Levitt, Kari. *Silent Surrender: The Multinational Corporation in Canada.* Toronto: Macmillan of Canada, 1970.

Main, O.W. *The Canadian Nickel Industry.* Toronto, University of Toronto Press, 1955.

Marshall, Herbert et al. *Canadian-American Industry.* 1936. Reprint ed. Toronto: McClelland and Stewart, 1976.

Moore, Steve, and Wells, Debi. *Imperialism and the National Question in Canada.* Toronto, 1975.

Naylor, Tom. *The History of Canadian Business.* 2 vols. Toronto: James Lorimer and Co., 1975.

Nelles, H.V. *The Politics of Development: Forests, Mines and Hydro-Electric Power in Ontario 1849-1941.* Toronto: Macmillan of Canada, 1974.

Neufeld, E.P. *A Global Corporation: A History of the International Development of Massey-Ferguson.* Toronto: University of Toronto Press, 1969.

———. *The Financial System of Canada.* Toronto: Macmillan of Canada, 1970.

Niosi, Jorge. *Canadian Capitalism: A Study of Power in the Canadian Business Establishment.* Toronto: James Lorimer and Co., 1981.

———. *The Economy of Canada: A Study of Ownership and Control.* Montreal: Black Rose Books, 1978.

Oglesby, J.C.M. *Gringos from the Far North.* Toronto: Macmillan of Canada, 1976.

Rannie, W.F. *Canadian Whisky: The Product and the Industry.* Lincoln, Ont., 1976.

Roberts, Leslie. *Noranda.* Toronto: Clarke Irwin, 1956.

Rosenbluth, Gideon. *Concentration in Canadian Manufacturing Industries.* Princeton, N.J.: Princeton University Press, 1957.

Sanger, Clyde. *Half a Loaf: Canada's Semi-Role among Developing Countries.* Toronto: Ryerson, 1969.

Skeoch, L.A., ed. *Restrictive Trade Practices in Canada.* Toronto: McClelland and Stewart, 1966.

Swift, Jamie et al. *The Big Nickel: Inco at Home and Abroad.* Kitchener: Between The Lines, 1977.

Taylor, A.J.P. *Beaverbrook.* London: Hamish Hamilton, 1972.

3.2 Articles

Garnier, G. "Les investissements du Canada à l'étranger." *L'actualité économique,* April-June 1973, pp. 211-36.

Litvak, Isaiah A., and Maule, Christopher J. "Canadian Multinationals in the Western Hemisphere." *Business Quarterly,* Autumn 1975, pp. 30-42.

————. "Canadian Small Business Investments in the United States: Corporate Forms and Characteristics." *Business Quarterly,* Winter 1978, pp. 69-79.

"Massey-Ferguson's Global Strategy." *International Management,* September 1968, pp. 44-49.

Mulqueen, F.J. "A Canadian Enterprise Abroad." *Canada Banker,* Winter 1952, pp. 34-55.

Myers, J.G. "Foreign Licensing: An Export Alternative." *Business Quarterly,* Autumn 1960, pp. 167-75.

Stevens, J.H. "Joint Ventures in Latin America: Corporate Philosophy and Practice." *Business Quarterly,* Winter 1974, pp. 66-71.

Wright, R.W. "Canadian Joint Ventures in Japan." *Business Quarterly,* Autumn 1977, pp. 42-51.

3.3 Official Documents and Sources

Canada. Energy, Mines and Resources Canada. *Copper.* Ottawa: Supply and Services Canada, 1976.

————. *Nickel.* Ottawa: Supply and Services Canada, 1976.

————. *Transfer Pricing, the Multinational Enterprise and Economic Development.* Ottawa: Supply and Services Canada, 1976.

————. *Zinc.* Ottawa: Supply and Services Canada, 1976.

Canada. Export Development Corporation. *Annual Reports.*

Canada. Royal Commission on Canada's Economic Prospects. *Report.* Ottawa, 1956-57.

————. *Studies.* Ottawa, 1956-57.

Canada. Royal Commission on Corporate Concentration. *Report.* Ottawa: Supply and Services Canada, 1978.

————. *Studies.* Ottawa: Supply and Services Canada, 1978.

Canada. Royal Commission on Farm Machinery. *Report.* Ottawa: Information Canada, 1971.

————. *Studies.* Ottawa: Information Canada, 1971.

Canada. Statistics Canada. *Statistics Canada Daily.* Cat. no. 11-001. Ottawa, daily.

————. *Canada Year Book.* Ottawa, annual.

————. *Corporations and Labour Unions Reporting Act.* Cat. no. 61-210. Ottawa, annual.

————. *Industrial Organization and Concentration in Manufacturing, Mining and Logging Industries.* Cat. no. 31-402. Ottawa, two-yearly.

International Finance Corporation (New York). *Annual Reports.*

United States. Department of Commerce. *Foreign Direct Investment in the United States: Report to the U.S. Senate.* Washington, 1976.

————. *Survey of Current Business.* Washington, monthly.

3.4 Private Documents

American Bureau of Metal Statistics. *Non-Ferrous Metals Data.* New York, annual.

Angel, J.L. *Directory of Foreign Firms Operating in the U.S.* New York: World Trade Academics, 1978.

Annual Financial Review, 1901-45. Toronto: Houston Publishing Co., annual.

Annual reports of companies studied.

Arpan, J.S., and Ricks, D.A. *Directory of Foreign Manufacturers in the U.S.* Atlanta: Georgia State University, 1979.

Financial Post Directory of Directors, 1931-80. Toronto: Maclean-Hunter Ltd., annual.

Financial Post Survey of Corporate Securities, 1928-46. Toronto: Maclean-Hunter Ltd., annual.

Financial Post Survey of Funds, 1962-80. Toronto: Maclean-Hunter Ltd., annual.

Financial Post Survey of Industrials, 1947-80. Toronto: Maclean-Hunter Ltd., annual.

Financial Post Survey of Mines, 1926-78. Toronto: Maclean-Hunter Ltd., annual.

Financial Post Survey of Oils, 1936-78. Toronto: Maclean-Hunter Ltd., annual.

Financial Post Survey of Resources, 1979-80. Toronto: Maclean-Hunter Ltd., annual.

Moody's Bank and Finance Manual. New York: Moody's Investors' Service, annual.

Moody's Industrial Manual. New York: Moody's Investors' Service, annual.

Moody's Public Utilities Manual. New York: Moody's Investors' Service, annual.

Moody's Transportation Manual. New York: Moody's Investors' Service, annual.

Morton Research Co. *The U.S. Distilled Liquor Industry.* New York, 1979.

————. *The U.S. Farm Machinery Industry.* New York, 1977.

Petrie, J.R. *Some Economic Facts About the Beverage Distilling Industry in Canada.* Montreal: Association of Canadian Distillers, 1961.

Stopford, J., et al. *The World Directory of Multinational Enterprises.* New York: Facts on File, 1980.

3.5 Newspapers, Magazines and Journals

Beama Journal, London (monthly).

Business Latin America, New York: Business International Corp. (weekly).

Business Quarterly, London, Ont.: University of Western Ontario (quarterly).

Canadian Banker, Toronto: Canadian Bankers' Association (quarterly).

Canadian Business, Toronto: CB media Ltd. (monthly).

Canadian Electrical News, Montreal (weekly).

Canadian Mining Journal, Montreal: Southam Business Publications (monthly).

Le Devoir, Montreal (daily).

Electrical World, New York (weekly).

Financial Post, Toronto: Maclean-Hunter Ltd. (weekly).

Fortune, Chicago: Time Inc. (fortnightly).

Monetary Times, Toronto (weekly).

Northern Miner, Toronto, magazine supplement, July 6, 1972.

La Presse, Montreal (daily).

Public Utilities Fortnightly, Washington: Public Utilities Report Inc. (fortnightly).

Wall Street Journal, New York: Dow-Jones (daily).

World Power, London (monthly).